ADALBERT STIFTER

ANGLICA GERMANICA SERIES 2

Founder Editor LEONARD FORSTER

Editors H. B. NISBET AND MARTIN SWALES

Other books in the series

D. Prohaska: Raimund and Vienna: A Critical Study of Raimund's plays in their Viennese Setting

D. G. Mowatt: Friedrich von Hûsen: Introduction, Text, Commentary and Glossary

C. Lofmark: Rennewart in Wolfram's 'Willehalm': A Study of Wolfram von Eschenbach and his Sources

A. Stephens: Rainer Maria Rilke's 'Gedichte an die Nacht'

M. Garland: Hebbel's Prose Tragedies: An Investigation of the Aesthetic Aspects of Hebbel's Dramatic Language

H. W. Cohn: Else Lasker-Schüler: The Broken World

J. M. Ellis: Narration in the German Novelle: Theory and Interpretation

M. B. Benn: The Drama of Revolt: A Critical Study of Georg Büchner

J. Hibberd: Salomon Gessner: His Creative Achievement and Influence

P. Hutchinson: Literary Presentations of Divided Germany

I. R. Campbell: *Kudrun:* A Critical Appreciation

A. T. Hatto: Essays on Medieval German and other Poetry

F. P. Pickering: Essays on Medieval German Literature and Iconography

L. Parshall: The Art of Narration in Wolfram's *Parzival* and Albrecht's *Jüngerer Titurel*

W. D. Robson-Scott: The Younger Goethe and the Visual Arts

R. Pascal: Kafka's Narrators: A Study of his Stories and Sketches

M. Beddow: The Fiction of Humanity: Studies in the Bildungsroman from Wieland to Thomas Mann

A. Bance: Theodor Fontane: The Major Novels

M. R. Minden: Arno Schmidt: A Critical Study of his Prose

D. Wellbery: Lessing's *Laocoon*: Semiotics and Aesthetics in the Age of Reason

ADALBERT STIFTER

A CRITICAL STUDY

MARTIN AND ERIKA SWALES

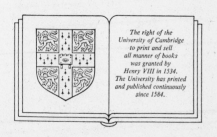

The right of the
University of Cambridge
to print and sell
all manner of books
was granted by
Henry VIII in 1534.
The University has printed
and published continuously
since 1584.

CAMBRIDGE UNIVERSITY PRESS

CAMBRIDGE

LONDON   NEW YORK   NEW ROCHELLE

MELBOURNE   SYDNEY

Published by the Press Syndicate of the University of Cambridge
The Pitt Building, Trumpington Street, Cambridge CB2 IRP
32 East 57th Street, New York, NY 10022, USA
296 Beaconsfield Parade, Middle Park, Melbourne 3206, Australia

First published 1984

Printed in Great Britain by New Western Printing Ltd.

Library of Congress catalogue card number: 83–20914

British Library Cataloguing in Publication Data
Swales, Martin
Adalbert Stifter. – (Anglica Germanica. Series 2)
1 Stifter, Adalbert – Criticism and interpretations
I. Swales, Erika II. Title III. Series
833′.7 PT2525.Z5
ISBN 0 521 25972 X

209909

IN MEMORIAM
ROY PASCAL
(1904 – 1980)

CONTENTS

CONTENTS

FOREWORD

A collaborative venture such as went into the writing of this book was a new enterprise for both of us. It derives from many years in which we discussed Stifter together, years in which both of us disagreed and shifted our critical ground very considerably – without ever quite finding that we, as it were, met in the middle. Indeed, rather than trying to iron out the differences between us, we concluded that the grounds for our disagreement had vitally to do with the particular tensions at work in Stifter's art – and in that sense provided a profitable framework for its analysis.

The book is collaborative in the precise sense that no part of it could have been written by one without the other. We greatly enjoyed working together: and we can only hope that the result of our labours does not read as though it had been written by a sub-committee.

Our debt to other Stifter scholars is great: and we are particularly grateful to our friends Eve Mason, Alec Stillmark, and Peter Stern for their hints and suggestions – very often for casual remarks that helped more than we (or probably they) knew at the time. Moreover, we are profoundly grateful to our students in London and Cambridge for the mixture of tolerance, enthusiasm, and dissent with which they greeted our attempts to teach Stifter.

Given that it will be many years before the new historical-critical edition of Stifter's works (edited by Wolfgang Frühwald and Alfred Doppler, Kohlhammer, Stuttgart, 1978ff.) is available in its entirety, we felt that it would be most helpful if all quotations from Stifter's works gave as their source one of the readily available compact editions: Adalbert Stifter, *Werke*, edited by Magda Gerken and Josef Thanner, five volumes, each with an afterword by Fritz Krökel, Winkler, Munich, 1949–61. A key to the location of Stifter's principal works in this edition, together with translations of titles, dates (following the chronology of the edition) and an explanation of the convention we have used for source references will all be found in the table given at the end of the Foreword. Where the source is given as *SW*, followed by a volume and page number, the edition cited is: Adalbert Stifter, *Sämmtliche Werke*, edited by August Sauer, Franz Hüller, Kamill Eben, Gustav Wilhelm, Prag/Reichenberg/Graz, 1901–60. References to the original versions, the *Urfassungen* (or, to quote the term preferred in the Doppler/Frühwald edition, the *Journalfassungen*), cite the three-volume edition by Max Stefl: Adalbert Stifter, *Erzählungen in der Urfassung*, Augsburg, 1950–2; the source is given as *Urf.* Letters are identified by the date of their composition and the name of the recipient. The translations throughout are our own.

Since Eric Blackall's *Adalbert Stifter: A Critical Study* (Cambridge, 1948) there has been only one general monograph in English on Stifter (Margaret Gump, *Adalbert Stifter*, New York, 1974), and a volume of essays on *Der Nachsommer* (Christine Sjögren, *The Marble Statue as Idea*, Chapel Hill, 1972). We are convinced that the time is ripe for another attempt to make Stifter known outside Germanist circles. We initially intended to write a large book, which was to include much more detailed analysis and extended comparisons of the early and late versions of Stifter's works. Finally (and reluctantly) we decided against such an enterprise: in our view, what is needed at the present time is a short critical study which highlights the major interpretative issues raised by Stifter's art and which attempts to make the connexion between these issues and the 'mainstream' of nineteenth-century European prose. In our analyses of individual texts we have paid particular attention to features of narrative and style. When it came to translating the quotations we were forcefully reminded how difficult it is to capture the 'feel' of Stifter's prose in English. We realize that this is another way of saying that Stifter's art may not travel well. But we are unrepentant in our conviction that this art represents a major voice in nineteenth-century European prose, and that the attempt to make Stifter accessible to an English-speaking audience is entirely justified by both the thematic and the stylistic character of his work. We can only hope that, warts and all, this study goes some way towards fulfilling that aim.

A final word of thanks – to the advisers of Cambridge University Press for the clarity and cogency of their criticisms, to Penny Souster, our exemplary sub-editor, and to Inge Mable for the unfailing patience and skill with which she typed more drafts of this study than we (and assuredly also she) care to remember.

We dedicate this book to the memory of a great teacher and friend who died as the first draft of our project was taking shape. We feel his loss keenly, and we can only hope that at least some parts of our study would have given him pleasure.

Source references

Most references to Stifter's works cite the Winkler Ausgabe. The sources are given in brackets after the individual quotation and indicate the volume by the initial letter or letters, followed by the page number.

Studien (*S*)	*Der Hochwald* (The Alpine Forest) 1841
	Abdias 1842
	Das alte Siegel (The Old Seal) 1843
	Brigitta 1843
	Der Hagestolz (The Recluse) 1844
Bunte Steine und Erzählungen (*BSt*)	*Granit* (Granite) 1853
	Kalkstein (Limestone) 1853
	Turmalin (Tourmaline) 1853
	Bergkristall (Rock Crystal) 1853

	Katzensilber (Myca) 1853
	Bergmilch (Mountain Quartz) 1853
	Prokopus 1848
	Der Waldgänger (The Walker in the Forest) 1847
	Zuversicht (Confidence) 1846
	Nachkommenschaften (Descendants) 1864
	Der Kuß von Sentze (The Kiss of Sentze) 1866
	Der fromme Spruch (The Pious Saying) 1867
Der Nachsommer (N)	Indian Summer 1857
Witiko (W)	Witiko 1865–7
Mappe, Schilderungen, Briefe (M)	*Die Mappe meines Urgroßvaters* (The Papers of my Great-Grandfather) 1867
	Wien und die Wiener (Vienna and the Viennese) 1844. This collection of essays includes *Ein Gang durch die Katakomben* (A Walk through the Catacombs) and *Der Tandelmarkt* (The Junk Market)
	Die Sonnenfinsternis am 8. Juli 1842 (The Eclipse of the Sun of 8 July 1842)
	Winterbriefe aus Kirchschlag (Winter Letters from Kirchschlag) 1866
	Aus dem Bayrischen Walde (From the Bavarian Forest) 1867

1 · BIOGRAPHICAL INTRODUCTION

Als die Unvernunft, der hohle Enthusiasmus, dann die Schlechtigkeit, und die Leerheit: und endlich sogar das Verbrechen sich breit machten und die Welt in Besitz nahmen: da brach mir fast buchstäblich das Herz.

(Stifter to Heckenast, 4 September 1849)

(When unreason, hollow enthusiasm, then wickedness, emptiness and finally even criminality spread everywhere and took possession of the world: then, almost literally, it broke my heart.)

Die einzige künstlerische Todsünde ist die gegen die ursprüngliche Gottähnlichkeit der menschlichen Seele.

(Stifter to Buddeus, 21 August 1847)

(The only artistic cardinal sin is that which offends against the original likeness between the human soul and Divinity.)

Es ist möglich, daß in mir viele Blumen getötet wurden, es ist aber auch möglich, daß sie vielleicht gar nie da waren.

(Stifter to Türck, 16 July 1852)

(It is possible that many flowers within me have been killed, but it is equally possible that they may never have existed at all.)

Das Herz möchte einem brechen bei Betrachtung gewisser Unmöglich-keiten.

(Stifter to Heckenast, 20 July 1857)

(One's heart could break at the thought of certain impossibilities.)

Adalbert Stifter was born on 23 October 1805 in the village of Oberplan in southern Bohemia, the first of five children. He was an intelligent boy, and his intellectual gifts soon became apparent in his early years at the local primary school. But in November 1817 his father, a linen weaver who also did a little farming on the side,[1] was killed in an accident, and Stifter had to leave school in order to work in the fields. However, his maternal grandfather felt that the boy deserved better than this: and he took him to the Benedictine monastery of Kremsmünster which was renowned for its grammar school. Stifter was accepted by Pater Placidus Hall, and in 1818 he began his studies. He enjoyed his time at Kremsmünster, being gifted both at academic work and at drawing and painting. He left in 1826 with an excellent school leaver's certificate which made possible his admission to the university. He went to Vienna and read law. Once again he proved himself a very good student, and his teachers helped him to find paid employment as a private tutor with respected families. While in Vienna he fell in love with Fanni Greipl, but her parents did not approve of the awkward and penniless student. Stifter continued to pine for Fanni long after it became clear that there was no hope of his marrying her; indeed, it would appear that the unhappy love affair made him lose interest in his studies. He became dilatory, strangely forgetful, even failing to present himself for an examination. He continued to lead a financially precarious existence, often changing his flat in Vienna in order to escape his creditors. Although his love for Fanni was in no way diminished, he turned his attentions to Amalia Mohaupt, and they were married on 15 November 1837. Amalia proved to be a capable administrator of the household, and Stifter gradually began to make a name for himself as a writer (the first volume of the *Studien* appeared in 1844). Not that the financial anxieties were lifted: he continued to work as a private tutor – even teaching Metternich's son physics and maths. In 1845 he and Amalia left for a journey to Oberplan, and the next two years or so saw a widening of Stifter's narrow circle of acquaintances (he met Robert and Clara Schumann and the singer Jenny Lind). He spent the summer of 1847 in Linz, suffering great deprivation because Amalia was not with him. When she joined her husband, she brought with her her niece, the pretty and high-spirited Juliane Mohaupt, who was to live with them and bring some life into their childless household. In March 1848 Stifter was in Vienna when the (abortive) Revolution began. He welcomed the liberation from the oppressiveness and censorship of the old regime, even allowing his name to go forward as a candidate to represent his district in the Frankfurt parliament. But his liberal aspirations were soon offended by what he saw as the chaos and violence of the revolutionary agitators. In May 1848 he withdrew to Linz: he became involved in journalism, writing a good deal about educational questions. After much delay, in March 1850, he was finally appointed to the post of Inspector of Primary Schools in Upper Austria. He seems to have welcomed the disciplined, orderly framework offered by the bureaucratic post, yet increasingly he came to resent its incursions into the time and psychological energy which he needed for his writing. There were, in addition, family anxieties. Juliane, having been beaten by Amalia, ran away from home and tried to work as a serving maid at an inn rather than return to Amalia's oppressive regime. Stifter was mortified by the gossip the incident caused and by the pedagogic failure entailed. Although he was now in relatively secure financial circumstances, monetary anxieties continued to plague him. He and his wife felt that they had a position to keep up, that a certain bourgeois grandeur was appropriate to their station in life. They ate and drank well, collected furniture and *objets d'art*, yet all the outward solidity failed to yield peace of mind. There were, in addition, frequent tensions with the ministry. Stifter was deprived of his inspectorate at the *Realschule* in Linz, his proposal for a school text book was rejected. His health began to decline: he was plagued by a variety of nervous ailments. In 1859 Juliane suddenly disappeared from the house: five weeks later her body was found in the Danube. Stifter was haunted by feelings of grief and guilt. Increasingly, he displayed a hypochondriac fascination with the symptoms of his own decline. On occasions he left Linz for a period of recuperation at a spa: but the improvement was always short-lived. Amalia, too, seems to have been fearful for her health. Stifter depended on her for comfort and solace and when he was separated from her, his need for her was acute. Yet, when he was with her, the combination of joylessness and oppressive bourgeois solidity seems to have taken its toll of his health and spirits. In

November 1865 he was pensioned off and awarded the title of 'Hofrat'. Various journeys followed to spas and resorts. But the promised Indian Summer did not come about. In December 1867 Stifter was confined to bed: the pain, caused by cirrhosis of the liver, was appalling. In the following month he cut his throat with a razor. He died two days later – on 28 January 1868.

How are we to define the essential signature of this outwardly so unadventurous life?[2] The temptation to pursue a psycho-analytical reading is very strong: one could point out that Stifter was determined to turn his back on the emotional turmoil of the early years, to stylize his experience within the strict channels of orderliness and integrity, to live and to create, as J. P. Stern suggests, the consciously maintained beautiful lie.[3] However justified such arguments may be, there is the danger that one dismisses the deliberation and deliberateness of Stifter's life as mere sham. In order to do justice to the complexities of his art, and to place that art within its nineteenth-century context, it is surely more fruitful to focus on the antinomies in Stifter, on those points where within the personal conflict there reverberate the tensions of his age. Stifter is steeped in the thought of the eighteenth century, the legacy of German Enlightenment and Classicism. The ideals of *Vernunft* (reason), *Humanität*, *Sittlichkeit* (morality), *Maß* (moderation), which were so dear to Herder, Kant, Schiller and Goethe, are inseparable from Stifter's personality as man and writer. Thus, time and again, he argues that the course both of an individual life and of human history is determined by man exercising his free will in accordance with the laws of Reason, and that, however negative the evidence at any given point may be, ultimately perfectibility will prevail. And yet: much in Stifter partakes of the pessimism that we associate with Arthur Schopenhauer. Not that Stifter ever consciously espoused the doctrine which, in place of supreme Reason, enthrones the dark, blind agency of the Will; but his creative personality absorbed impulses from the decade (the 1840s) in which *Die*

Welt als Wille und Vorstellung (The World as Will and Idea) became a bestseller – the first edition of 1819 sold so few copies that it was pulped. In terms of his discursively proclaimed attitudes Stifter was constantly at pains to keep at bay any notion of man and world as driven by no more than the blind, unmotivated 'Wille zum Leben' (will to live); yet, as we shall see, there are many passages in his work where the tenaciously held ground of Reason suddenly gives and there are flashes of perception which recall Schopenhauer. Indeed, the very vocabulary can be reminiscent: thus, on the opening page of *Abdias*, Stifter reflects on the possibility of the 'letzte Unvernunft des Seins' (ultimate unreason of being).

That Stifter walks a precarious tightrope emerges perhaps most clearly from three central aspects of his inner biography which highlight his fierce, yet ever threatened, will towards equilibrium.

First, there is the conflict between the needs of passionate man and the demands of 'established' morality – a conflict which may account for the striking polarization of Stifter's erotic experience. Most commentators agree in describing the marriage to Amalia if not as loveless, then as little more than an emotional and intellectual 'second best'. This view is corroborated by the letter which Stifter wrote to Fanni in August 1835. He reports his engagement to Amalia:

Gekränkte Eitelkeit war es – zeigen wollt' ich eurem Hause, daß ich doch ein schönes, wohlhabendes und edles Weib zu finden wußte – ach und hätte über dem Experimente bald mein Herz gebrochen! Je weiter zur Vermählung hin ich es mit Amalien kommen ließ, desto unruhiger und unglücklicher ward ich. Dein Bild stand so rein und mild im Hintergrund vergangener Zeiten, so schön war die Erinnerung und so schmerzlich, daß ich, als ich Amalien das Wort künftiger Ehe gab, nach Hause ging, und auf dem Kissen meines Bettes unendlich weinte – um Dich.[4]

(It was wounded vanity – I wanted to prove to your family that I was after all able to find a beautiful, prosperous and noble wife – alas and the experiment nearly broke my heart! The closer I let things come to an engagement with Amalia, the more restless and unhappy did my heart become. Your image stood so clear and gentle as the background of times past, the memory was so beautiful and so painful that, after I had given Amalia my promise of marriage, I went home and wept unending tears on the pillow of my bed – for you.)

Amalia was a beautiful, sensuous woman of very little culture, and she hardly understood her husband's literary aspirations. Yet it has been suggested that Amalia, precisely because she was a woman of few intellectual and imaginative gifts, was able to channel and fulfil Stifter's powerful sexuality, in the sense that he could only find physical release with a partner whom he could not respect intellectually. There is, for example, the telling comment on the marriage by a contemporary observer: 'und wenn er müde[ist], wartet seiner im Nebenzimmer eine junge, hübsche, Frau, die er sehr liebt, obwohl sie eher spießbürgerlich als poesieempfänglich scheint'[5] (and when he is tired, there is waiting for him in the next room a young pretty wife whom he loves greatly, although she seems to be a pretty-bourgeois philistine rather than a lover of poetry).

Stifter's letters to Amalia make fascinating reading. They document his overpowering need for her: he frequently reproaches her in near panic for not writing and torments himself with fears for her health and well being. There is, then, the sense of an obsessive passion, but, typically, he associates that very passion with feelings of guilt and sin:

Ich wäre ja ruhig, es wäre ja alles recht, wenn diese schreckliche Liebe nicht wie eine Strafe Gottes auf mich läge. Es muß wirklich eine Strafe des Himmels für begangene mir nicht mehr erinnerliche Sünde sein, daß ich Dich gar so liebe.[6]

(I would be calm, all would be well, if this terrible love did not weigh upon me like a punishment from God. It must truly be a punishment from Heaven for some sin, which I have committed but can no longer recall, that I love you so greatly.)

In this context, it is not surprising that Stifter at times interprets the fact that their marriage was childless as a judgment on their relationship. Furthermore, the undercurrent of guilt feelings helps to illuminate the sheer frequency with which Stifter stylizes his feelings for Amalia into endlessly reiterated assertions of the sanctity of marriage:

Dein einfacher Wandel voll Rechtlichkeit, Deine Dir fast unbewußte Ausübung der häuslichen und weiblichen Tugend, Deine Zurück-gezogenheit, Dein Fernsein von jedem Prunken und Anmaßen verbunden mit der Güte Deines Wesens hat mich immer mehr und mehr mit Achtung erfüllt, und hat mein Herz an Dich gefesselt mit den stärksten Ketten, die es für einen guten und redlich wollenden Menschen gibt.[7]

(Your simple way of life, full of righteousness, your unselfconscious exercising of domestic and wifely duties, your reticence, your abhorrence of all vanity and pretentiousness, coupled with the goodness of your character, has filled me more and more with respect and has bound my heart to you with the strongest chains which a good and right thinking man can know.)

The hectoring sacramentalism of such passages surely connotes the determination to transmute passion into morality. This same process of forcing affective drives into channels of ethical legitimation is mirrored in the opening section of *Brigitta* where the narrator speculates on the laws of attraction:

Daß zuletzt sittliche Gründe vorhanden sind, die das Herz heraus fühlt, ist kein Zweifel, allein wir können sie nicht immer mit der Waage des Bewußtseins und der Rechnung hervor heben, und anschauen. Die Seelenkunde hat manches beleuchtet und erklärt, aber vieles ist ihr dunkel und in großer Entfernung geblieben. (*S*, 735)

(That ultimately there are ethical reasons which the heart divines cannot be doubted, but we cannot always isolate them and explore them with the scales of consciousness and calculation. The science of the soul has illuminated and explained many things, but much has remained obscure and beyond its grasp.)

This same syndrome of legitimizing passion by investing it with an ethical function can be observed in Stifter's relation-ship to the theatre. He was greatly attracted to the theatre, repeatedly speaks of its physical appeal, but, in direct con-tinuation of eighteenth-century mainstream aesthetics and in sharp contrast to a Büchner, he also insists that the passions which the theatre unleashes must be in the service of morality.

Clearly, the conflicting demands of passion and morality explain a great deal of Stifter's mentality as private man and public writer, but they also touch on the fundamental tension of his age. One thinks of Grillparzer, who is suspended between moral judgment on and psychological sympathy with his characters, one thinks of Droste, her self-torment in the *Geistliche Lieder*, above all her poem 'Am Turme' which so perfectly expresses the restlessness within the largely self-imposed confines of a strict morality:

> Nun muß ich sitzen so fein und klar,
> Gleich einem artigen Kinde,
> Und darf nur heimlich lösen mein Haar
> Und lassen es flattern im Winde!

> (Now must I sit so delicate and clear
> Like a well-behaved child,
> And only secretly may I undo my hair
> And let it flutter in the wind!)

The second crucial aspect of Stifter's biography is his response to the public events of his time. A precarious, but determined faith in Reason informs Stifter's conception of history and society, in particular his relationship to, and role within, the social world of mid-nineteenth-century Vienna and the events of 1848. His collection of essays *Wien und die Wiener* bespeaks the charm which the sheer scale and bustle of the metropolis held for him. But, equally, there is the fear at the anonymity of the urban world, and it was in Vienna that Stifter saw, with anguish and horror, the threat of mass political movements. His letters of 1848 frequently express despair. Thus he writes to Heckenast in May:

Betrübend ist die Erscheinung, daß so viele, welche die Freiheit begehrt haben, nun selber von Despotiegelüsten heimgesucht werden; es ist auch im Gange der Dinge natürlich: wer den Übermut anderer früher ertragen mußte, wird, sobald er frei ist, nicht etwa gerecht, sondern nun seinerseits übermütig.[8]

(The phenomenon is troubling that so many people who craved freedom are now themselves prey to despotic desires; it is also a natural ingredient of the course of things: whoever had earlier to suffer under the arrogance of others becomes, once he is free, not righteous but arrogant in his turn.)

Such words recall the pained questioning of Büchner's *Dantons Tod* – and one wonders what perspective Stifter would have chosen for his planned novel on Robespierre. In January 1849 he writes again: 'daß das Volk im allgemeinen den Beweis geliefert hat, daß es unmündig sei, . . . daß es als Opfer seiner eigenen Leidenschaften nur Stürme und Verwirrungen stiften kann'[9] (that the people in general have provided the proof that they have not come of age . . . that they, as victims of their own passions, are only able to bring about turmoil and confusion). Stifter, then, was only too aware of the negative evidence offered by history, and yet, as is the case with Kant, Schiller or indeed Hegel, this awareness serves to strengthen the resolution to uphold the postulates of Reason and Perfectibility: it is man's unending task 'seine reine Menschlichkeit zu entwickeln, das heißt, so gut und volkommen zu werden als es einem Menschen möglich ist'[10] (to develop his pure humanity, that is, to become as good and as perfect as is possible for a human being). Stifter is predisposed to see history as a purposive agency, as a process which, for all its waywardness, is driven by the mainspring of Reason. Hence throughout his essays of 1848 and 1849, he pleads for moderation and patience, for politics to be conducted with respect for the gradual rhythms of natural growth, and he advocates the stabilizing functions of the family, school, and religion as bastions against the inroads of disorder. The essay of March 1849 *Die octroierte Verfassung* (The Imposed Constitution) is very typical: Stifter concedes that the constitution which the Emperor has decreed, thus preempting any parliamentary decision, may lack democratic legitimation, but he defends the Emperor's action because time is short, and a clear lead is necessary in the heady atmosphere of the times:

Laßt uns die Gabe unseres jungen edlen Kaisers freundlich und treu aufnehmen, laßt uns die so notwendigen Gesetze für die Ordnung der

Länder zu Stande kommen machen, und laßt uns zuletzt die Veränder-
ungen, die in der Verfassung Not tun mögen, in dem neuen, edlen,
starken, gesinnungsvollen Reichstage, der zusammenberufen wird, in
Vorschlag, in Beratung und Wirksamkeit bringen.[11]

(Let us receive the gift of our young and noble Emperor in a friendly
and faithful spirit, let us help to bring about those laws which are so
necessary for the order of the realm, and let us, finally, take up the
reforms to the constitution which may well be necessary and bring
them before the new, noble, strong, and principled parliament which
will be called into being, there to propose, to deliberate on them, and
to enact them.)

There is, then, the embattled determination that the course
of contemporary politics and history overall shall vindicate
Reason. He even at times comes close to a Hegelian vision;
thus he perceives the struggles of the French Revolution, the
crime and fall of Robespierre, in terms of 'eine erschütternde
moralische Größe, und der Weltgeist schaut uns mit den
ernstesten Augen an'[12] (a shattering moral greatness, and the
world spirit observes us with the most earnest gaze). But
Stifter does not absolutize the present in the name of Reason's
self-objectification. 1848 was such a profound shock that no
Hegelian notion of the 'ruse of reason' ('List der Vernunft')
could have afforded any comfort. And yet, he does not
relinquish the teleological vision. In 1849 he writes: 'Die
Menschheit wird einstens doch ihren höchsten, vollendetsten
Gipfel erreichen...Weil Gott das höchste Wesen ist, muß
die Menschheit sich einst zur höchsten Höhe erschwingen'[13]
(Mankind will one day reach the highest summit of supreme
perfection...Because God is the highest being, man will one
day manage to scale those most exalted heights). The teleological promise is asserted in the repeated 'einst(ens)' – 'one
day'. But, characteristically, Stifter inserts a sentence between
the two quoted above: 'Ich glaube das selber, und ich müßte
verzweifeln, wenn ich es nicht glaubte' (I believe that myself,
and I would have to despair if I did not believe it). The
promise is not a given truth: it is an act of will.

This constellation of embattled faith, resolution, and despair, informs Stifter's work as journalist, school inspector and writer. To take his professional career first: he was a most hard-working official of the School Inspectorate, although he resented the inroads that the administrative load made into his time and creative energies. His reports have been published by Kurt Vancsa, tellingly juxtaposed with letters written at the same time.[14] The upshot is a dualism: on the one hand we have the painstaking administrator, and on the other the creative writer longing for deliverance from daily servitude so that he can write. Yet despite all his frustration, he persists: 'Ich gebe den Schmerz nicht her, weil ich sonst auch das Göttliche hergeben müßte' (I will not surrender the pain because otherwise I would also have to surrender the divine).[15] It is a pain endured in the name of a divinely vouchsafed perfectibility of man – a faith which his horror at the events of 1848 only served to intensify. The painstaking bureaucrat, who repeatedly demands free schooling for all and decent salaries for the teachers, contributes in his own small way toward the 'Bildung' (education) of mankind on which he pins all his hopes. Thus he writes to Heckenast in March 1849:

Das Ideal der Freiheit ist auf lange Zeit vernichtet, wer sittlich frei ist, kann es staatlich sein, ja ist es immer: den andern können alle Mächte der Erde nicht dazu machen. Es gibt nur eine Macht, die es kann: Bildung. Darum erzeugte sich in mir eine ordentlich krankhafte Sehnsucht, die da sagt: 'Lasset die Kleinen zu mir kommen.'[16]

(The ideal of freedom has been destroyed for a long time, whoever is ethically free can be politically free – indeed always is so. No earthly power can make the others free. There is only one power that can do that: education and culture. Hence there has grown up in me a frankly obsessive longing which says 'Suffer the little children to come unto me.')

This same sense of task, if not mission, informs Stifter's conception of his own writings. They parallel his work as school inspector in that they, too, function as an educative agency. A typical example of this evaluation is to be found in the preface to the *Studien* (Studies, 1843) where he expresses his hope, so often repeated in his letters, that the stories will further 'ein sittlich Schönes' (a morally beautiful aim) and thus contribute to the 'ganze Bau der Ewigkeit' (the whole edifice of eternity), although they are but tiny granules. We find thus in Stifter a striking interdependence of office and art: both are tied to a religious-cum-moral aim which in turn carries socio-political implications. The essay *Über Stand und Würde des Schriftstellers* (On the Position and Value of the Writer, 1848) is precisely concerned with this double aim. It begins by defining the essential task of the writer, which is that he 'die Dinge in ihrer objektiven Gültigkeit (nicht in einseitigen Beziehungen zu unsern Leidenschaften) kennt'[17] (knows things in their objective validity – and not in their one-sided relationship to our passions). This strikes one as an all too global definition of the artist's task, but it soon becomes clear that, in context, it has a precise temporal significance: 'Alles Unheil, welches die Weltgeschichte erzählt, entsprang daraus, daß man die Gegenstände wider ihre Natur behandeln wollte'[18] (all evil which world history recounts stems from the attempt to treat objects in defiance of their nature). Reverence for the natural being of objects is not only an artistic, but also a political maxim: common to both is the conservative stance which invokes the notion of a God-given organic necessity. Thus, if Stifter in his art is at pains, both in thematic and stylistic terms, to enshrine gradualness as a moral and artistic value, he provides what he sees as the necessary corrective to the turmoil of his times. The less commerce there is between his creativity and the public affairs of his country, the more that creativity serves as an antidote to the threat of mass unrest and primitivism. In a letter to Heckenast he speaks of *Der Nachsommer* as a deliberate affront to the wickedness of his age:

Ich habe wahrscheinlich das Werk der Schlechtigkeit willen gemacht, die im Allgemeinen mit einzigen Ausnahmen in den Staatsverhältnissen der Welt in dem sittlichen Leben derselben und in der Dichtkunst herrscht. Ich habe eine große einfache sittliche Kraft der elenden Verkommenheit gegenüber stellen wollen.[19]

(I probably made the work on account of the rottenness that in general, and with only few exceptions, prevails in the public affairs of the world, in its ethical life, and in its literature. I wanted to confront the most wretched depravity with a great, simple ethical force.)

We may fruitfully compare these words with another letter in which Stifter defines the attraction of a civil service office: 'das Höchste, was bei Staatsstellen locken könnte, wäre die Aussicht, das Hohe, das Göttliche, das eigentliche Reich des Himmlischen auf der Welt fördern zu können'[20] (the most exalted appeal that a post in the public service can have would be the chance to further the sublime, the divine, the true kingdom of heaven on this earth). What emerges here is the full interdependence of the administrative and creative mentality within Stifter. One wonders, incidentally, if this is not representative of an Austrian ethos, of that strange hypostatization of the ideal of bureaucratic service which, for Claudio Magris, is one of the cornerstones of the 'Habsburg myth in Austrian literature'.[21] One thinks particularly of Grillparzer, not only of his Emperor Rudolf (in *König Ottokars Glück und Ende*) who is 'merely the Emperor who never dies', all office and no man, but of the fact that Grillparzer (like Stifter) was rewarded with the title of 'Hofrat'. And, in our century, we are reminded of Kafka; in a recent essay, Roy Fuller has suggested that Kafka the artist needed to devote his day-time hours to the seemingly alien demands of painstaking office work.[22] At issue is not the fact that certain Austrian writers had bureaucratic jobs: but the fact that that kind of work was invested with a cultural and political pathos that did not, for example, apply to T. S. Eliot's time as a bank employee in Lombard Street or to Wallace Stevens's work as a lawyer with an insurance company.

And yet – behind all this determined self-discipline, there is a haunting sense of futility. Not only does Stifter often despair and ask himself whether his work as school inspector will yield results, but there is also the fear that his artistic aspirations may be doomed. He writes and rewrites endlessly – 'Sie glauben nicht, wie ich mich abquäle, ich weiß das Höhere, und es gestaltet sich nicht'[23] (You would not believe what I go through, I know of higher things, but they will not take shape). Throughout his creative life, he carries with him the project of *Die Mappe meines Urgroßvaters*, which he typically describes to Heckenast as 'eine heillose Geschichte',[24] a hopeless story, lacking in wholeness. In four major attempts, Stifter tried to heal the novel, but it was not to be. The futility, the deadening compulsion of art, finds richly comic expression in the story *Nachkommenschaften*. Here, for six pages, Stifter reports the anguish of a painter who finds himself and the world drowning in a flood of landscape pictures. The painter also reflects on the absurdity of writing books. Why tell a tale when all has been told? The only virtue of books, he finds, is that they are at least small, can be torn up and their covers used as saucepan lids. Such passages are the comic counterpart to those points in *Der Nachsommer* where Risach distances himself from his earnest cultural pursuits, refers to them as 'Spielereien' (trifles), and sees them as ultimately pointless: 'Wer wird dann nach zehntausend Jahren noch von Hellenen oder von uns reden? Ganz andere Vorstellungen werden kommen, die Menschen werden ganz andere Worte haben' (*N*, 457) (In ten thousand years, who will still talk of the ancient Greeks or of us? Totally different ideas will come along, human beings will have totally different words).

Here we come to the third aspect of Stifter's mental biography: that his sense of futility is anchored in a metaphysical questioning which at times comes astonishingly close to that of a Schopenhauer or a Büchner. There is the notion, anticipating Darwin, that the world, the universe, may not be a divinely underwritten and sustained creation, but simply a self-sufficient mechanism, revolving in eternal cycles of destruction and recreation. This vision is most acutely expressed in the essay *Ein Gang durch die Katakomben*, where Stifter reflects on the horror of mass decay. The experience of death under the paving stones of the metropolis does not yield the gentle *memento mori* as vouchsafed by a village churchyard. Instead, there is stark horror in the brutal, anonymous destruction. Indeed, the conjoining of the anonymity of the metropolis and of death prefigures Rilke's Malte Laurids Brigge in Paris. Stifter writes:

Mir war, als sei ich in ein fabelhaftes Gebiet des Todes geraten, in ein Gebiet, so ganz anders, als wir es im Leben der Menschen erfahren, ein Gebiet, wo alles gewaltsam zernichtet wird, was wir im Leben mit Scheu und Ehrfurcht zu betrachten gewohnt sind – wo das Höchste und Heiligste dieser Erde, die menschliche Gestalt, ein wertlos Ding wird, hingeworfen in das Kehricht, daß es liege, wie ein anderer Unrat. – Ach! welch eine furchtbare, eine ungeheure Gewalt muß es sein, der wir dahin gegeben sind, daß sie über uns verfüge – und wie riesenhaft, all unser Denken vernichtend, muß Plan und Zweck dieser Gewalt sein, daß vor ihr millionenfach ein Kunstwerk zu Grunde geht, das sie selber mit solcher Liebe baute, und zwar gleichgültig zu Grunde geht, als wäre es eben nichts! – Oder gefällt sich jene Macht darin, im öden Kreislaufe immer dasselbe zu erzeugen, und zu zerstören? – es wäre gräßlich absurd! (*M*, 312)

(It seemed to me that I had entered some fabled region of death, a region utterly different from the way we experience death in the life of man, a region where everything that we in life are accustomed to regard with awe and reverence is brutally destroyed – where the highest and holiest thing on this earth, the human form, becomes a worthless object, flung into the garbage and left to lie like another piece of refuse. Ah, what a terrible and enormous power it must be to which we are totally subjected and which dictates to us – and how immense, destructive of all our thinking, must be the plan and purpose of this power before which a work of art which it has made with such love is destroyed in its millions, is indifferently destroyed as though it were nothing! Or does that power take pleasure in creating and destroying always the same life in a barren cycle? – it would be appallingly absurd!)

But shattered by the Unreason of mass death and a mindless, ever regenerative nature, Stifter takes a desperate, last minute leap into meaning: 'Mitten im Reich der üppigsten Zerstörung durchflog mich ein Funke der innigsten Unsterblichkeitsüberzeugung' (*M*, 313) (In the midst of this realm of abundant destruction the spark of an intense conviction of immortality shot through my being).

At first sight, *Ein Gang durch die Katakomben* strikes one as a direct nineteenth-century reworking of Baroque thought: the intense experience of transience, *vanitas mundi*, serves to highlight the one and only reality of Christian transcendence. This much emerges from the essay's initial polemic against the prevailing climate of religious indifference and the stated aim that the reader may be encouraged 'über Gott, über Weltgeschichte, Ewigkeit, Vergeltung usw. nachzudenken, und vielleicht ein anderer zu werden' (*M*, 304) (to think about God and world history, eternity, retribution etc., and perhaps become a different person). But, on reflection, the text confronts us with a considerable problem of interpretation, a difficulty which we encounter repeatedly in Stifter's major works: Is this 'conviction of immortality' absolutely anchored in the reason of Christian faith? Or are we to interpret the above passage, and the essay as a whole, much more along the lines of Schopenhauer's *Die Welt als Wille und Vorstellung*, above all of the chapter 'Über den Tod und sein Verhältniß zur Unzerstörbarkeit unsers Wesens an sich' (On Death and its Relationship in the Indestructibility of our Being as such). Here, Schopenhauer defines death as 'die große Zurechtweisung' – the profound reminder to heed, not Christian teaching of the Beyond, but the 'große Unsterblichkeitslehre der Natur'[25] (the great doctrine of natural immortality): man can attain immortality by transcending selfhood and submerging himself in the general, the eternal cycle of Life, the Will itself. At one point Schopenhauer argues that 'die Individualität der meisten Menschen eine so elende und nichtswürdige ist, daß sie wahrlich nichts daran verlieren, und daß was an ihnen noch einigen Werth haben mag, das allgemein Menschliche ist'[26] (the individuality of most people is so wretched and worthless that they in truth will lose little by forfeiting it, for if anything about them has any value, it is their human generality). As regards both the vocabulary and the central notions, the similarities between Schopenhauer and Stifter are indeed striking: it is in the preface to *Bunte Steine* (Coloured Stones, 1853) that Stifter stresses the general, rejects the particular, individual, and demands that we focus on the sustaining powers of the natural and the moral law – 'das welterhaltende', 'das menschenerhaltende'. Of course, Stifter argues largely in terms of classical humanism, with all its Christian undertones; but nevertheless, the proximity to Schopenhauer deserves our attention, particularly as the analysis of individual works will cause us to return to these issues. Many of the major texts seem to hang in the balance between transience as understood within the Judaeo-Christian tradition and that transience which, according to Schopenhauer, points precisely to 'zeitliche Unsterblichkeit' (temporal immortality). In other words, these texts tend to view the lot of man and his world as does the Psalmist who laments the withering of the grass: but at the same time, by stressing the ultimate continuity of nature, they admonish us as does Schopenhauer when he writes: 'Erkenne doch dein eigenes Wesen...erkenne es wieder in der innern, geheimen, treibenden Kraft des Baumes, welche, stets *eine* und die selbe in allen Generationen von Blättern, unberührt bleibt vom Entstehn und Vergehn'[27] (Know your own being...recognize it in the secret, inward, thrusting force of the tree which, in all generations of leaves, is one and the same force, unaffected by the waxing and the waning). The following example may serve to anticipate the interpretative problems which abound in Stifter's creative work. The closing lines of the story *Der Hagestolz* fully acknowledge the futility of all life – 'wie jedes Irdische erlischt – und...in dem Ozean der Tage endlich alles, alles untergeht, selbst das Größte und Freudigste' (*S*, 910) (as all earthly things fade – and...in the ocean of days finally everything, everything is swallowed up, even the greatest and most joyous of things). Yet the bachelor is condemned for his treachery of foresight, that is, for not entering life at all:

17

Aber er ist...ausgetilgt, weil sein Dasein kein Bild geprägt hat, seine Sprossen nicht mit hinunter gehen in dem Strome der Zeit...So geht er eher unter, weil an ihm schon alles im Sinken begriffen ist, während er noch atmet und während er noch lebt. (*S*, 910)

(But he is eradicated because his existence has left no image, no scions of his join those who are borne down the mighty river of time...He will go under more swiftly because everything about him is sinking even as he lives and draws breath.)

If, in conclusion, we take all these tensions into account – Stifter's struggle to reconcile passion and morality, to uphold, in the face of a problematic reality, Reason as inherent in both nature and history, to worship that double deity of Religion and Art despite latently persistent doubts – then we may view his suicide as the toll which these long endured stresses and strains exacted. We must be careful not to invoke the fact of his suicide as proof that the basis of his whole life was melancholy and despair – he was after all desperately ill and in great pain. But equally, it is surely difficult to insulate his life from the reverberations of its catastrophic close. It is in this sense that we would read the lines which he wrote to Heckenast in 1865:

Ich habe zu manchen Zeiten zu Gott das heißeste Gebet getan, er möge mich nicht wahnsinnig werden lassen, oder daß ich mir in Verwirrung das Leben nehme (wie es öfter geschieht).[28]

(Many times I have uttered the most heartfelt prayer to God that He will not let me go mad or take my life in a moment of disorientation – as can so often happen.)

2 · STIFTER CRITICISM

Ausgerüstet mit einem Schatze moderner Kenntnisse, namentlich naturwissenschaftlicher Art, begabt mit einem ungewöhnlich ruhigen Forscherblick und einem glücklichen Kombinationstalent, greift der Verfasser mit einer Hand in das Menschenleben, mit der andern in das ihn umgebende Schaffen der Natur und bringt beides in eine glühende Vermischung, in die die Seele des Lesers mit Erquickung sich taucht.

(*Telegraph für Deutschland*, 1844)

(Endowed with a wealth of modern knowledge – specifically of a scientific kind – blessed with an unusually dispassionate capacity for objective observation and a fortunate talent for combination and synthesis, the author digs deep with one hand into human life, and with the other into the activity of nature all around him, and brings both into an incandescent fusion in which the soul of the reader plunges with refreshment and delight.)

The processes and appearances of external nature occupy so prominent a place in these tales that they might almost be described as 'landscapes with figures'.

(*Westminster Review*, 1853)

Wer sich darüber unterrichten will, wie man seine Privatwohnung, seine Bibliotheken, seine Gärten, seine Werkstätten usw. ebenso geschmackvoll als zweckmäßig ausstatten kann, findet [in dem *Nachsommer*] die reichhaltigsten Notizen. Die Poesie des Luxus ist selten so anschaulich und einsichtsvoll dargestellt worden.

(Julian Schmidt, *Die Grenzboten*, 1858)

(Whoever wants to inform himself as to how one can equip one's home, one's libraries, gardens, workshops etc. both tastefully and functionally will find abundant hints [in *Indian Summer*]. The poetry of luxury has seldom been so vividly and perceptively portrayed.)

Despite the fact that there is no shortage of secondary literature on Stifter – indeed, the last twenty years or so have seen a boom in criticism devoted to him – the overall placing of his art remains uncertain.[1]

If we begin by commenting on the vagaries of Stifter criticism, this is because the ebb and flow of his fortunes in the literary market place tells us something both about Stifter's creative achievement and about the currents of German intellectual and cultural history from the mid-nineteenth century on.

Moriz Enzinger's superb compilation[2] of critical reactions to Stifter during his lifetime enables us to chart the responses of contemporary readers. The early stories, which were written in the 1840s and appeared in various almanachs before they were collected in the volumes entitled simply *Studien*, enjoyed very considerable critical acclaim. Stifter was not uncommonly hailed as the propounder of eighteenth-century humanist values, of *Vernunft* and *Sittlichkeit*. In 1846 the poet Eichendorff praised the essential wholeness of the *Studien:* 'nicht eine Spur von moderner Zerrissenheit, von selbstgefälliger Frivolität oder moralisch experimentierender Selbstquälerei ist in dieser gesunden Poesie'[3] (there is not a trace of modern dislocations, of self-satisfied frivolity or of the self-torture of moral experimentation in this healthy prose). Yet by the early 1850s the picture begins to change. Hebbel, in his notorious onslaughts on Stifter, accuses him of myopia and triviality. But his is by no means the only dissenting voice. Where previously Stifter's gift for objective, almost scientific, observation had been welcomed, increasingly his work was criticized for an excessive reliance on set pieces of exhaustive, static description, and the later prose was by and large rejected as ponderous and mannered. Certainly, it cannot be denied that from *Bunte Steine* on, Stifter's work became increasingly stylized and he sought to make his art function as an intact aesthetic construct which would provide a counterweight to contemporary dislocations. The charge levelled at Stifter that he was anachronistic, *unzeitgemäß*, was not, after all, imperceptive.

While the nineteenth-century evaluation of Stifter was anything but unanimous, there was nevertheless a measure of agreement on the import (intended or otherwise) of his art. The integrity of his fiction (in moral and aesthetic terms) was never called into question. He was seen as the defender of the values of order, decency, the family, the organic community, peace and quiet. He was felt to be, as it were, a moral arbiter, a writer whose art was informed by a consistent vision of man's true humanity. The problem for us today is that, viewed under this aspect, Stifter seems an irredeemably provincial writer – a maker of lofty, sublimely intentioned *Heimatliteratur*. One could, of course, quote passages from the letters which would endorse this image:

Wenn meine Bücher mit ihren Mängeln, die ich nur zu tief fühle, doch so reine hohe und begabte Menschen zu rühren vermögen, so muß etwas Edleres und Höheres in ihnen sein, das menschlich und erhebend fortwirkt, und das ist der einzige und höchste Lohn, den ich anspreche.[4]

(If my books with all their faults which I feel only too keenly are yet able to move such pure, lofty and gifted people, then there must be some grain of nobility and sublimity in them which can continue to have a humane and uplifting effect: and that is the only – and it is the highest – reward which I could ever claim.)

Those of Stifter's contemporaries who were hostile to him dissented little in terms of the overall understanding of his work: they disagreed in so far as its evaluation was concerned.

In the closing decades of the nineteenth century a more complex image of Stifter's work and creative personality emerges. It is formed initially by Nietzsche's enthusiasm for Stifter. At first sight it would seem an unlikely meeting of minds: but then, perhaps the author of the *Unzeitgemäße Betrachtungen* (Untimely Meditations) was particularly attuned to the *unzeitgemäß* impulses of Stifter's art. It must, of course, be admitted that we know very little of what Nietzsche thought of Stifter: we only have scattered remarks to go on. But we can hazard a number of conjectures.[5] Nietzsche was enthusiastic about Stifter because of what he perceived as the embattled integrity of his art, its uncompromising transcendence of the tangle and turmoil of human passion, its willed calm and repose beyond heartbreak and weariness. Nietzsche was drawn to Stifter because in his art Stifter over and over again rejects the oddity, the man who stands apart from the ceaseless continuity of the living process. If Stifter's art can be seen as an onslaught on the aberrations of the individual heart, on the foolishness and inadequacy of those who cannot submerge their own longings and desires in the necessary service of being, then perhaps we can understand why Nietzsche felt him to be a kindred spirit. Much of this is implicit in Ernst Bertram's work on Stifter. Bertram was, of course, very much a disciple of Nietzsche's. And in his book on Nietzsche, Bertram devotes a whole chapter to the philosopher's enthusiasm for *Der Nachsommer*, stressing the novel's autumnal melancholy, its sadness at human fulfilment forfeited beyond recall, its willed, utopian character, its affirmation in spite of the odds.[6] Bertram also wrote a book on Stifter which made much of the tension in the man and his art: the tension between a volcanic temperament and an affirmation of order, orderliness.[7] And in an article written in the 1920s, Bertram comments on Nietzsche's reading of Stifter's letters, suggesting that Nietzsche esteemed Stifter's fierce resistance to his times, to their banality and meretriciousness.[8]

Twentieth-century criticism equally perceives stress and difficulty as vibrating presences behind the Stifterian serenity of self-deprecation and self-abnegation. One thinks of a number of biographies or psychologically and biographically based literary analyses – of, for example, Erik Lunding's famous book which takes an existentialist view of Stifter,[9] insisting on the titanic drama of being that the man's life and art enshrines, a drama compounded of will, *Angst*, unbearable loneliness. The virtue of the biographical inquiry is that it has called into question the image of Stifter as the high-minded pedagogue, the man of undifferentiated calm and self-possession. And much of this perception of conflict has produced fruitful studies of his work in which the smug, monolithic quality of the *Heimatdichter* is undermined by the perception of dark forces. The argument has been cogently

22

advanced by Fischer, Kaiser, Klatt, Muschg, Reddick, Roedl.[10] Such critics have important insights to offer, and twentieth-century Stifter scholarship would be unthinkable without them. One should mention, as a footnote to this particular strand of Stifter criticism, that there is one voice from the nineteenth century that prefigures the post-Nietzschean view. In the *Allgemeine Theaterzeitung* for 1844, J. Märzroth wrote the following of *Der Hagestolz*: 'Wie die meisten aus Stifters Feder entwickelt diese Novelle ein gewisses wohltuendes Still-eben, aber nur scheinbar; denn unter all diesen zahllosen Blumen und Schmetterlingen dringt oft gewaltig das Rauschen menschlicher Leidenschaft, das Hämmern menschlichen Kummers hervor'[11] (as with most of the *Novellen* from Stifter's pen, this story spreads before us a particular and reassuring still life – but only apparently so: for amongst all these innumerable flowers and butterflies the roar of human passion, the hammering of human grief often forces its way through). To such intimations of the tension at the heart of Stifterian orderliness we are greatly indebted: at this stage we would simply wish to point out (in answer particularly to the Freudian de-stabilizers of Stifter's art) that, while tension can, of course, produce structural cracks and fissures, it may also serve to hold an edifice together.

Hitherto we have been discussing contradictory, but helpful responses to Stifter. One should also mention the less legitimate ones. From the late 1920s on we have a nationalistic, indeed explicitly Nazi, Stifter. J. W. Storck has shown how the conservative ideologists of the time could welcome *Witiko* (1867) as enshrining the 'deutsch-böhmisch' basis of the Imperial Dream.[12] And Nadler and Kühn claimed Stifter as a spiritual leader of the Germanic nation, as a writer who upheld the values of nature, soil, *Heimat*, and family, or, as Kühn puts it, 'das blutmäßig Reine, bodenständig Echte'[13] (the racially pure, the rootedly authentic). In one sense, of course, this is a politicized version of the *Heimatdichter* image. But it is also the politicized heir to the Nietzsche/Bertram view

of Stifter: in the titanism with which he confronts the dae-
monic Stifter is seen to prefigure the will and the ideology of
spiritual strenuousness of the German nation in the 1930s.
These are appalling distortions. But to condemn the aberrations
of the 1930s may impute a false clarity and stability to our
present vantage point. In fact, we still seem remarkably
uncertain as to what to make of Stifter.

Some well-nigh contemporary examples will serve to suggest that the history of Stifter criticism is still a long way
from achieving a point of consensus. Arno Schmidt has denounced the inhumanity of Stifter; the manic austerity of his
style and theme.[14] But he has *also* praised Stifter for precisely
that artistic integrity which militates against cheap excitement,
detective-story sensationalism in literature.[15] And in this –
admittedly volatile – response to Stifter as one of the great
bourgeois classics, Schmidt is by no means alone. Other modern
writers have voiced their approval, even indebtedness. Handke
has praised Stifter's purity, the extent to which his art, as it
were, makes no concessions: it is uncompromisingly what it is,
exhaustive, exhausting of course, but simply there in hermetic
splendour. Similar approval has been expressed by Thomas
Bernhard.[16]

If we, then, look back over the history of Stifter criticism,
it would seem that

(a) Stifter is either felt to be a didactic writer, one who
teaches and edifies – and this can either be welcomed (Rehm,
Staiger)[17] or denounced as a monstrous piece of bourgeois self-
stylization (Glaser);[18]

(b) or Stifter is hailed as the creator of fictional texts which
display an almost unapproachable (and unassailable) artistic
integrity, a utopian pitting of style and structure against the
tangle and banality of common experience (Hermann Bahr,
Curt Hohoff);[19]

(c) or Stifter is felt to be neither the bourgeois pedagogue
nor the high priest of *l'art pour l'art*: rather, the deepest truth
of his art resides in the fact that the art he produces is

essentially a house of cards interesting by virtue of the fissures and tension that threatens to tear it asunder (i.e. his art is interesting because it consists of the emblems of a neurotic mind).[20]

We are, in other words, still left with the problem of what can and should be claimed for this extraordinary, austere, yet curiously eloquent oeuvre.

In this study we want to make a case for Stifter's art by focusing on formal, stylistic, narrative aspects of his prose. Rudolf Wildbolz has spoken[21] of a strange discrepancy in Stifter's fiction between an explicit, almost didactic, will towards the transcendence of subjectivism on the one hand and on the other the fact that, stylistically and thematically, the subjectivism refuses to be banished. Wildbolz is right to highlight Stifter's artistic irresolution, in our view: but on the face of it, such irresolution would seem to be the recipe for artistic failure. To this issue we will return later. Certainly one has to beware of that simple modern orthodoxy which equates the discovery of ambiguity with the proof of literary quality. Yet equally there can be no doubt that, for modern readers, the fascination of Stifter's prose is inseparable from that sense of strain and paradox to which Thomas Mann drew attention in a famous passage from the *Entstehung des Doktor Faustus* (Genesis of Doctor Faustus):

Man hat oft den Gegensatz hervorgekehrt zwischen Stifters blutig-selbstmörderischem Ende und der edlen Sanftmut seines Dichtertums. Seltener ist beobachtet worden, daß hinter der stillen, innigen Genauigkeit gerade seiner Naturbetrachtung eine Neigung zum Exzessiven, Elementar-Katastrophalen, Pathologischen wirksam ist... Stifter ist einer der merkwürdigsten, hintergründigsten, heimlich kühnsten und wunderlich packendsten Erzähler der Weltliteratur, kritisch viel zu wenig ergründet.[22]

(The contrast has often been highlighted between Stifter's bloody, suicidal end and the gentle nobility of his creative writing. But it has been less frequently noticed that behind the quiet, heartfelt accuracy of his natural descriptions especially there is at work a predilection for the excessive, elemental, catastrophic, pathological... Stifter is one

25

of the most remarkable, profound, secretly bold and strangely exciting story-tellers in world literature: one who has received too little critical analysis.)

This is a wonderfully suggestive observation. But, in our view, the most appropriate way of explicating and building on Thomas Mann's comment is to eschew biographical decoding – and to insist on those stylistic and structural features of Stifter's art which account for both the 'secrecy' and the 'boldness'.

3 · THEME AND STRUCTURE

Stifter schreibt weder im Sinne eines 'poetischen' Realismus – dazu fehlt ihm die 'Gemütlichkeit' – noch eines 'kritischen' noch eines Realismus des Tatsächlichen – den verachtet er. Er geht – mit einem Begriffspaar Ernst Blochs ausgedrückt – nicht auf das 'empirisch Tatsächliche', sondern auf das 'utopisch Tatsächliche' aus: seine gegenständliche Darstellungskraft steht im Dienst eines Realismus des Möglichen.

(Wilhelm Dehn, 1969)

(Stifter's writings belong neither to 'poetic' realism – he lacks the 'cosiness' for that – nor to a 'critical' nor to a factual realism – the latter he despises. He pursues – to borrow terms from Ernst Bloch – not 'empirical actuality' but 'utopian actuality': his power of objective description is placed in the service of a realism of the possible.)

Der 'Realismus' seines Erzählens aber ist die konkrete Gestalt jener Haltung zur Wirklichkeit und ihrer Problematik: *Anerkennung* der Eigengesetzlichkeit der Natur und zugleich *Beglaubigung* eines Menschenbildes, das seine geschichtliche Verbindlichkeit zu verlieren beginnt.

(Hans Dietrich Irmscher, 1971)

(The 'realism' of his narrative art is the concrete expression of [his] attitude towards reality – and of its problematic: *recognition* of the fact that nature follows her own laws, and at the same time the *validation* of a view of man which is beginning to lose its historical cogency.)

Stifters eigentliche schriftstellerische Entdeckung...ist nicht die Kunst der Naturbeschreibung, sondern die Poesie des Allgemeinen, von der jene lebt.

(Martin Selge, 1976)

(Stifter's essential creative discovery is not the art of nature description, but that poetry of the general from which such description derives its life.)

Looking back on his life, Stifter writes in 1867 to Leo Tepe that even as a child he was obsessed by the desire to learn about 'den Grund aller Dinge, die uns umgaben'[1] (the basis of all things which surrounded us). Indeed, this quest is central to his discursive and creative writings: time and again, his texts revolve around the question of what constitutes and determines the elements, both human and non-human, that make up the world. Such expressions as 'ergründen', 'erforschen' (explore), 'Wesenheit' (essence), 'Eigenheit' (particularity) are strikingly recurrent throughout his work. Thus the above quotation touches on the very core of Stifter's being as thinker and writer. But it is important that we note how indeterminate the actual vocabulary of this phrase (and of many similar examples) is. Is 'Grund' to be understood in a quasi-scientific sense as explicable basis or is it rather a philosophical category to do with 'Grund' as the principle of sufficient reason? Does 'Dinge' also include human beings? And what is the specific gravity of 'umgeben'? Is it mere contingency, or does it also suggest a firm framework, a solid housing of individuated man? The answer surely is that we must contend with the multivalency of this terminology: as we shall see, many Stifter texts enact precisely the uncertainties, if not antinomies, inherent in this one brief phrase.

True, Stifter is very much embedded in the values of the Catholic, Baroque tradition of Austria and the classical legacy of the eighteenth century, and thus perceives nature as a divine agency. Hence the scientific inquiry into the human and non-human spheres of nature largely coincides with a philosophical quest, indeed with an act of Christian worship – in contrast to his contemporary Darwin. To discover the laws of material processes, of physical 'Grund', is to discover step by step the divine design, the *Ordo*, the metaphysical 'Grund' of supreme reason.

Stifter frequently speaks of the limitations of science. Both the 'Natur– und Menschenforscher' (natural and human scientist) may come to understand a good deal, but inevitably there comes the point where scientific inquiry must yield to a sense of wonder and worship: 'Nur Weniges...ist unser Eigentum, das andre ruht in Gott'[2] (only a small part...is ours, the rest is with God). Similarly, on the opening page of *Brigitta* from which we have already quoted, Stifter writes:

Die Seelenkunde hat manches beleuchtet und erklärt, aber vieles ist ihr dunkel und in großer Entfernung geblieben. Wir glauben daher, daß es nicht zu viel ist, wenn wir sagen, es sei für uns noch ein heiterer unermeßlicher Abgrund, in dem Gott und die Geister wandeln. (*S*, 735)

(The science of the soul has illuminated and explored many things, but much has remained obscure and beyond its grasp. We do not believe that it is going too far if we say that all this is a serene unfathomable abyss to us, in which God and spirits walk.)

Such passages make it clear that the gaps in man's cognitive capacity do not call into question the notion of an ultimately meaningful order; on the contrary, the gaps point beyond, towards the whole. The darkness in which man may find himself reinforces the faith in ultimate light. The cognitive struggle strengthens the reverence for the divine order as yet shrouded in mystery. Hence we find that typical interplay of scientific and religious vocabulary in Stifter. This tenor is, for example, central to the *Winterbriefe aus Kirchschlag*. Stifter's description of the area is scientific, and contains precise geological and climatic statistics, but the scientific stance is fused with the spiritual sensibility in man: the scale of the universe can, to some degree at least, be scientifically charted, yet ultimately scientific measurement yields to awe:

Und doch kann auf der Spitze des Berges unter der ungeheuren Himmelsglocke, wenn in klaren Winternächten die millionenfache und millionenfache Welt über unsern Häuptern brennt, und wir in Betrachtung unter ihr dahin wandeln, ein Gefühl in unsere Seele kommen, das alle unsere kleinen Leiden und Bekümmernisse majestätisch überhüllt und verstummen macht, und uns eine Größe und Ruhe gibt, der man sich beugt. (*M*, 537f.)

(And yet, when we stand on a mountain peak under the massive dome of the sky, when on clear winter nights, the millionfold and millionfold world burns above our heads and we walk contemplatively below it, a feeling steals into our souls which throws a majestic veil over all our pretty sorrows and anxieties, reducing them to silence, which gives us an exaltation and calm before which we bow the knee.)

Stifter's most celebrated discursive statement on nature and

man is to be found in the *Vorrede* (preface) to *Bunte Steine*.[3]
And it is here that his indebtedness to the eighteenth century,
in particular Herder, is most evident. In many respects, the
Vorrede reads like a shorthand version of Herder's *Ideen zur
Philosophie der Geschichte der Menschheit* (Ideas on the
Philosophy of Human History, 1791) – particularly as regards
the central assertion of a universe of Reason and the principle
of equilibrium. Herder holds for example that although there
do occur moments of profound disturbance, ultimately the
harmony of the whole will prevail:

Alle zerstörenden Kräfte in der Natur müssen den erhaltenden Kräften
mit der Zeitenfolge nicht nur unterliegen, sondern auch selbst zuletzt
zur Ausbildung des Ganzen dienen.[4]

(All the destructive powers in nature must not only yield in the course
of time to the maintaining powers, but must ultimately be subservient
to the development of the whole.)

Similarly, Stifter places the general law, the ever-continuous
processes of nature, above the singular, disruptive event however sensational that may be. He argues that the power which
moves the seasons forward in their cycle is greater than the
power manifested in such freak events as thunderstorms or
earthquakes. And accordingly, challenging the common
evaluative conception of 'groß' and 'klein', he postulates that
we need a sensibility and a vocabulary that can cherish timeless
processes rather than discrete events:

das Wehen der Luft, das Rieseln des Wassers, das Wachsen der
Getreide, das Wogen des Meeres, das Grünen der Erde, das Glänzen
des Himmels, das Schimmern der Gestirne. . .(*BSt*, 8)

(the moving of the air, the rippling of water, the ripening of the corn,
the flowing of the sea, the greening of the earth, the glowing of the
sky, the shimmering of the stars.)

It is no accident that all the substantives here are verbal
nouns: these grammatical structures perfectly reflect pure
continuity with no beginning and no end, the laws of nature
which sustain 'das Ganze und Allgemeine' (the whole and the

general). The scientist plays a vital role here: by the cumulative observation of details he will find significance where it truly resides – in the generality, in the 'welterhaltend' (sustaining) laws and causes of the physical universe. Artists, Stifter argues, are in a sense at a disadvantage: they can 'immer nur das Einzelne darstellen...nie das Allgemeine, denn dies wäre die Schöpfung' (*BSt*, 9) (always only portray the individual,... never the general – for that would be creation itself). But the task of the artist is clear: he must illuminate individual phenomena in such a way that the generating laws are both implied and validated.[5]

Stifter also follows Herder's footsteps in so far as he asserts that the natural laws which sustain the cosmos have their correlative in the moral law which regulates and sustains the world of man.

Übrigens beruhet sowohl die Vernunft als die Billigkeit auf *Ein- und demselben Naturgesetz*...Ein und dasselbe Gesetz also erstrecket sich von der Sonne und von allen Sonnen bis zur kleinsten menschlichen Handlung.[6]

(Both reason and justice rest on *one and the same natural law*...One and the same law extends therefore from the sun and from all suns to the most modest human action.)

Similarly, Stifter argues in the *Vorrede*: 'So wie es in der äußeren Natur ist, so ist es auch in der inneren' (*BSt*, 9) (as it is in external nature, so it is with inner nature). Human greatness is to be found not in exceptional deeds, not in unique feelings and actions, but rather in those modest, everyday activities and values that serve the generality of mankind. The human scientist ('der Menschenforscher') will perceive and uphold 'nur dieses Gesetz allein, weil es das einzig Allgemeine, das einzig Erhaltende und nie Endende ist' (*BSt*, 11) (only this law because it alone is the generality, it alone is all-preserving and unending). Human greatness resides, then, in affirming the continuity of human life, in selfless service to the family and the community. In this sense, Stifter's famous 'sanftes Gesetz' (gentle law) is a condensed version of Herder's *Ideen*, Book 15, with its central concept of *Humanität*.

There is no doubt that Stifter's creative work reflects the legacy of the eighteenth century both thematically and structurally. The notion of a sustained and sustaining equilibrium finds expression, for example, in the symmetry of the plot line, in that typical *Rundgang* (circular) movement from order into threat and back into order, as we find it in *Granit* or *Bergkristall*. It is no accident that Stifter is fond of the *Rahmenerzählung* or frame narration as an artistic device: many Stifter texts deal with profoundly disturbing, even catastrophic, occurrences, but precisely because they are embedded in a circular structure, be that thematically or narratively,[7] these disruptive moments point beyond themselves toward ultimate continuity. Negativity is made to intimate positivity. There is a revealing parallel to be found in Stifter's essay *Die Sonnenfinsternis am 8. Juli 1842*. For Stifter, the eclipse highlights the beauty and significance of those fundamental, but inconspicuous, facts which man all too easily takes for granted, namely that the earth and the life that it sustains need light in order to exist. For one brief moment, when the moon obliterates the sun, it is as though the everyday laws of the world's operation are suspended, and Stifter comments:

Warum, da doch alle Naturgesetze Wunder und Geschöpfe Gottes sind, merken wir sein Dasein in ihnen weniger, als wenn einmal eine plötzliche Änderung, gleichsam eine Störung derselben geschieht? (*M*, 511)

(Why, given that all laws of nature are miracles, are God's creation, are we less able to perceive His existence in them than when a sudden change – as it were, a disturbance of their working – occurs?)

In so far as Stifter, following the eighteenth-century tradition, equates 'Klarheit des Lichtes' with 'Klarheit der Seele' (*M*, 520) ('clarity of light' with 'clarity of soul'), we may argue that many of his works enact eclipses in order to vindicate the light. The reader is made to experience dark moments, but it is precisely in these dark moments that, like the plant, the mind will struggle to 'irgend wo durch eine Ritze oder ein Loch hinaus in das freudige Licht zu gelangen' (*M*, 520) (find a path somewhere – through a gap or a hole – in order to reach the joyous light).

This dominant aim to celebrate 'das freudige Licht' both as physical and metaphysical principle illuminating this world helps to account for the sheer weight which – both quantitatively and qualitatively – Stifter assigns to the narrative illumination of things. Literary criticism has repeatedly focused on this aspect of his art and Michael Böhler may be seen as a representative voice when he says 'es ist keine anthropozentrische Kraft, sondern eine, die die Dinglichkeit ins Zentrum rückt'[8] (it is no anthropocentric force but one which puts the essential nature of things at the centre). As we shall see, Stifter's texts are not as simple as this structural model would imply, but there is no denying that in one sense, for Stifter, man is not the measure of all things, but rather, all things are the measure of man.[9] Things, in this context, are not mere contingent objects: they function as emblems of a supreme, divinely underwritten order of being which is largely denied to passion-torn man, but which nevertheless stands as a constant reminder that the individual should be integrated into the cohesiveness and continuity of being. Here we may recall Rilke's conception of 'Dinge' as ciphers of undivided being, which by indicting us yet point to our potentiality:

> Und alles ist einig, uns zu verschweigen, halb als
> Schande vielleicht und halb als unsägliche Hoffnung.[10]

> (And everything conspires against us with silence,
> Half as disgrace perhaps and half as unutterable hope.)

The celebratory naming of pure being, of saying the world, as Rilke would put it, lies at the heart of that litanesque style that we associate with Stifter's work. Just as his descriptions prevent us from rushing forward into the distracting experience of action, so the weighty, often repetitive rhythms, rhetorical parallelisms, and tautological sequences force our reading metabolism down and make us experience the semantics of 'Langeweile' – boredom: make us stay as long as possible with the being of things, with the being of the word itself. An essential part of this syndrome is Stifter's fondness for paratactic style, for 'und' clauses, for the constatation of what simultaneously is – without recourse to complex modalities of subordination whereby one fact is dependent upon another. Particularly noteworthy in this context is what J. P. Stern has defined as Stifter's 'ontic' mode, a predilection for the verb 'to be' used not in a predicative way, but on its own, as a full verb that records existence.[11]

It is such thematic and structural properties which in their interplay reflect the 'Grund aller Dinge' as both a physical and metaphysical category and which suggest that, potentially, man can perceive things, the set of circumstances surrounding individual life, not as random, but as a metaphysically anchored, solid housing. On this level, Stifter's emphasis on the significance of things and man's relationship to them is deeply indebted to Herder's concept of an overall divine cohesion (even the formulations are strikingly similar). Herder writes 'Vernunft heißt der Charakter der Menschheit; denn er vernimmt die Sprache Gottes in der Schöpfung, d.i. er sucht die Regel der Ordnung, nach welcher die Dinge zusammenhängend auf ihr Wesen gegründet sind. Sein innerstes Gesetz ist also Erkenntnis der Existenz und Wahrheit, Zusammenhang der Geschöpfe nach ihren Beziehungen und Eigenschaften'[12] (Reason is the very character of mankind; for man hears the language of God in creation, that is, he seeks the rules, the organization according to which things are coherently grounded in their very essence. Man's innermost law is comprehension of existence and truth, is the coherence of all creatures according to their relationships and qualities). Such echoes are representative of Stifter's general indebtedness to the eighteenth century: time and again, his discursive statements in prefaces or letters invoke the central tenets of classical humanism. One thinks above all of his conception of aesthetics as an adjunct to ethics, of art as being 'neben der Religion das Höchste'[13] (after religion the supreme human activity), 'das Göttliche im Kleide des Reizes'[14] (the divine clothed in a physically appealing garb). He often expressed his faith in the educative function of art, and by implication in the perfectibility of man. The aim of that educative process can perhaps be best summed up in terms of the preface to *Bunte Steine* as the attainment of 'Überblick über ein Größeres' (*BSt*, 12) (overview over a greater whole) that is, a state of being that has transcended subjectivity and gained a perception which sees, beyond the particular and disruptive, the order of ultimate Reason: 'wo durch unmeßbar große Kräfte in der Zeit oder im Raume auf ein gestaltvolles vernunftgemäßes Ganzes zusammen gewirkt wird' (*BSt*, 11) (where, by means of immeasurably great forces in time and in space a shaped, reasonable whole is woven). It is precisely this 'vernunftgemäßes Ganzes' which the thematic and aesthetic organization of Stifter's work seeks to intimate by means of such features as those discussed above.

And yet, in the act of reading, so many Stifter texts tell another story, one that does not convey the sense of man being embedded in a metaphysically underwritten set of circumstances, but, on the contrary, sees man as merely surrounded by contingencies. On this level, the phrase 'Grund aller Dinge, die uns umgaben' signals no more than the sheer givenness of facts, both non-human and human, which do not vouchsafe any inherent meaning.

As regards nature, the most striking example of this perspective is to be found in the opening section of *Abdias* where Stifter reflects:

Es liegt auch wirklich etwas Schauderndes in der gelassenen Unschuld, womit die Naturgesetze wirken, daß uns ist, als lange ein unsichtbarer Arm aus der Wolke und tue vor unseren Augen das Unbegreifliche. Denn heute kommt mit derselben holden Miene Segen und morgen geschieht das Entsetzliche. Und ist beides aus, dann ist die Natur die Unbefangenheit, wie früher. (*S*, 581)

(There is really something terrifying about the calm innocence with which the laws of nature function, such that we believe that an invisible arm reaches out of the cloud and performs before our eyes the inconceivable. For today blessing comes with the same peaceful countenance and tomorrow the dreadful occurs. And when both are over, then nature is as imperturbable as before.)

Here we have a nature concept free from any ideology of Reason, and it is indeed very telling that later in the story, Stifter abandons this notion of 'Unbefangenheit' and suggests that the time will come when man will be able to unravel the workings of natural forces, to perceive 'das Liebesband zwischen diesen Kräften und unserm Leben' (S, 652) (the loving bond between these forces and our life). The contradiction – 'Unbefangenheit' versus 'Liebesband' – strikingly illuminates Stifter's philosophical uncertainty: suspended between Reason and Unreason, he perceives nature on the one hand as a self-sufficient mechanism, radically indifferent to the fate of man, and on the other hand, he maintains the notion that ultimately there is a benevolent causality at work, that there is a meaningful whole. Such tensions are by no means restricted to Stifter's early work. In the last version of *Die Mappe meines Urgroßvaters*, we find the same syndrome at the end of Part I. Here Stifter is very close to Schopenhauer when he reflects on the indifference of fate, the expendability of individual lives and even of nations, the splendour of a totally amoral, ever regenerative nature:

Und wenn ganze Ströme von Völkern dahin gegangen sind, die Unsägliches und Unzähliges getragen haben, so werden wieder neue Ströme kommen, und Unsägliches und Unzähliges tragen...Und wenn du deinem Herzen wehe getan hast, daß es zucket und vergehen will, oder daß es sich ermannt und größer wird, so kümmert sich die Allheit nicht darum, und dränget ihrem Ziele zu, das die Herrlichkeit ist. (M, 203)

(And if whole streams of people have come and gone, who have borne unsayable and innumerable things, so new streams will come and will bear unsayable and innumerable things...And if you have bruised your heart so that it twitches and threatens to collapse – or so that it takes courage and grows stronger, the totality is not concerned, and presses on towards its goal which is splendour.)

But, with that typical inconsistency, the passage ends by postulating that man is responsible for his fate and that there is an overall meaning in so far as some law of cause and effect is at work:

Du aber hättest es vermeiden können, oder kannst es ändern, und die Änderung wird dir vergolten; denn es entsteht nun das Außerordentliche daraus. (*M*, 203)

(But you could have avoided it, or you can change it, and the change will be credited to you: for what now emerges in the process is something remarkable.)

Such tensions in the philosophical fabric of *Die Mappe* suggest that the late Stifter is not as secure as is commonly held by critics,[15] that he still struggles with the problems posed by that phrase 'Grund aller Dinge, die uns umgaben'.

Let us now turn to the man-made 'Dinge', both concrete and abstract, that constitute the immediate world of man. Time and again, these are narratively so organized as to suggest a close parallel with the 'Dinge' of nature's realm, that is, they are presented as a second frame containing and securing individual existence. There is no doubt that Stifter partakes of the *Biedermeier* in so far as the idyllic intention is central to his work. One need only think of his contribution to the *Gartenlaube für Österreich* (1866), in which he reflects on the beauty of the arbour as a concept. He makes the point that, while man often seeks wide, open spaces, he also needs, on frequent occasions, to feel enclosed and sheltered:

So geht er auch wieder sehr gerne in kleine und beengte Gelasse, um mit sich selber allein zu sein, er geht in ein Gebüsch des Waldes oder Gartens, er geht in ein kleines schmales Tal, er geht in sein Kämmerlein ...Und je begrenzter und in sich geschlossener so ein Räumchen ist, um desto lieber sucht man es auf...(*M*, 544)

(So he also likes entering small, enclosed shelters, to be alone with himself, he goes into a forest or garden thicket, he goes into a small, narrow valley, he goes into his chamber...And the narrower and compacter such a room is, the more eagerly does he seek it out...)

Idyll means 'little picture', and clearly the idyllic in Stifter's work is the secularized domestic version of that overriding faith in a philosophical housing, the universe of Reason. And yet, so often and so tellingly, the idyll will not work. As Jens Tismar suggests in his admirable study, the idyll becomes problematic in Stifter's hands.[16] The aspirations in that direction are there – the fondness for the small, encapsulated space, the cave, the valley, the cottage, the box, the drawer within a cabinet, and so on. The idyllic intention is manifest in the seemingly endless layering of protection, of shell upon shell, wall upon wall, frame upon frame. Yet – as in Kafka's *Der Bau* (The Burrow) – the centre remains problematic, not insulated against heartbreak and tragedy. Tismar at one point acutely suggests that the overprotectiveness can be felt in the language, and his analysis of the idyll significantly concludes with Thomas Bernhard, a countryman of Stifter's and a writer who has expressed admiration for Stifter. What they have in common is a particular line in narrative claustrophobia, in exhaustiveness, in bureaucratically monomanic *Akribie*. One might also add the name of another contemporary Austrian writer, Gert Friedrich Jonke, who has created a richly comic version of this 'idyllic' tradition. His *Geometrischer Heimatroman* (1969) explores both thematically and stylistically a totally bureaucratized ruralism, one in which the recurring patterns of agrarian life issue in a veritable plethora of notices, questionnaires, forms. The commingling of the measured and the menacing is something that he shares with Adalbert Stifter.

The syndrome of the disturbed idyll becomes particularly acute if we examine the value and function which Stifter ascribes to man-made objects. These are for him, ideally, emblems of sound being. No one tried harder to give all things that human radiance and loveliness, that 'aura' of which Walter Benjamin spoke when he talked of the intimacy which ownership, collecting, involves.[17] This intention informs for example Stifter's essay *Der Tandelmarkt* from *Wien und die Wiener* where we find the following remark:

Jeder, der da weiß, wie ihm als kleinem Knaben wohl war, wenn etwa die Truhe der Großmutter aufgemacht wurde, und nun ein Haufen alten Zeugs hervorkam...: jeder, der das weiß, wird gerne durch die Gassen dieses Marktes gehen, wo derlei Sachen in Massen aufgehäuft sind. (*M*, 372)

(Anyone who knows how happy he felt as a little boy when, for example, the grandmother's chest was opened and a jumble of old things appeared...anyone who remembers that will gladly go through the alleyways of this market, where such things are piled high.)

And in that same essay Stifter describes the treasures to be found in the ironmonger's stall:

dann sind die Tragherde, Kochöfen, die Zangen, Hauen, Haken, Klammern, die Schaufeln, Sägen, Bohrer, die Feilböcke, all das kleinere Volk der Lichtputzen, Scheren, Beschläge, dann sind die Torsos, die Fragmente von einstigen Ganzen, die bloßen Eisenstücke, Aushängeschild, Stiefelsund Krückenbeschläge, und endlich die Sachen, die gar niemand mehr kennt. (*M*, 375)

(then there are the portable stoves, ranges, the tongs, axes, hooks, clips, the spades, saws, drills, filing clamps, all the little bits and pieces for lamp cleaning, scissors, metal plates, then there are the torsos, the fragments of what were once entireties, iron pieces, display signs, metal tips for boots and sticks, and finally the things that are beyond recognition.)

And yet, such passages also suggest the inherent precariousness of the idyllic undertaking: if they essentially aim to convey the sense of still-life in praise of life's plenitude, they are also in danger of collapsing and enacting the stark semantics of the term, which is so overtly there in the French: *nature morte*. The problem can perhaps be best highlighted by reference to *Die Mappe*. Early on we discover that the narrative impetus behind the text is the discovery of a 'Mappe', a portfolio of notes, jottings from a life that is now over and done with. This portfolio is the palpable distillate of a man's experience and, lest we be disposed to dismiss it as bits and pieces, we are told that there is an inherent poetry, a distinction and value to all this humble bric-à-brac. We are to be offered 'Dichtung des Plunders'[18] (poetry of clutter). And it is this poetry of clutter which informs the opening sections where Stifter describes the trunk that harbours the relics from the past. These pages embody the celebratory still-life which Heinrich Böll, who admires Stifter and sees in him a potential 'Vater eines neuen humanen Realismus' (father of a new humane realism), invokes in his essay 'Großeltern gesucht' (Grandparents wanted). Here, he nostalgically pits the poetry of the 'Rumpelkammer' (lumber room) against the prose of modern clean living:

Da standen Schränke mit abgebrochenen Beinen, zerbrochene Spiegel, lagen in Schachteln abgelegene Hüte, von Motten zerfressene Kleider, eine alte Geige, Zeitschriften; Kinderwagen standen da, Kisten und Koffer. Es gibt keine Rumpelkammer mehr: in unseren Wohnungen ist kein Raum dafür frei.[19]

(There were cupboards with broken legs, shattered mirrors, discarded hats lay in boxes, moth-eaten clothes, an old violin, magazines; prams stood around, boxes and trunks. There is no such thing as a lumber room any more: in our flats no room is available for such things.)

But this poetry of clutter is balanced on a knife edge, for, without an inherent meaning to them, such objects are a dead and deadening presence. Once our assent to the sacramentalism of things is disturbed, then the clutter threatens to congeal into junk, the celebratory impetus threatens to collapse and move alarmingly close to the unregenerate world of Flaubert's *Bouvard et Pécuchet*. One man's collection may be another man's rubbish; the collected and collecting life may be the sterile life, as Grillparzer with his key psychological and moral concept of 'Sammlung' knew all too well. The idyllic, protected world may turn into the emblem of reification. If we look at Stifter's work as a whole, we must conclude that he never thematized this knife edge in any overt sense. Critics may have done it for him – in the case of *Turmalin* for example where the solidly furnished rooms of the 'Rentherr' and his wife have been interpreted negatively, as ciphers of a sterile life, although the text itself does not invoke any moral criteria and the first version explicitly praises the couple's ordered life which was then so irresponsibly ruined by the actor Dall. We do, however, find a considerable number of stylistic phenomena which suggest a latent antimony, a sense of unease on the part of Stifter within his self-imposed ethos of solid order. Privately, he formulates his ambivalent feelings in a letter to Karl Donberger, who had offered to buy an antique table on his behalf. There is a strange interplay of genuine need and a critical distance which evaluates the collecting of *objets d'art* as a questionable preoccupation, and sees beautiful things as mere fetishes of an unfulfilled life:

Es ist fast ein lächerlicher Gedanke, daß ein ernsthafter deutscher Autor und Schulrat und ein ernsthafter deutscher Doktor der Medizin sich um ein dem Zerfalle entgegen gehendes deutsches Geräte im Ernste Mühe geben..., aber es tut nichts, ich mache meiner Frau das Vergnügen...Es ist einmal so. Sie hat keine Kinder und sonst keine Unterhaltung. Da schleppt sie mir auch die ältesten abenteuerlichsten verschollensten und schiefmäuligsten Porzellanschalen zusammen, von denen sie den hundertjährigen Staub abwaschen muß, daß dann eine altmodische gespreizte Blume zum Vorscheine kommt. Nach unserem Tode wird bei unserer Lizitation ein schreckliches Gelächter sein.[20]

(It is a well-nigh laughable thought that a serious German author and School Inspector and a serious German doctor of medicine are, in all seriousness, concerned with a German household object which is heading for complete decay...but it does not matter, I will do my wife this favour...It is the way things are. She has no children and no other amusements. She lumbers me with the oldest, queerest, most old-fashioned and repulsive china dishes which she washes free of their hundred-year-old dust in order that a dated, stilted flower appears. After our death, when our will is opened, there will be a burst of terrible laughter.)

In the creative work, this ambivalence becomes a stylistic issue, and it expresses itself most typically in a dual perspective. To take one striking example: in *Der Hochwald*, the narrator invites the reader to recreate in his mind the seventeenth-

century setting, the castle of the Wittinghauser. We are asked
to imagine the various rooms: 'und ziere sie mit all dem lieben
Hausrat und Flitter der Wohnlichkeit' (S, 188) (and adorn
them with all the beloved homely objects and trappings of
domesticity). We note the tension here; beloved objects versus
mere trappings of domesticity, and this tension haunts a great
many Stifter texts. Time and time again he will lovingly and
painstakingly create *intérieurs*, scenes which spell stability, yet
this detailed, weighty circumstantiality can erode itself: the
'lieber Hausrat' may emerge as mere 'Flitter'.

The same syndrome applies if we regard 'Dinge' in their
abstract connotations, that is, as those norms and values which
constitute the ethos of 'das sanfte Gesetz'. In this respect, too,
the private Stifter displays a striking ambivalence when he
evaluates his duties as a school inspector. On the one hand,
the endless paperwork is the emblem of a meaningful, morally
responsible life, on the other hand it is but dead weight,
fettering the self. Thus he writes to Heckenast in the letter of
13 May 1854 from which we have already quoted:

wenn ich dann in meine Amtsstube trete, stehen wieder Körbe voll
von jenen Dingen für mich bereitet, die ich mir in das Haupt laden
muß...Ich glaube, daß sich die Dinge an mir versündigen...die
kleinen Dinge schreien drein, ihnen muß von Amtswegen und auf
Befehl der Menschen, die sie für wichtig halten, abgewartet werden,
und das Große ist dahin. Glücklich die Menschen, die diesen Schmerz
nicht kennen! und doch auch unglücklich, sie kennen das Höchste des
Lebens nicht. (M, 726)

(when I step into my office, there are always baskets waiting for me
full of things which I have to load into my head...I think that things
are sinning against me...little things clamour for attention, the
dictates of the job and the insistence of people who regard them as
important, mean that they have to be heeded, and everything that is
great and good is done for. Happy those who do not know this pain!
And yet also unhappy, for they do not know the highest things in life.)

Clearly, in his creative work, it is Stifter's intention to convey,
by means of inconspicuous, regular narration, the inconspicuous
workings of the moral law as it manifests itself in the regular

acts of family loyalty and constancy. Yet, to use the terms of his preface to the *Studien*, 'das Gewirkte', the effect, as opposed to 'das Gewollte', the intention, is not nearly as clear cut. There are many passages where this social morality as sustaining frame, as 'Dinge, die uns umgaben', comes in for implicit, if not explicit, questioning. There is for example the constancy of the village Gschaid in *Bergkristall*, which Stifter, although maintaining a slightly humorous distance, essentially affirms, but then inserts the unsettling sentence: 'Sie sind sehr stetig und es bleibt immer beim alten' (*BSt*, 164) (they are very constant and everything always stays the same). Suddenly, the regular rhythm of this village life takes on a deadening element. The same may be said of *Katzensilber* where the text on the one hand assents to the orderliness of the family's lifestyle, and on the other highlights its sheer monotony. Furthermore, obedience, based on a loving trust in authority, proves to be a far more volatile value than the preface to *Bunte Steine* with its emphasis on familial and communal cohesion, on 'Ordnung und Gestalt' (order and shape), suggests. In *Granit*, Stifter celebrates this sense of obedience, above all in the litanesque exchanges between grandfather and child which function as veritable speech acts of faith. In *Bergkristall*, however, the same device begins to generate speech acts of bad faith as Sanna follows her brother into the snow storm and with each 'Ja, Konrad' (Yes, Konrad) they move closer into potential disaster. In the first version of *Kalkstein*, there is the disturbing moment when the narrator reflects that children brought up to obey parental authority are likely 'etwas zu tun, woraus auch der Tod folgen könnte' (*Urf*, 241) (to do something which could result in death). This one sentence suffices to ruffle the thematic tranquillity of the story in so far as it makes the reader reflect on the priest, who is the exemplar of obedience and whose morally grounded self-discipline bears the imprint of a deadly routine. Even the monumental novel *Der Nachsommer* leaves some room for questioning. For several hundred pages, Heinrich Drendorf essentially enacts obedience by listening to and following his mentor Risach, yet as the chapter 'Rückblick' makes clear, it was precisely obedience to parental authority which led Risach to forfeit the fulfilment of an existential summer. Thus, even this text which is so organized as to speak of a solid life within a solid housing, generates questions about its very premises.

To convey the 'Grund aller Dinge' remains, then, for Stifter an unending, challenging task. He was determined to create texts which would stem the flux of random being and set it in frames of meaning. And yet, with the possible exception of *Witiko*, there are constantly tensions at work which threaten to tear these structures asunder as much as they hold them together. The exhaustive constatation of circumstances, both natural and man-made, clearly strives to create the 'Überblick über ein Größeres' which, in terms of the preface to *Bunte Steine*, is not only the scientific, but also the moral stance of seeing beyond: the particular is to intimate the general, the discrete is to suggest the cohesive. The things which house a specific life are to be seen as ciphers which point to that ultimate housing of Reason. Yet there is always the risk that the particular will not yield the general, that facticity will not yield transcendence. The problem is strikingly formulated in *Der Nachsommer* when Risach elaborates on the term 'Einerlei' (sameness) and ascribes to it two radically different values and functions:

Das gesellschaftliche Leben in den Städten, wenn man es in dem Sinne nimmt, daß man immer mit fremden Personen zusammen ist, bei denen man entweder mit andern zum Besuche ist, oder die mit andern bei uns sind, ist nicht ersprießlich. Es ist das nämliche Einerlei wie das Leben in Orten, die den großen Städten nahe sind. Man sehnt sich ein anderes Einerlei aufzusuchen; denn wohl ist jedes Leben und jede Äußerung einer Gegend ein Einerlei, und es gewährt einen Abschluß, von dem einen Einerlei in ein anderes über zu gehen. Aber es gibt auch ein Einerlei, welches so erhaben ist, daß es als Fülle die ganze Seele ergreift, und als Einfachheit das All umschließt. (*N*, 456f.)

(Social life in the towns, if we understand it to mean that one is constantly together with strange people whom one either visits with other people or who visit us with other people, is not rewarding. It is indistinguishable from that sameness to be found in places which are close to the great cities. One longs to find another kind of sameness; for, of course, every life, every expression of an area is a sameness, and the only cessation it promises is the transition from one sameness to another. But there is also a sameness which is so sublime that, in its abundance, it captures the whole soul and with its simplicity encircles the totality.)

Here, 'Einerlei' is poised on the dividing line between a Schopenhauerian vision of man and world, the drab monotony of existence, and the notion, so dear to German Idealism, of the 'en kai pan', the sublime simplicity of an all-cohesive universe. By analogy, we may argue that Stifter's work is poised precisely on that critical point where the 'Einerlei' of mere facts is to be lifted into that higher 'Einerlei' of Reason. It is an enormous gamble: it may come off – and if it does, then the Stifter register of ritualistic weightiness will speak of plenitude and cohesion. But equally, the task may prove too great, the 'Einerlei' of the here and now may prove too resistant to be redeemed – in which case that same style may strike us as the desperate incessancy of a magic formula that has lost its spellbinding force.

And there is a further problem: the relationship between frame and centre, between the circumstances of this world and the human experiential core. Clearly, it is Stifter's philosophical and artistic aim to bridge that gap. At one point in *Der Nachsommer*, Heinrich reflects that there is only one story worth exploring: 'die Geschichte der Erde, die ahnungsreichste, die reizendste, die es gibt, eine Geschichte, in welcher die der Menschen nur ein Einschiebsel ist' (*N*, 291) (the story of the earth, the one that is most rich in implication, the loveliest story there is, a story in which the story of man is but an intrusion). These words perfectly sum up the essence of Stifter's undertaking: to tell of individuation as an inset story within the massive frame-narration of this earth, to embed human experience in the continuity of non-individuated processes. Yet, as we shall see, this aim can only in exceptional cases be

45

achieved. Most of Stifter's stories chronicle dislocations, fissures between man and the things of this world. The surrounding frame, the detailed descriptive mode may – not redeem, but – highlight the isolation, the strangeness of the centre. If the centre is human need and pain which engages our sympathy and concern, then, however laconic its pathos, it will outweigh all the gradualness that surrounds it. In *Der Waldgänger*, for example, the spare dialogue – a mere few lines – between Georg and Corona is enough to make the whole frame a desert, a compilation of facts, of being and living that is irrelevant, if not inhuman. And the *Novelle* of passion in *Der Nachsommer* opens a gap which no amount of loving cataloguing of plants, cacti, roses, gardening, restoring old furniture, will quite close. To borrow Wolfgang Iser's term, there is a 'Leerstelle', a hiatus in the narrative intimation of Stifter's major creations.[21] Iser uses the term to designate a property of all narrative texts: that the rhetoric is never completely closed, never simply a self-validating intactness. He suggests that a text may set up certain expectations which it only incompletely fulfils, and the point at which the expectations break down may well be decisive for the interpretation of the text. As we shall see, Stifter's work often enacts this 'Leerstelle' in a radical and specific sense: it will invoke, be that explicitly or by stylistic implication, such expectations as are, for example, inherent in the genre of the moral tale, the fairy tale, or the *Bildungsroman*; but at crucial points it will modify and subvert them. It sets out to create solid union of frame and centre, but then produces tensions which threaten to fracture that very will to harmony in which the work is grounded.

The discursive Stifter may ceaselessly advocate that human greatness resides in affirming the continuity of life, in submitting selfhood to the demands of the common good. But Stifter also knows of that capacity for choice which is the measure of man's individuation. If human beings can submerge their individuality in selfless service then this is, precisely, a choice and there may be much wrenching and heartache involved in that choice. No one rendered that struggle with greater compassion and astringency: the conflict between the particular ('das Einzelne') and the general ('das Allgemeine'), between centre and frame, is the very life-blood of his creative work. It generates the strangely haunting tension of Stifter's style. There is, for example, the conflict between the assurance of those weighty, often repetitive cadences, and the laconic pathos, the brutally abrupt constatation of horror and catastrophe. One thinks of the blind Ditha in *Abdias* – 'sie war eine Lüge' (she was a lie); of the death of the Obrist's wife in the *Mappe* – 'sie lag unten zerschmettert' (she lay there broken); of Brigitta who takes 'das aufgequollene schreiende Herz gleichsam in ihre Hand und zerdrückte es' (the swollen, screaming heart, as it were, in her hand and crushed it). The combination of the reassuring and the catastrophic is unique to Stifter. It can produce such unsettling paradoxes as 'überall blühte der Haß sachte auf' (on all sides hatred gently bloomed), 'die Verbindung blieb getrennt' (the relationship remained separated') or 'heiterer Abgrund' (bright abyss). It is such tensions that make his prose so fascinating. In this sense, the English critic who, in the *Athenaeum* for August 1848, reviewed *Abdias*, touched on the very nerve-centre of Stifter's work when, baffled by the antinomies of this story, he coined the phrase 'a highly finished doorway leading into vacant space'.[22]

4 · THE TRAGEDY OF INDIVIDUATION

denn unter all diesen zahllosen Blumen und Schmetterlingen dringt oft gewaltig das Rauschen menschlicher Leidenschaft, das Hämmern menschlichen Kummers hervor.

(Allgemeine Theaterzeitung, 1844)

(for amongst all these innumerable flowers and butterflies the roar of human passion, the hammering of human grief often forces its way through.)

In this chapter we wish to consider a number of stories which suggest that man's individuation is an essentially tragic condition, and yet, which also show a Stifter determined to countermand this central perception. He may, as for example in *Abdias*, weave in discursive passages or stylistic elements which seem to intimate that there is an ultimate meaning even though that insight may be denied to the characters concerned. At other times, Stifter attempts to soften the sting of irremediable tragedy by following the eighteenth-century legacy, in particular Herder's *Ideen*, and asserting that human destiny is not at the mercy of some mysterious force, but that the onus of responsibility rests solely on man. Yet in such stories as *Das alte Siegel* and *Der Waldgänger*, Stifter suggests that precisely the human capacity for choice, for ethical responsibility, can contradict and deform the deepest affective needs of the person. In other words, the faculty of Reason, on which Stifter's image of man and world largely rests, can sometimes prove to be the very source of aberration. This philosophical uncertainty can and does produce moments of narrative irresolution which, by traditional aesthetic standards, may be regarded as artistic blemishes on the text in question. But that uncertainty also makes possible a range of theme and stylistic register that one would be loath to exchange for that artistic perfection which stems from a refusal to take risks. One might recall a comment which Raymond Williams makes about George Eliot.[1] In his analysis of her novels he draws attention to the contradiction that occurs when a particular kind of discursive moralizing clashes with the sympathetic imaginative comprehension of a social world which refuses simply to function as illustrative material for the discursive voice. In these areas of friction, Williams discerns the vital 'creative disturbance'[2] of George Eliot's art, a disturbance that, he insists, is infinitely richer and more challenging than is the seamless competence of Trollope's novels. If we apply Williams's term to Stifter's work, we may argue that, as in the case of George Eliot, the imaginative impulse frequently reaches out to comprehend that which the discursive voice seeks to repudiate. And these moments of disturbance seem a small price to pay for the illumination vouchsafed.

Moreover, in certain stories the narrative friction serves ultimately to sustain a complex argument, with the result that the theme is differentiated and deepened beyond the reach of simple narrative summary or evaluation. Therein resides the particular challenge of Stifter's art, a challenge which, as we hope to show in the concluding chapter, has precisely to do with his historicity – and his modernity.

Der Hochwald begins with a leisurely description of the setting, the Bohemian forests. The narrator gradually focuses on a ruined castle. He then takes the reader back some two hundred years to the time of the Thirty Years War when the castle was inhabited by Wittinghauser and his two daughters, Clarissa and Johanna. The two girls are sent by their father to live in the safety of the forest until all dangers of war have passed. Protected by old Gregor, a close friend of their father, they spend weeks by the forest lake, in a specially built wooden house. To reassure themselves they look every day at their castle through a telescope. One day, Ronald, a young Swede who is in love with Clarissa, seeks them out. Although she is haunted by a sense of unease, she returns his love and they become engaged. Ronald then departs, promising to use his influence so that the Swedish troops will spare Wittinghauser.

Soon after his departure, the telescope reveals the castle to be roofless and burnt out. Finally, the girls return to the ruin and live in one still habitable corner for the rest of their lives. Eventually they learn what has happened: the Swedes laid siege to the castle, and Ronald attempted to negotiate. But Wittinghauser, who recognized him, misunderstood his intentions and hurled a lance at him. A pitched battle ensued: the castle was taken, the father, the brother and Ronald lost their lives. Old Gregor remains in the forest, he destroys the wooden house and eventually nature reclaims the land.

In typical Stifterian manner, the human drama is embedded in and set against the unending presence of nature. This is strikingly reflected in the seven chapter headings: 'Waldburg' (forest castle), 'Waldwanderung' (forest walk), 'Waldhaus' (forest house), 'Waldsee' (forest lake), 'Waldwiese' (forest meadow), 'Waldfels' (forest rock), 'Waldruine' (forest ruin). We note how the second component in these compound nouns registers the ebb and flow of human life: the need for security and home ('Burg'), the urge to move out into experience ('Wanderung'), the return to the domestic impulse ('Haus'), the attempt at the idyll within nature ('See', 'Wiese', 'Fels'), and finally the doomed end to all these aspirations – 'Ruine'. This flux and change stands in sharp contrast to the ceaseless continuity of 'Wald'. The forest functions quite literally as the alpha and omega of the story: the narration begins with a detailed description of the landscape, and to it we return at the end when the forest retreat is destroyed:

Die Ahornen, die Buchen, die Fichten und andere, die auf der Waldwiese standen, hatten zahlreiche Nachkommenschaften und überwuchsen die ganze Stelle, so daß wieder die tiefe jungfräuliche Wildnis entstand, wie sonst, und wie sie noch heute ist. (*S*, 276)

(The maples, beeches, and firs and other trees which stood on the forest meadow had numerous descendants and grew over the whole area so that once again the deep virgin wilderness came into its own as before, and as it still is today.)

Given the sequence of the chapter headings and the circular

narration, there is, then, a sustained aim to create a structure within which the frame, unindividuated nature ('Wald'), holds and embraces the centre, individuated nature, the realm of man. But, in fact, there is a crucial tension between the statement of the aesthetic organization and the actual story told. The gesture of encompassing is deceptive: the centre, human fate, remains starkly isolated. Nature has her unending chain of descendants, but this continuity is denied to the human sphere: the lives of the characters are blighted forever and, in the end, the house of Wittinghauser is extinct. This overall tension informs the thematic and stylistic fabric of the story at almost every turn. Above all, there are two contrasting images and concepts of nature: on the one hand we have Mother Nature, sheltering and supporting man who is the crowning glory of the divinely ordained world; and on the other hand we have nature seen in its radical otherness, as the realm of integral organic matter. Roy Pascal has finely analysed the latter strand:[3] he shows how the narrator perceives the sombre, powerful drama of death and renewal at work in the landscape: –

Es ist eine wilde Lagerung zerrissener Gründe, aus nichts bestehend, als tiefer schwarzer Erde, dem dunklen Totenbette tausendjähriger Vegetation, worauf viele einzelne Granitkugeln liegen, wie bleiche Schädel von ihrer Unterlage sich abhebend, da sie vom Regen bloßgelegt, gewaschen und rund gerieben sind... Keine Spur von Menschenhand, jungfräuliches Schweigen. (S, 184)

(It is the chaotic precipitate of decomposed layers, consisting of nothing but deep black earth, the dark bier of thousand-year-old vegetation on which are to be found many separate granite blocks, standing out from their background like pale skulls, for they have been bared by the rain, washed and rubbed smooth... No trace of the hand of man, virgin silence.)

But this sober, dispassionate tone of almost scientific constatation is not sustained throughout the story. For time and time again we find that nature is anthropomorphized; similes, metaphors, personifications incorporate nature into the realm of human cognition and volition. One thinks of the moment when the two girls ride into the forest:

Clarissas edles Angesicht lag liebreich ruhevoll dem Himmel offen, der zwischen den Ästen festlich wallend sein Blau hereinhängen ließ, und erquicklich seine Luft um ihre lieben sich färbenden Wangen goß; – – wie ein schöner Gedanke Gottes senkte sich gemach die Weite des Waldes in ihre Seele. (205)

(Clarissa's noble face lay in peaceful loveliness open to the sky which allowed its festal blue to billow down between the branches and poured its air soothingly around her lovely, flushing cheeks; like a beautiful thought from God the expanse of the forest gradually descended into her soul).

Everything in this passage suggests a unity between men and nature which the story itself will not enact. The description turns nature into a divine, mythical entity endowed with animate, caring properties which the 'scientific' tenor of the opening pages and of the closing lines of the story do not endorse.

The conceptual and hence stylistic uncertainty is also strikingly reflected in Stifter's portrayal of old Gregor. On the one hand, he can appear as a figure not unreminiscent of St Francis of Assisi, as the pious old man who discerns in nature the handiwork and purposes of God:

sehet, da fing ich an, allgemach die Reden des Waldes zu hören, und ich horchte ihnen auch, und der Sinn ward mir aufgetan, seine Anzeichen zu verstehen, und das war lauter Prachtvolles und Geheimnisreiches und Liebevolles von dem großen Gärtner, von dem es mir oft war, als müsse ich ihn jetzt und jetzt irgendwo zwischen den Bäumen wandeln sehen. (211)

(see, then I began gradually to hear the speech of the forest, and I harkened to it, and the sense was revealed to me, to understand the signs, and it was always splendid and secret and lovely things that I heard from the great Gardener, and I often thought that I should one day see him walking somewhere amongst the trees.)

On the other hand Gregor also appears as a huntsman – at one point he is sorely tempted to shoot down a beautiful vulture.

And this huntsman is the spokesman of an almost Darwinian view of nature. He sees it as a realm where all creatures prey on one another and thus he defends the animal who

ißt Fleisch, wie wir alle auch, und er sucht sich seine Nahrung auf, wie das Lamm, das die unschuldigen Kräuter und Blumen ausrauft. Es muß wohl so Verordnung sein in der Welt, daß das eine durch das andere lebt. (229)

(eats meat, as we all do, and he seeks out his food as does the lamb when he uproots the innocent herbs and flowers. There must be such an ordained order in the world that each lives off the other.)

These two concepts – nature as paradisal garden and nature as the realm of a fierce struggle for survival – stand alongside one another in unresolved tension. At one point Stifter even formulates this tension in a moment of narrative reflection. As Gregor guides the two girls deeper into the forest, the narrator comments:

Es liegt ein Anstand, ich möchte sagen ein Ausdruck von Tugend in dem von Menschenhänden noch nicht berührten Antlitze der Natur, dem sich die ganze Seele beugen muß, als etwas Keuschem und Göttlichem, – – und doch ist es zuletzt wieder die Seele allein, die all ihre innere Größe hinaus in das Gleichnis der Natur legt. (209f.)

(There is a decency, I might almost say an expression of virtue, in the face of nature undisturbed by human hands before which the whole inner man must bow as before something chaste and divine – and yet it is ultimately the soul alone which projects its inner greatness into the symbol of nature.)

This passage first asserts the divine and paradisal quality of nature, but then suggests that any such notions of religious and moral categories are but pathetic fallacies. The passage formulates the irresolution, but does not resolve it, for the argument remains curiously open-ended:[4] the term 'innere größe' vibrates with ambivalence. If it signals ethical integrity, then nature functions as a religiously anchored pathetic fallacy; but if 'innere Größe' has to do with the conflicting energies in the human psyche, then nature would stand as that strife-torn

53

realm which is the extension and corroboration of the human drama.

This conceptual uncertainty at the heart of *Der Hochwald* has many ramifications. It affects in particular the narrator's attitude towards the loving couple, Clarissa and Ronald. Within the perspective that perceives nature as a paradisal state, their love emerges as the sinful act of individuation, the Fall of Man. It is seen to destroy the peace of the forest retreat and is directly responsible for the catastrophic outcome. There are passages where Stifter openly laments Clarissa's passion. At one crucial point, Clarissa's bad conscience is underpinned by a particularly censorious comment from the narrator:

Sie blickte fast mit Wehmut darnach zurück, wie sie so gegangen war durch die Stellen des Waldes mit Gregor, mit Johannen unschuldig plaudernd, selbst so unschuldig wie die Schwester und der Greis, die so schön an sie geglaubt hatten, dann abends kosend und lehrend und einschlafend mit Johannen, deren einfältigem Herzen sie Schatz und Reichtum dieser Erde gewesen – und jetzt: ein schweres süßes Gefühl trug sie im Herzen, hinweggehend von den zwei Gestalten an ihrer Seite, den sonst geliebten, und suchend einen Fremden, und suchend die Steigerung der eignen Seligkeit. – – O du heiliges Gold des Gewissens, wie schnell und schön strafst du das Herz, das beginnet, selbstsüchtig zu werden. (259)

(She looked back almost with melancholy to the time when she had walked through the forest places with Gregor, talking innocently with Johanna, as innocent as her sister and the old man who had put the loveliness of all their trust in her, then in the evening embracing and teaching and falling asleep with Johanna to whose simple heart she was the whole priceless treasure of the earth – and now: she bore a heavy sweet feeling in her heart as she moved away from the two figures at her side whom she had loved so dearly, and sought out a stranger, and sought the increase of her own happiness. – – O holy gold of conscience, how swiftly and beautifully do you punish the heart which begins to grow selfish.)

Years later Clarissa will agonize 'Ich war es, die Vater und Bruder erschlagen' (293) (I it was who killed father and brother). On this level, the story endorses the view held by Ronald's father who had rejected his son's love for Clarissa with the words: 'laß lieber fahren das Scheinding' (248) (let go of that false thing). By extension, this dictum of fatherly authority reverberates with the judgment of the biblical Father warning against the Tree of Knowledge.

However, within that other perspective which suggests an amoral, vitalistic conception of nature, the two lovers are not morally condemned. Their love and sexual attraction are quite simply natural. Gregor says:

Es ist so der Wille Gottes – darum wird der Mensch Vater und Mutter verlassen, und dem Weibe anhängen – es ist schon so Natur –. (252)

(Such is the will of God – that man will leave father and mother and cleave to the woman – such are the ways of nature –.)

This dual evaluation which sees sexuality both as sin and as rightful element within the divine design must not simply be dismissed as conceptual confusion on the part of Stifter. For the inherent ambivalence touches on the central problem which sexuality poses within Christian thinking: the paradox that life is holy, yet sex is sinful (see Genesis 1. 27; Mark 10.7; Matthew 19.5) has not been resolved, but has, rather, been formalized within certain Christian traditions by that division of function whereby the priest remains celibate and the secular community has the task of propagating divine life. Stifter's attempt to synthesize the two breaks down in the human sphere; it is only in the realm of unindividuated nature that he can exorcise the paradox. Thus in the closing section of the story he can celebrate both the fecundity ('zahlreiche Nachkommenschaften') and the virginity ('die tiefe jungfräuliche Wildnis') of nature.

There are further, closely related, manifestations of this central ambivalence. At one level, there is a narrative commitment to the deliberate creation of the perfect image, the framed idyll. One thinks of the moment when the narrator invites the reader to imagine the castle as it was two hundred years ago: 'geh mit mir die mittlere Treppe hinauf in das erste Stockwerk, die Türen fliegen auf – Gefällt dir das holde Paar?' (188)

(come with me up the middle staircase to the first floor, the doors fly open – do you like the lovely couple?). There follows a description of the world in which the two girls live: every detail is described and so organized as to convey a secure, narratively validated, domestic order which clearly parallels the conception of nature as a divinely ordered garden. Things are neatly framed: Johanna looks a picture, quite literally;[5] her head 'schaut fast wunderselig jung aus der altväterischen Kleiderwolke' (189) (looks in wondering youthfulness out of the old-fashioned cloud of clothes). Her eyes are 'rund und rein in ihrem Rahmen' (round and pure within their frame), and the view from the window 'liegt in den zwei Fenstern wie in einem Rahmen' (rests in the two windows as in a frame). Needless to say, the frequent use of diminutives is an essential part of the painterly quality which informs these scenes and figures. However, at another level the text suggests a critical distance toward this domestic order. To take one crucial example: when the narrator invites us to participate in the creation of the idyllic *intérieur*, we read: 'teile die Gemächer und ziere sie mit all dem lieben Hausrat und Flitter der Wohnlichkeit'. Beloved objects or trappings? Which is it to be? The answer must be: both. The narrative as a whole enacts precisely this tension: lovingly and affirmingly it evokes domestic order and yet also intimates that this order may be but thin veneer. Thus, sometimes the two girls are stylized into figures of *Märchen* simplicity, one fair haired, the other dark. Yet the willed simplicity of the *Märchen* register is in constant danger of erosion as the narrator insists on the complexity and abundance of feeling in the girls (and demands emotional empathy from the reader). We have, for example, the fulsome – almost sexual – intensity in the description of the affection between the sisters: 'Clarissa küßte sie [Johanna] zweimal recht innig auf die Kinderlippen, an deren unbewußter schwellender Schönheit sie wie ein Liebender Freude hatte' (191) (Clarissa kissed Johanna twice fervently on the childish lips in whose innocently swelling loveliness she de-

56

lighted like a lover). Furthermore, in contrast to the neatly dressed Johanna, Clarissa is 'noch nicht angezogen...Eine Fülle äußerst schwarzer Haare ist aufgelöst' (189) (not yet dressed...An abundance of extremely black hair hangs loosely down). This image of woman free from the constraints of costume and hairstyle runs counter to the dominating impression of stable order; and indeed, the term 'aufgelöst' anticipates the final dissolution of all order and stability.

Thus time and again, we see a Stifter turning his back on the neat setting which he has so carefully built up. He lends considerable poetic sympathy to Clarissa as a creature of passion; he gives her speeches which soar way above her sister's virgin imagination. He tells us a good deal about the explosive tensions underneath the idyllic surface – but then, quite suddenly and inconsistently, he changes tack and calls the two sisters 'zwei Engel' (two angels) and describes their room as 'geweiht und rein wie eine Kirche' (194) (holy and pure like a church).

What are we to make of this narrative unease? It must be conceded that *Der Hochwald* is an early – and a flawed – work. The story overall oscillates between a potentially search- ing study of man, his place within the natural order, and a moralistic fate-tragedy in which passion is punished as a Fall from Grace. By means of various juxtapositions the text sets out to deliberate to what extent nature is a realm of integral harmony denied to individuated man and to what extent it is itself a battlefield of conflicting processes. As regards the human sphere, the story asks how far it is man's nature to build his own solid circle ('Kreis'), both socially and morally, and how far it is equally man's nature to break out of tradi- tional loyalties. In this sense the story touches on some key issues of the nineteenth century, but as both a thematic and an aesthetic organization it does not fully succeed in transform- ing irresolution into a sustained ambivalence, into the tensions of a consistent dialectical illumination.

In *Abdias*, we see Stifter recognizing the gulf which he has endeavoured to bridge in *Der Hochwald*. On the opening pages we find a series of philosophical reflections which signal that the ensuing story is set up almost as a test case: that it will ask whether there is any link between the continuity of natural processes and the fate of man; and further, whether individual fate can at all be interpreted and by what criteria one may invest it with meaning. As we shall see, the story poses these questions with a narrative reticence that is the polar opposite of the effusiveness that characterizes *Der Hochwald*.

We learn the life story of the Jew Abdias, a man whose experience is marked by a chain of disasters which finally reduce him to helpless insensibility. Each section of the tale bears the name of a woman: the mother, the wife, the daughter. Each woman would seem to represent the possibility that Abdias can find shelter within the continuity of family life. But each promise proves a rebuff. First we see Abdias growing up as a typical product of a Jewish community which, in the early nineteenth century, lives among ancient Greek and Roman ruins in the African desert. His father Aron is wealthy and when Abdias is old enough, he sends him, in the traditional manner, out into the world to fend for himself and to learn the trade on which this community depends. Fifteen years later, Abdias returns, hardened by experience. He marries Deborah, but the promise of happiness comes to nothing: when his face is disfigured by pockmarks, Deborah turns inwardly away in disgust. Thus Abdias loses both beauty and love. His only compensation is his wealth and warrior skills. But even these prove to be disastrous for they provoke an attack by his enemy Melek, who destroys the Jewish settlement. The community blames Abdias and turns on him in fury and contempt. At this point of utter desolation, hope suddenly seems to return: Deborah gives birth to Ditha, a beautiful baby girl, and she also rediscovers her original love for Abdias. But then, in childbirth, she bleeds to death. In the third and by far the longest chapter, we find Abdias heaping all his attention on the one remaining, beloved possession,

Ditha. He leaves with her for Austria where he hopes to found a new life in a secluded valley. But disaster pursues him: when Ditha is four years old, he discovers that she is blind. In order to secure her future, he resumes trade and accumulates riches. Once again, good fortune strikes: when Ditha is fourteen, a flash of lightning restores her eyesight. A deeply happy time ensues: Abdias guides and teaches his daughter and cultivates the land. Then, at the age of sixteen, Ditha is killed by a flash of lightning. Abdias is broken – he lives on for more than thirty years, but with all energy and purpose drained.

Abdias is an extraordinary story: its hectic graph of fortune and misfortune is quite unique in mid-nineteenth-century German fiction. If it has a predecessor it must surely be in the works of Heinrich von Kleist. There is above all one particular similarity: *Abdias*, like *Das Erdbeben in Chili* (The Earthquake in Chile) thematizes the issue of interpretation only to withhold a guiding answer. In the introduction, Stifter puts essentially three interpretative possibilities before us: first, the 'Fatum' of the Greeks, 'furchtbar letzter starrer Grund des Geschehenden' (S, 581) (horrifyingly unyielding bedrock of everything that happens); secondly, the notion of a personal destiny, of something that is sent by some higher power to individual man; and thirdly, a transcendentally anchored Sufficient Reason thanks to which the discrete phenomena of our world could acquire coherence and sense;

eine heitere Blumenkette hängt durch die Unendlichkeit des Alls und sendet ihren Schimmer in die Herzen – die Kette der Ursachen und Wirkungen – und in das Haupt des Menschen ward die schönste dieser Blumen geworfen, die Vernunft, das Auge der Seele, die Kette daran anzuknüpfen, und an ihr Blume um Blume, Glied um Glied hinab zu zählen bis zuletzt zu jener Hand, in der das Ende ruht. Und haben wir dereinstens recht gezählt, und können wir die Zählung überschauen: dann wird für uns kein Zufall mehr erscheinen, sondern Folgen, kein Unglück mehr, sondern nur Verschulden. (S, 582)

(a serene chain of flowers is suspended through the infinity of the universe and sends its shimmering radiance into human hearts – the chain of cause and effect – and into the head of man was cast the loveliest of these flowers, reason, the eye of the soul, to which we can attach the chain, in order to count back along it, flower by flower, link by link, until we reach that hand in which the end rests. And if at some future time we have counted properly, and if we can survey the whole sequence, then there will be no such thing as chance for us any more, but consequences, no misfortune but simply guilt.)

The possibility of transcendental reason-giving is held out to us: but as with Kleist, the possibility is tormentingly distant. The events of our world, of our lives must in the meantime remain an enigma. And Stifter raises – but leaves unanswered – the crucial question: whether the pain that man feels is 'eine Blume in jener Kette' (a flower in that chain), whether, in other words, suffering is metaphysically underwritten as the guarantor that such knowledge will one day be vouchsafed to man – or whether (by implication) such pain is simply the necessary condition of (and on) man's humanity.

Particularly unsettling is the moment when these reflections come to a sudden stop. The narrator states 'Wir wollen nicht weiter grübeln, wie es sei in diesen Dingen' (582) (we do not wish to brood further on these matters); he turns to the life of Abdias, but immediately admits that it forces one to ask: ' "Warum nun dieses?" und man wird in ein düsteres Grübeln hinein gelockt über Vorsicht Schicksal und letzten Grund aller Dinge' (583) ('Why should this happen?', and we are enticed into dark broodings on providence, fate and the ultimate ground of all things). The narrator is as good as his word: he tells of a life marked by a series of extraordinary turning-points – 'Wendungen' is the recurrent term – but he does not attempt to explicate them. As in the work of Kleist, the laconic narration only serves to highlight these bewildering changes. Thus at the beginning of Chapter 2 we read that Abdias 'tat den Tieren, den Sklaven und den Nachbarn Gutes. Aber sie haßten ihn dafür' (592) (was good to the animals, the slaves, the neighbours. But they hated him for it). And at the end of Chapter 2, the narrator says of Deborah: 'Sie hatte wenig Glück in dieser Ehe gehabt, und als es angefangen hatte, mußte sie sterben' (612) (in this marriage she had had little good fortune, and when it began, she had to die). If the narrator comments at all, it is simply to register the perversity and cruelty of what happens, the fact that 'sich die Dinge zu den seltensten Widrigkeiten verketteten' (650) (things combined to form the strangest perversities). There are moments in the story when moral judgments are made, but they stem not from the narrator, but from the characters. When Abdias is struck down with smallpox, it is his neighbours who say 'das sei der Aussatzengel Jehovas, der über ihn gekommen wäre' (592) (it was the avenging angel of Jehovah who had come over him); likewise it is the neighbours who interpret Melek's attack as God's judgment on Abdias for his vanity and greed. When the news of Ditha's blindness becomes public, human judgments are again in evidence: 'das Unglück, in welchem sein Mädchen gefangen war, schrieb man dem gerechten Urteile Gottes zu, der den maßlosen Geiz des Vaters strafen wollte' (649) (the misfortune in which his daughter was entrapped was attributed to the righteous judgment of God who wished to punish the immediate avarice of the father). And that censorious voice is not lacking when the thunderbolt kills Ditha: 'das neue Wunder und Strafgericht, wie sie es nannten, flog sogleich durch das Land' (672) (news of the recent miracle and, as it was called, divine judgment spread immediately throughout the land). But these interpretations cannot be accepted by the critic because the characters that pronounce them are as compromised as are their counterparts in Kleist's work. And so, we are faced with a text that both invites and withholds judgment and interpretation. This stance is crystallized in the narrator's insidiously distanced invitation to the reader: 'urteile er über den Juden Abdias, wie es ihm sein Herz nur immer eingibt' (583) (let him judge the Jew Abdias in whatever way his heart prompts him).

If anything, the facts of the story enact the sheer Unreason of nature on which, as we have seen, the narrator comments in the opening sections:

Es liegt auch wirklich etwas Schauderndes in der gelassenen Unschuld, womit die Naturgesetze wirken, daß uns ist, als lange ein unsichtbarer Arm aus der Wolke und tue vor unseren Augen das Unbegreifliche. Denn heute kommt mit derselben holden Miene Segen und morgen geschieht das Entsetzliche. Und ist beides aus, dann ist die Natur die Unbefangenheit, wie früher.

Nature simply follows the laws of her being. She does not respect the wishes of man; her splendour is inseparable from her indifference; her beauty has nothing to do with ethical values, let alone transcendental religious values. She revolves in radical 'Unbefangenheit'. Thus the narrator describes the thunderstorm at the end of the story:

Das Gewitter, welches dem Kinde mit seiner weichen Flamme das Leben von dem Haupte geküßt hatte, schüttete an dem Tage noch auf alle Wesen reichlichen Segen herab, und hatte, wie jenes, das ihr das Augenlicht gegeben, mit einem schönen Regenbogen im weiten Morgen geschlossen. (673)

(The thunderstorm which, with its soft flame, had kissed the life from the child's head, poured that same day abundant blessing on all creatures and, like the one which has given her her eyesight, had closed with a lovely rainbow in the wide morning sky.)

There is no reason given here: simply a registering of an awesome power. There is no meaning: only an integral organization of natural phenomena. The story intimates that perception to us, and it intimates the havoc which that being wreaks in the individuated sphere of one man's affective and ethical needs. Abdias does not achieve insight: he and his story are too close to the 'Unvernunft des Seins' ('Unreason of being') for that. Indeed, at the end of his life he seems to join that very Unreason – 'denn nach glaublichen Aussagen war er wahnsinnig gewesen' (673) (for according to reliable reports, he has gone mad). He is seen for several years more sitting on the bench in front of his house:

Eines Tages saß er nicht mehr dort, die Sonne schien auf den leeren Platz und auf seinen frischen Grabhügel, aus dem bereits Spitzen von Gräsern hervorsahen. (673)

(One day he was no longer sitting there, the sun shone down on the empty place and on the mound of his freshly dug grave from which already the tips of blades of grass were appearing.)

In this sense he becomes one with the unreasoning continuity of being. There is a release here, a release from knowing, from pain, in a word, from individuation.

At the level of surface statement, then, *Abdias* is a story of radical disjunction between self and world, centre and frame. And when one looks back at the opening of the story, with its reflections on the chain of flowers, one cannot help thinking that Stifter could have hardly selected a tale more guaranteed to disprove any such comforting speculations. What are we, then, to make of Stifter's postulation that within the universe there is a chain of cause and effect? And what of his intervention just before Ditha gains her eyesight:

Es geschah eine wundervolle Begebenheit – eine Begebenheit, die so lange wundervoll bleiben wird, bis man nicht jene großen verbreiteten Kräfte der Natur wird ergründet haben, in denen unser Leben schwimmt und bis man nicht das Liebesband zwischen diesen Kräften und unserm Leben wird freundlich binden und lösen können. (652)

(There occurred a wondrous event – an event which will remain wondrous as long as we are unable to understand the great, widespread forces of nature in which our life floats, as long as we cannot with friendly hand tie and release the loving bond between these forces and our life.)

Are we to dismiss such lines as typical, but utterly futile, attempts on the part of Stifter to rescue the story out of its overwhelming darkness? We may in the end come to this very conclusion and invoke that freedom of interpretative choice which is granted by Stifter's initial invitation to the reader to judge 'wie es ihm sein Herz nur immer eingibt'. But, equally, one can argue that in the course of rereading, the text begins to yield a historical, philosophical perspective which makes the possibility of ultimate meaning not simply a tormenting mirage. We note, for example, the great emphasis that is placed on the specific social and cultural situation in which Abdias grows up. The physicality and harshness of his environment produces paradoxically (Hegel would say dialectically) the longing for another way of being, for a spirituality that is denied any present accommodation. Abdias's father Aron is the first to feel this: he is successful and wealthy, yet he feels 'als gäbe es noch andere Seligkeiten' (586) (as though there were yet other kinds of happiness). Like that other successful businessman, Thomas Buddenbrook, Aron fears these moments because they could be detrimental to his practical capability and he avoids them as much as he can. They are only glimpses, soon forgotten under the pressures of a harsh socio-economic reality. But in Abdias, these intimations are stronger. His temperament is gentle; the laws of survival in his community may toughen him both outwardly and inwardly, yet he retains, we are told, angelic eyes. He may excel as a member of his society, but he displays an increasing longing for inwardness, a more spiritual way of being. At one point, after a highly successful battle, he throws away his sword in disgust. But again, we are told that these are but fleeting intimations, 'flatternde Gedanken'. The birth of Ditha strengthens his intuitions of a different kind of happiness – 'so wurde ihm in seinem Herzen, als fühle er drinnen bereits den Anfang des Heiles, das nie gekommen war, und von dem er nie gewußt hatte, wo er es denn suchen sollte' (600) (so it was in his heart as though he felt there already the beginnings of a redemption that had never come and for which he had never known where to look). He thanks God 'daß er einen solchen Strom sanften Fühlens in das Herz des Menschen zu leiten vermöge' (600) (that He was able to direct such a stream of gentle feeling into the hearts of men). As Ditha grows up, she brings out a dimension of his being which is utterly foreign to his socio-cultural make-up. More and more he comes to understand this 'redende Blume' (662) (talking flower) – the echo of the introduction is unmistakable. Her speech is poetic, because it is untouched by the crude referentiality of everyday language, and it leads Abdias back to his earliest childhood before the brutal process of growing up began: 'Sie sagte die Worte nach und erfand andere, welche aus ihrem inneren Zustande gekommen waren, die er nicht verstand, und die er wieder lernte' (649) (she repeated the words and invented other ones which issued from her inner condition, which he did not understand and which he learnt again).

This whole thematic strand is more accentuated in the first version (*Journalfassung*) of the story, which stresses the hidden spiritual potential of this man in a world that militates against it. We learn of the 'Schatz der Liebe' (*Urf*, 1), (treasure of love) which slumbers in his heart; in the midst of his worldly success he feels 'bitterste Verachtung aller Dinge, die da sind . . .und. . .Hohn über die Nichtigkeit und Erbärmlichkeit der menschlichen Dinge' (18), (the bitterest contempt for all things that are,. . .and scorn for the emptiness and vanity of human things). He is bitterly disappointed by the mechanistic values of Europe, whose people strike him as 'abgerichtete Wesen, eines dem anderen gleich. . .wie ihre Maschinen, die er auch haßte. . .leblose Zieger einer Uhr' (50) (drilled creatures, one like the other. . .like their machines, which he also hated. . .lifeless hands of a clock). In the first version the narrator actually meets and stays with Abdias in his valley: there is a greater personal involvement on the part of the narrator, a recognition of the abundant spiritual potential in Abdias. It is this narrator who describes Ditha as a miracle from God: 'so blühte das Wunder Gottes in der Verlassenheit und Öde auf' (54) (thus this miracle from God bloomed in the forsaken desert). Implicitly, then, Ditha expresses the flowering of a new spirit out of the ruined layers of Greek, Roman, Jewish civilization. Not that that promise can be fulfilled: Europe is a sadly mercantile culture. And yet the possibility of a culture that could accommodate the needs and promptings of Abdias and Ditha is not simply chimerical: however doomed in practical terms, Abdias's journey from North Africa to Europe has the dignity and the purpose of a spiritual pilgrimage.

The second version is much more cautious about asserting this metaphorical design. All those intimations of 'Heil' are presented as mere feelings on the part of Abdias. Frequently they are couched in such qualifying phrases as 'ihm war, als ob' (he felt as if), 'er dachte, er sehne sich' (he thought that he felt a longing). Yet even so, behind the facts and circumstances of Abdias's life story, there is a network of metaphors which intimate a possible pattern. One thinks of the antithetical pairings in the story: drought versus life-bringing rain; barren desert versus the green valley which is a 'Wiege', a cradle harbouring new life; the iron constraints of Abdias's life in trade and war versus the secret flow of his tears; the persistent motif of the withered palm-trees versus the abundantly blue flax, the colour of the sky, that Ditha loves so much.

At one level, all these elements are presented to us as mere facts and events of Abdias's life. In this sense, they are, in terms of that opening page, simply part of the 'furchtbar letzter starrer Grund des Geschehenden, über den man nicht hinaussieht und jenseits dessen auch nichts mehr ist' (*S*, 581). But at another level, these same elements are so arranged as to suggest a metaphorical, that is, transcendent, reading. They invite us to look beyond their bedrock of mere factuality and ascribe to them a symbolic function. If read on this level, they can suggest that from within the narrow socio-cultural confines of Abdias's life, this life set in the nineteenth century, there may emerge some higher state of being. The metaphorical mode perfectly captures the conjectural spirit of those introductory remarks: 'eigentlich *mag* es weder ein Fatum geben' (but ultimately there *may* be neither fate). And metaphor is as much reason-giving as *Abdias* can offer in the face of the brutal indifference of natural phenomena.[6]

In conclusion, we may argue that *Abdias*, in its textual organization, is critically poised between the perspectives of Schopenhauer and Hegel. The reader may feel that this life is mere toil and suffering, but he may also conclude that the text points beyond immediate facts and experience – that the text enacts both facticity and transcendence. In this sense, the story, thematically and stylistically, deepens and enriches the stance of *Der Hochwald*: irresolution is heightened into a sustained dialectic. The two strands of reading *Abdias* are fully interwoven. In the first version, there is a phrase which describes Abdias's life, and that phrase defines superbly the text as it now stands: 'doppelt geschlungenes Leben' – 'doubly woven life'.

The category of 'das Unbegreifliche' (the incomprehensible), as defined in the opening sections of *Abdias*, is taken up in *Prokopus*, and radicalized: this text yields no alternative way of reading that would vouchsafe some meaning. Instead it offers a laconic constatation of that indiscriminate law of being which no amount of human willing can countermand.

It begins with Prokopus taking his young wife Gertraud to his castle. They are attended by relatives and well-wishers. They themselves are physically beautiful – and deeply in love. They stop at an inn in the 'Fichtau': they are welcomed and toasted with due ceremony. On all these formalities – as on the clothes and appearance of the various participants – time and narrative space are expended. At the end of this day, a day replete with public circumstances, Prokopus is glad to be alone with his young wife:

Es war nach dem geräuschvollen Tage, in welchem den Menschen ihr Tun wie eine Rolle im Schauspiele war vorgeschrieben worden, eine Last von ihm genommen, da er allein war. (*BSt*, 491)

(After the noisy day in which people's behaviour was prescribed for them like a part in a play, a weight was lifted from his shoulders when he was alone.)

Yet, with that same abruptness that we have found in *Abdias*, the second section of the story begins with the laconic phrase: 'das versprochene Glück ist nicht gekommen' (497) (the promised happiness did not come). We are given details of the life in the castle, the husband showing his wife all the things that are now part of their life: there is no hint of jealousy, of ill-will, of deliberate wounding. All circumstances would seem to conspire to suggest peace, harmony, fulfilment, yet everything that surrounds these two people becomes a frame housing despair and anguish – 'die Spaltungen erschienen wieder und wurden tiefer' (506) (the cracks appeared again and became deeper). The disjunction between actual things and inner processes becomes an abyss. And that is all there is to the story. No reasons are given, no moral evaluation is supplied: it simply seems to be that those in the 'Fichtau' find happiness, those in the castle do not. The story is pervaded by a sense of the sheer perversity of destiny: 'andere Eheleute hätten sich gefügt und nach ihrer Art glücklich gefühlt. Sie waren höher, liebten sich und machten sich unglücklich' (514) (other married people would have come to some arrangement, and found happiness according to their lights. But they were higher, they loved one another and made themselves unhappy). Is the fault an excess of love? Or simply that their 'Inneres grundverschieden sei' (514) (that inwardly they were totally different)? The narrator does not explicate, and the occasional moments of sententious comment seem totally misplaced in a story that is about the perversity of human unhappiness. In their misplacement, such comments invalidate themselves. Take the following example:

Die natürlichen Dinge gehen ihren Lauf, wir mögen noch so großen Schmerz darüber empfinden. Es ist aber in unsere Macht gegeben, die Wesenheit dieser Dinge zu ergründen, und sie nach derselben zu gebrauchen. Dann gehorchen uns die Dinge. (512)

(Natural things take their course, however great the pain may be which we feel at this. But it is given to us to fathom the being of these things, and to use them accordingly. Then things will obey us.)

One is hard put to it to know what this phrase might actually mean, and the lives set before us are at no point given the chance to bow before the being of natural things. For this story inhabits a territory beyond moral argument, beyond cause and effect.[7] The circumstances seem propitious, but they are all cancelled out by a radically resistant reality. Linguistically, this is reflected in that stark sequence of passages beginning with 'aber' (but) or 'und dennoch' (and yet), which chronicle the fact that human happiness will not oblige, will not be dictated to by circumstances. The frame is simply unable to legislate for the centre. The slow, detailed narration almost feels like a parody of Stifterian gradualness: for this is gradualness to no avail.

As we shall see in the course of this study, Stifter remains haunted by the sense of 'das Unbegreifliche' to the very end of his creative life. Even texts that are largely, and determinedly, informed by a moral argument are not always proof against the inroads of the incomprehensible, and the more determined a text is to drive home the 'moral of the tale', by adopting the mode of the moral fable or the didactic fairy-tale, the more unstable it will become at such moments of attempted sententiousness.

Turning to *Der Waldgänger*, we shall have occasion to refer again to this phenomenon, although in the following we wish to focus particularly on the moral issues. We hope to show that in contrast to the serenity and comfort which emanate from Stifter's philosophical deliberations as found in the preface to the *Studien, Bunte Steine* and elsewhere, a story such as *Der Waldgänger* explores the extent to which man's ethical capability and deliberation can lead him astray and be the very source of a diminished life.

The structure of *Der Waldgänger* is familiar from much of Stifter's prose: the narrator begins with a leisurely depiction of present circumstances, of a figure and of the world that figure inhabits. Gradually we are taken into the past, we learn of the experiences that have made that figure what he is, we learn of the human centre at the heart of the circumstances with which we have begun. We are told of the 'Waldgänger', of his isolated existence, of his painstaking education of a little boy, the 'Hegerbub'. The man does have a name – it is Georg:

Aber ganz abkommen konnte der Name Waldgänger nie mehr, weil

69

abgeschlossene und einsame Menschen an ihren einmal angenommenen Dingen haften, wie die Wurzeln ihrer großen Tannen im Grunde ihrer Berge...(*BSt*, 375)

(But the name 'the forest walker' was not to be shed any more, because isolated and lonely people depend on things that have once become a habit, as the roots of their great pine trees are sunk into their mountains...)

This is, we gather, despite the isolation which surrounds it, a rooted life, one anchored in the natural circumstances that define it. But even that rootedness brings only cold comfort. The boy grows up. At one point he promises the older man that he will never leave him, but Georg replies:

Es bleiben ja nicht einmal die eigenen Kinder bei den Eltern, geschweige denn fremde; sondern sie gehen alle fort, um sich die Welt zu erobern, und lassen die Eltern allein zurück, wenn ihnen diese auch alles geopfert, wenn sie ihnen ihr ganzes Glück und das Blut ihres Herzens gegeben hätten. Es wird auch schon so das Gesetz der Natur sein. Die Liebe geht nur nach vorwärts nicht zurück. Das siehst du ja schon an den Gewächsen: der neue Trieb strebt immer von dem alten weg in die Höhe, nie zurück, der alte bleibt hinten, wächst nicht mehr und verdorrt. (393)

(Children do not even stay with their own parents – let alone with adoptive ones; they all leave, they set out to conquer the world and leave their parents behind them, alone, even though they would have sacrificed everything for them, their whole happiness, even their heart's blood. That is presumably the law of nature. Love only moves forwards, never backwards. You can see it in growing things: the new shoot always strains away from the old one, upwards, never back. The old branch is left behind, ceases to grow and withers.)

The rooted life is, then, grounded in the 'Law of Nature': but there is nothing gentle about this law, there is no compassion, no respect for human feelings, for individual vulnerability. And the gloomy prophecy of the 'Waldgänger' comes to pass: the boy leaves him, and shortly afterwards, the man himself is seen no more. Even his beloved forest, with which he is identified to the point of forfeiting the emblem of his individuated existence, his name, is simply a further proclamation of his own expendability.

There follows a lengthy flashback which chronicles the youth of Georg and his wife Corona. Both have known loneliness: indeed, it is the dark background of emotional impoverishment that draws them together: 'die verödete Größe, die in ihrem [Coronas] Wesen lag, lockte ihn an' (416) (the blighted greatness which informed her being attracted him). The deprivation of their childhood serves to unite them more closely. But their happiness is marred by one thing: they have no children. Finally, Corona suggests divorce. She speaks of a sacred duty that man has, 'die Welt in einem kleinen Teilchen durch seine Kinder fort blühen zu machen' (436) (to help the world in one small particular to continue to flourish – by producing children). Georg finally acquiesces. He and Corona meet many years later. Georg has remarried and has two sons. But Corona, in spare, simple words reveals her inability to carry out the plan to serve the world, to subdue the needs of her individuated selfhood – 'Ich habe es nicht vermocht' (445) (I wasn't able to do it). Her embarrassment is compounded of shame, sorrow, and a fierce declaration of love. She has sought out a landscape which is similar to the one where she and Georg lived when they were married – 'hier lebte sie nun, weil sie die Erinnerung der Vergangenheit nicht wegtun konnte in einem Teile dieser Vergangenheit' (445) (here she now lived because she could not banish the memory of the past, living as she did in part of this past). She needs so to live because that past is the sole foundation of her being. The meeting with Corona leaves Georg shattered. In rapid succession the closing two pages chronicle the fact that Georg never finds stability: eventually his wife dies, his sons leave him, just as years later the 'Hegerbub' leaves him. The narration, cursorily dismissing the central characters, mirrors the law of expendability operating in nature:

Wir wissen nicht, wo der alte Waldgänger jetzt ist. Er mag noch irgend wo leben, er mag gestorben sein – wir wissen es nicht. Von seiner Gattin Corona wissen wir auch nichts. (446)

(We do not know where the old walker in the forest now is. He may still be living somewhere, he may be dead – we do not know. Of his wife Corona we also know nothing.)

The central section of the story presents us with a tragedy whose mainspring is firmly located within a moral framework: in the name of a 'sacred duty' (435), of a 'higher purpose' (437) to beget children and thus serve the continuity of being, two people sunder their marriage and override their deepest emotional needs. This is their fatal error, for their sacrifice brings no fulfilment, but only loneliness in its train. After his meeting with Corona, Georg comes to recognize the enormity of what they have done: 'jetzt erst stand die Größe der Sünde vor ihm, die er begangen hatte' (445) (only now did the magnitude of the sin which he had committed stand before him). In this sense, the story follows the pattern of classical tragedy: there is the central flaw, in this case too rigid an adherence to moral principle, and the characters come to recognize the error of their ways. This strand is rather clumsily underpinned by the concluding reflections of the narrator who yet again stresses that Georg and Corona had erred and should have been content with their lot. But the text is more complex than this; and it is also far richer than the narrator initially suggests when he introduces the story of the 'Waldgänger' as follows:

Nach vielen Jahren sind seine Verhältnisse bekannt geworden . . . und wir wollen uns dieselben zu unserer eigenen Erinnerung aufzeichnen, wenn sich anders etwas so wenig Gegliedertes darstellen läßt, das eher durch sein einfaches Dasein, als durch seine Erregung wirket. (363)

(After many years his circumstances became known . . . and we wish to record these for the sake of our own memory, if something that has so little structure can be depicted, for it affects us more through its simple being than through its excitation.)

We are promised something that is pure being rather than excitement, that is not particularized, but is simplicity itself, existence rather than individuation. But this is not the case. The reminiscences do coalesce to form a story and that story has quintessentially to do with a core of individuated experience which blights these lives irredeemably. If Kafka pronounces 'Im Kampf zwischen dir und der Welt, sekundiere die Welt'[8] (In the struggle between yourself and the world, take the part of the world), then Georg and Corona do precisely that. However, as it turns out, to respect the duty to propagate life is a sin – but not to respect it is also a sin. Indeed, it would seem that man's consciousness leads him radically astray: whatever goal he pursues, whether the greater glory of the whole or of the individual components, he is doomed to forfeit any sense of fulfilment.

In this sense Georg and Corona experience in heightened and exceptional form the tragedy of individuation as formulated by Schopenhauer and as Stifter himself expresses it in *Ein Gang durch die Katakomben*. And this realization is shared by the narrator when, in the opening pages, he appears as a figure in his own right. He first looks back on his own past when he was 'ein Jüngling mit stürmendem Herzen und voll fliegender Hoffnungen. Jetzt sind die Wünsche in das Geleise des Möglichen zurückgekehrt' (357) (a youth with a pounding heart and full of exalted hopes. Now his wishes have returned to the more modest track of what is possible). But he goes beyond the simple framework of renunciation and growing maturity when he reflects on the course of his life:

was er sonst anstrebte, erreichte er nicht oder erreichte es anders als er gewollt hatte, oder er wollte es nicht mehr erreichen; denn die Dinge kehrten sich um, und was sich als groß gezeigt hatte, stand als Kleines am Wege, und das Unbeachtete schwoll an und entdeckte sich als Schwerpunkt der Dinge, um den sie sich bewegen. (362)

(what he otherwise intended he did not achieve, or he achieved it in a different way from that intended, or he no longer wanted to reach it; for things changed their design, and what had appeared as great now stood as a triviality by the edge of the road, and that which had been ignored expanded and revealed itself as the centre of gravity round which things move.)

Here, the text touches again on that category of 'das Unbegreifliche', the radical disjunction between the human centre with its wishes and needs ('wollen' is a key term), and the ways of things, 'die Dinge'. And as in *Der Hochwald*, discontinuity within the human sphere is contrasted with the unending continuity of nature as reflected in the chapter headings: 'Am Waldwasser' (At the Forest Stream), 'Am Waldhange' (On the Forest Slope), 'Am Waldrande' (At the Edge of the Forest). The narrator's account operates with that same litanesque register which in a work like *Der Nachsommer* sustains the notion of gradualness guaranteeing meaning, but here it takes on the opposite function; stylization stands as a confession of total disorientation. The reader is forced to ask what that 'Schwerpunkt der Dinge' means and the answer is as much denied to him as it is to the characters. Georg and Corona leave one such centre of gravity (their marriage) for another (the begetting of children). Corona says:

Ich glaube, es ist überall das Rechte, wo ein Ding, das wir anstreben, verweigert wird, es rasch ändern, und den Weg einschlagen, den die Gesetzmäßigkeit der Dinge vorschreibt. (438)

(I believe it is always right, where a thing that we have striven for is denied us, that we change it, that we follow the path that the order of things prescribes.)

Yet, as the story shows, the laws of natural, organic existence do not coincide with those of moral consciousness and may radically conflict with the equally natural laws of man's emotional centre. Unwittingly, Corona touches on this point when she rejects the possibility of adopting children:

Wer eine Pflicht übernimmt, ohne die Grundlagen der Pflicht erzeugen zu können, der macht ebenfalls ein Mißverhältnis der Dinge, das sich in den Folgen rächt. (438)

(Whoever assumes an obligation without being able to fulfil the bases of that obligation produces likewise a misrelationship of things which will exact its revenge in the consequences.)

What she does not foresee at this point is that their separation is also 'ein Mißverhältnis der Dinge', a human aberration.

It would appear that man is simply denied that centre of

gravity which would vouchsafe firm anchorage. Even if he retreats into nature as Georg does, he will not find accommodation, but will experience the law of expendability even more acutely. After the 'Hegerbub' has left Georg, the narrator comments:

Georg ist wieder allein, wie er es ja, wenigstens von den erstrebten Kindern aus, sein mußte – der rückgelassene verdorrte Ast, wenn die neuen voll Kraft und Jugend zu neuen Lüften emporwachsen, in ihr Blau, in ihre Wolken, in ihre Sonne emporschauen, und nie zurück auf den, woraus sie entsprossen. (446)

(Georg is alone again, as he, at least as far as the passionately desired children are concerned, had to be – the abandoned, withered bough, while the new shoots, full of strength and youth, grow up to new air, look upwards to their azure, to their clouds, to their sun – and never back to him from whom they have their being.)

The law of nature legislates for being, not for meaning, nor for human fulfilment. And if that integral being is the ultimate 'Schwerpunkt der Dinge', then it follows that to be individuated is to be banished from the centre of things: to strive to reach that centre of things is to forfeit the human centre, selfhood itself.

In the works discussed so far, one detects a particular, deep-seated ambivalence on Stifter's part: in his detailed descriptions of human activities he underwrites the characters' search for a stable life, in material, psychological, and moral terms; and yet the plot-line and certain discursive comments from the narrator frequently suggest a critical distance whereby all these attempts are viewed as futile, if not erroneous. This ambivalent stance is particularly in evidence in the last two stories which we want to discuss in this chapter: *Das alte Siegel* and *Der Hagestolz*.

Das alte Siegel tells the story of how Hugo, following the mysterious invitation of an old man who requests him to go to a church at a certain time, meets Cöleste, a young woman. Gradually they fall in love. But Cöleste forbids him to ask about the past. The Napoleonic Wars break out and some eleven years pass before they are reunited. Now she can tell her secret: when they first met, she was married, but separated from her husband. He was cruel, blaming her for their childlessness. She promised to pray every day for a child, hence her presence in church. Dionys, her servant, arranged for Hugo and Cöleste to meet. When Hugo learns all this, he is appalled: he feels that he has been drawn into a shameful union, and he leaves without acknowledging the young girl who appears in the doorway as his own daughter by Cöleste. Years afterwards, he comes to regret what he has thrown away, but it is too late.

The story makes it abundantly clear why the relationship breaks down. The cause is psychologically motivated and evaluated in moral terms. We learn that Hugo is brought up by his father, a man of unshakable rectitude, who bequeathes to his son a fearsome sense of honour and principle – symbolized in the old seal which passes from father to son on the former's death. We know little of the father, except that he was a soldier who

in bedeutend vorgerückten Jahren in die Gefangenschaft eines schönen Mädchens geriet, welcher er nicht entging; daher er das Mädchen zur Frau nahm, dieselbe auf seinen Landsitz ins Hochgebirge führte, und mit ihr sein Söhnlein Veit Hugo erzielte. (*S*, 677)

(in decidedly advanced years fell under the spell of a beautiful girl and could not escape: accordingly he took the girl for his wife, conducted her to his estate in the mountains and with her produced his little son Veit Hugo.)

The formulation of the father's emotional life is especially telling: he 'could not escape' the spell of the girl, he 'erzielt' (literally: achieves) a son by her. The seeds are sown for the son's life, which will be blighted by the incapacity to deal with emotion, with passion – above all with sexuality. The farewell between father and son is significant. The boy's eyes fill with tears:

so kam auch in die starren, eisengrauen Züge des alten Mannes ein so plötzliches Zucken, daß er nicht mehr zurück halten konnte. Er sagte nur die ganz verstümmelten Worte: 'Dummer Hasenfuß', und kehrte sich um, indem er heftig mit den Armen schlagend in den Garten zurückging. (679)

(and then there came into the rigid, iron-grey features of the old man such a sudden twitching that he could not control himself. He simply said the broken words 'stupid coward', and turned round, flailing violently with his arms, and went back to the garden.)

There is something straitjacketed about this existence: the father passes on to the son those qualities of orderliness and self-control which will lead him to repudiate his and Cöleste's relationship, their passion as dishonourable. The thought that his love should have been drawn into an illicit affair is unbearable to him: it does not belong in his scenario of principled existence. Cöleste pleads with him – 'Ich hatte Angst, dich zu verlieren' (729) (I was afraid of losing you). But his rhetoric of honour is terrifyingly proof against the simplicity of Cöleste's words. And as the perverse rigidity of his character dawns on her, she dismisses him: ' "Setze nichts mehr auseinander," sagte sie, "es ist ja deutlich. Gehe nur" ' (729) ('Do not explain any further,' she said, 'it is clear. Just go'). The story ends by chronicling Hugo's regret, and, almost in relief, the narrator in the final paragraph turns away from human affairs to the natural world:

Nur die Berge stehen noch in alter Pracht und Herrlichkeit – ihre Häupter werden glänzen, wenn wir und andere Geschlechter dahin sind...Wie viele werden noch nach uns kommen, denen sie Freude und sanfte Trauer in das betrachtende Herz senken, bis auch sie dahin sind, und vielleicht auch die schöne freundliche Erde, die uns doch jetzt so fest gegründet, und für Ewigkeiten gebaut scheint. (732)

(Only the mountains still stand in their old splendour and majesty – their heads will still glow when we and other generations are gone... How many will come after us, whose hearts will feel joy and gentle sadness at the sight of them, until those generations too will fade, perhaps together with the lovely, friendly earth which seems to us so firmly founded, and built for all eternity.)

This closing paragraph is concerned with change and decay.

If such is the law of being, it serves to highlight the folly of men who forfeit happiness in the brief span allotted to them.

Like *Der Waldgänger*, this story enriches and differentiates Stifter's familiar denunciation of human error. Individuation produces a whole spectrum of aberrations, one of which is the one-sidedness of passion, excess, of subjectivity: but, equally, ethical man can go drastically astray. Hugo's sense of principle is such that he can no longer trust – nor even acknowledge – the truth of feeling, 'da es sich von den Dingen der Wirklichkeit auch keine entfernt ähnliche Vorstellung zu machen verstand' (683) (because it was not able to achieve even an approximately adequate conception of the things of reality). Man's sexuality can lead him to mistake intensity of feeling for truth of feeling: but, in Hugo's case, it is the capacity for reflectivity and scruple that leads him to distrust – and ultimately deform – his capacity for sexual response.

In this sense, the import of *Das alte Siegel* is clear – even to the point of didacticism. It is a tale with a moral, symbolized in the 'old seal' of the title. When, at the end of the story, we learn that Hugo throws the seal away, we take this to mean that he has come to recognize the truth of Cöleste's anguished cry of self-justification: 'meine Sünde ist menschlicher als deine Tugend' (729) (my sin is more human than your virtue). The story would appear to be a psychological study of an emotionally crippled life. Yet careful examination of the text reveals that Stifter as narrator is implicated in this ethos of repression. One thinks, for example, of the revealing passage in which the narrator comments on the father's legacy to the son. Two years have passed since the father's death, but Hugo's diary still consists of letters to the old man:

Anders wußte sich seine Liebe nicht zu helfen; wie hold Mutterliebe sei, hatte er nie erfahren, und wie süß die andere, davon ahnete ihm noch nichts, oder, wenn man es so nimmt, die Briefe an den Vater sind mißgekannte Versuche derselben. (687)

(His love could find no other outlet; he had never known the beauty of a mother's love, and of the sweetness of the other kind of love he was still utterly unaware, or – if one wishes to take it that way – the letters to the father were unwitting attempts at that love).

The passage offers a sharp psychological illumination, but we must note that in the same breath the narrator understates and forbears to pursue ('wenn man es so nimmt') the psychological issue.[9] This exercise in narrative reticence is one of many, and they all entail the refusal to drive home the psychological analysis of Hugo. Thus, towards the end of the story the narrator withdraws from any intimacy with the psychological state of the main character: 'Hugo hatte kein Wort mehr gesagt, kein einziges; es ist unbekannt, ob er nicht konnte, oder ob er nicht wollte' (730) (Hugo had said not another word – not one; it is not known whether he could not or would not). The night after the disastrous interview with Cöleste he writes her a long letter – 'was er ihr in demselben schrieb, wie sanfte, gute oder starke Worte er in demselben an sie richtete, ist nie bekannt geworden' (731) (what he wrote to her in the letter, what gentle, good, or strong words he addressed to her, has never been discovered). Indeed, far from being strictly analytical, the narrative viewpoint manifestly partakes of that dialectic of suppression and revelation which is central to the text. When Hugo sees Cöleste in church, she is wearing a cumbersome, old-fashioned dress and is heavily veiled. When he gives her the picture she has dropped, her hand has to struggle to free itself from the enveloping folds: 'Als sich aus den weiten schwarzen Falten die junge Hand hervor arbeitete...' (698) (as the young hand worked its way out of the full black folds). The hand, like its owner, is youthful, oppressively hidden by the heavy material. The key verb – and it recurs throughout Stifter's work – is 'sich lösen' – 'Ihr Schleier legte sich zurück, und ein wunderhaft schönes Mädchenantlitz löste sich aus seinen Falten' (699) (her veil was drawn back and a wonderfully beautiful girl's face freed itself from its folds). When he visits her in her house, he finds her 'leicht und mit den Kleiden der Jugend angetan' (705) (lightly dressed and in youthful clothes). Her hands are not gloved. The sexuality is hinted at, but not explored.

It is noteworthy that in the first version (the *Urfassung* or *Journalfassung*) the narrative stance does not force us into this tacit collusion with the repressive consciousness of the protagonist. It devotes little time or narrative space to the ethos of the 'old seal', and, significantly, there is an explicitness and intensity to the depiction of the physical passion of Hugo and Cöleste which has no parallel in the later version. Compare the following two passages:

Und wieder war es heute wie das letztemal – wieder war es, als hätten sie sich noch nie gesehen, als müßten sie die kargen Stunden benützen, um nur der Wonne sicher zu werden, daß sie sich haben, ohne die Frage zu tun, wer bist du, und wie wird es werden. Wie ein goldenes, zauberisches Rätsel hatte sich die Pracht dieser Glieder aus der unheimlichen Kleiderwolke gelöset, daß er sie in den Armen halte, und den Gedanken gewöhne, sie ist mein – – und wie ein Glück, das sie sich schwer errungen, wie ein märchenhaftes Glück, sah sie ihn mit aller Trunkenheit der Liebe an, und fragte die erste Zeit gar nicht einmal nach seinem Namen. (*Urf*, 259f.)

(And again today it was like the last time – it was again as though they had never seen each other before, as though they had to use the scarce hours in order to be sure of the bliss of possessing each other – without asking the question 'who are you?' or 'how will it turn out?' Like some golden, magic enigma the splendour of those limbs had been released from the uncanny cloud of clothes so that he had held her in his arms and grew accustomed to the thought she is mine – like some good fortune that they had fought hard for, like some fairy-tale happiness, she looked at him with all the drunken absorption of love, and initially did not even ask his name.)

Wie das erste Mal führte ihn das Mädchen durch die Vorzimmer hinaus, er ging die Treppe hinab, sah den alten Türsteher, ging über den Sandweg des Gartens hinvor, und schritt durch das Eisengitter auf die Straße hinaus. Der Gegensatz des Alltäglichen mit dem, was er so eben erlebt hatte, drängte sich ihm auch heute auf. Sie war wieder sehr schön gewesen, und in dem schlanken zarten dunkelgrünen seidenen Kleide, das die kleinen Fältchen auf dem Busen hatte, sehr edel. Es war ihm, wie ein Rätsel, daß sich die Pracht dieser Glieder aus der unheimlichen Kleiderwolke gelöset habe, und daß sie vielleicht sein werden könne. (S, 709)

(As the first time, the girl led him through the ante-rooms, he went down the stairs, saw the old porter, went over the sandy path of the garden and stepped through the iron gate and into the street. The contrast of the everyday world with what he had just experienced was borne in upon him today as well. She had again been very beautiful and very noble in the slim, delicate dress of dark green silk with the small folds at the breast. It was like an enigma to him that the splendour of those limbs could have been released from the mysterious cloud of clothes, that she might perhaps one day be his.)

One obvious difference is a syntactical one: the first passage has a breathless, almost incoherent feel to it as it evokes the urgency of sexual desire. Moreover, the first passage describes the act of love between Hugo and Cöleste (and it is not the first time that they sleep together). The second passage describes Hugo's leaving the house after their meeting: the references to their love-making occur as a recollection in Hugo's mind, moreover as a recollection of something that is, by contrast with the everyday world around him, fantastic and unreal (one notes the subjunctives of 'gelöset habe', 'könne'). In the *Urfassung* sexual passion has the sting of an actual, lived experience: in the later version it is a mysterious, unfocused possibility, a promise rather than a binding fact. The facts are the rooms, the path, the stairs, the familiar world of the street. It is no accident that, in the first version, the servant Dionys thoroughly merits his name: he is a pander figure, someone who unleashes the dionysian truth of sexuality in Hugo. The later version understates this issue by remaining close to the repressions of Hugo's consciousness. Although the text mentions the sexual contact so discreetly, there can be no doubt of the intensity of Hugo's feelings: 'wenn er durch die zarte Seide ihre Glieder fühlte, die er sich sonst kaum anzusehen getraut hatte, so floß es wie ein Wunder durch sein Leben' (S, 713) (when through the delicate silk he felt her limbs which he had scarcely dared to look at, it was like a miraculous current through his life). The final meeting between them lifts the veil of secrecy. As Cöleste says, 'alles, alles hat sich gelöset' (723) (everything, everything has been resolved). But the truth that is revealed – that Dionys, the old servant, had sought to pair them in an illicit union that would give Cöleste a child – is something that, for Hugo, blights their relationship although both he and Cöleste were innocent of the plan. The simple truth behind the enveloping clouds of secrecy, a truth to do with mutual need, with sexual desire, is both inadmissible and unacceptable. The fierce austerity of Hugo's upbringing and background proves too strong.

In one sense the narrator denounces Hugo for what almost amounts to perversion, but in another, he seems to admire Hugo for his adherence to principle and even shows this to be part of the man's spiritual and physical beauty. In other words, the psychological category of repression is turned into a moral category of praiseworthy self-restraint. One thinks of the passage where the narrator talks of father and son:

allein neben dem Unterrichte gab er seinem Sohne unversehens auch ein anderes Kleinod mit, welches ein Fremder nicht hätte geben können, nämlich sein eigenes einfältiges, metallstarkes, goldreines Männerherz, welches Hugo unsäglich liebte, und unbemerkt in sich sog, so daß er schon als Knabe etwas Eisenfestes und Altkluges an sich hatte. (677)

(But in addition to the instruction he unwittingly gave his son a further jewel which a stranger could not have handed on: his simple manly heart of golden purity and metallic strength, which Hugo loved beyond words and unknowingly made part of himself so that, already as a boy, he had something precocious, a kind of iron strength about him.)

The key metaphors are those of metallic strength and fixity, metaphors which seem to be applied approvingly. The narrator may point out the emotional impoverishment entailed, but at the same time he suggests that this impoverishment is inseparable from very real moral qualities.

This ambivalent stance has disturbing ramifications because the deformation of natural feeling is not confined to Hugo alone, but touches the lives of a whole generation. We recall the father's words of advice to the son which are in praise of war as something that can steel the will and purpose of a whole people:

Aber es kann nicht lange so dauern; wenn das Kraut fort wachsen wird, dann wird [der Feind] sich über die Blume wundern, die ganz oben stehen wird. Sie muß Ingrimm heißen, diese Blume, und alle alten Sünden müssen getilgt werden. (682)

(But it cannot last much longer like this; as the plant continues to grow, [the enemy] will be astounded at the flower which crowns it. This flower will be called wrath, and all old sins will be purged.)

The yoking together of hatred, militarism, with images of natural growth is, within the didactic scheme of the story, a perversity. But it is a perversity that becomes public reality of which the narrator partakes: his report of the growing war-fever echoes the image patterns of the father's admonition: 'der Haß war sachte und allseitig heran geblüht, und die geschmähte Gottheit der Selbständigkeit und des eigenen Wertes hob allgemach das starke Haupt empor' (699) (hatred had softly bloomed on all sides, and the scorned deity of self-assertion and self-esteem gradually raised its mighty head). The divided allegiance of the narrator can be traced time and time again. He points out that Hugo's hardness, inherited from his father, is intensified by the war, but typically continues: 'Aber dennoch wurde sein hartes Antlitz und sein strenges Auge von den Untergebenen fast abgöttisch geliebt, weil er immer gerecht war' (719) (but even so, his hard face and his stern eyes were almost idolized by his inferiors because he was always just). We are given to understand that this hardness relaxes its grip when Hugo and Cöleste are reunited – here the metallic metaphor is negated: 'das ganze eherne Rad des Krieges war von seinem Herzen' (722) (the whole bronze ring of the war was lifted from his heart). But the grip cannot be broken: it has become inseparable from Hugo's selfhood, and while on one level the story condemns his iron restraint, on another it endorses it. The hardness is linked with beauty: 'Diese Scheu zierte den Mann nun unendlich schöner, als sie einstens den Jüngling geziert hatte' (723) (this reticence graced the man even more than it had done the youth). What we hear in this comment is a note of narrative approval – just as later we sense a flicker of disapproval when we are told that Hugo loses his hardness with the passing of time: 'da er alt geworden, da sich die Härte des Krieges verloren hatte, und da er weich-herzig geworden war, hat er oft bitterlich geweint' (731) (and as he grew old, and as the hardness of the war had faded, and as he had grown soft-hearted, he often wept bitterly). The strange rhetoric to this sentence, with its thrice repeated 'da' clause, scarcely asserts the rightness of Hugo's 'soft-heartedness'. Yet, within the didactic import of the story, that weakening ought, surely, to constitute a value.

Clearly, *Das alte Siegel* cannot simply be regarded as a cautionary tale that advocates life, emotion, passion over principle, reticence, discipline. The narrator is significantly implicated in the cast of mind which he portrays in Hugo and thereby suggests that the human psyche enacts an unsettling dialectic of spontaneity and repression. Images of the metallic, the constricting, the rigid, intertwine with images of warmth and physicality. Love may bloom like a flower – but so does hatred and militarism. And this invoking of the natural as part and parcel of both emotion and rigidity is at the centre of the story's disturbing implications. Section Three begins with a lengthy set-piece description in which the narrator evokes the gradual, almost imperceptible start of an avalanche. And he then spells out the metaphorical implications: 'so wie die Sage das Beginnen eines Schneesturzes erzählt, ist es oft mit den Anfängen eines ganzen Geschickes der Menschen' (702) (as the legend recounts the beginning of an avalanche, so it is with the beginning of the whole destiny of men). The reference is to Hugo's decision to go to the church: the natural image of inevitable processes is linked with Hugo's 'destined' meeting with Cöleste. The very next section of the story begins with another set-piece description of nature – cobwebs shining with dew in the morning sunlight. Once again the metaphor is made clear:

so hatte sich ein Schleier gewoben durch das ganze deutsche Land, an jedem Jünglingsherzen war ein Faden angeknüpft – und längs dieses Fadens lief die Begeisterung. Wohl ahneten und wußten einzelne Herzen um den Schleier, aber es fehlte nur noch die Sonne, die da aufgehen, das Geschmeide plötzlich darlegen, und allen weithin sichtbar machen sollte, daß es da sei – gleichsam ein Kleinod für das Vaterland, und ein verderbliches Totenhemd für den Feind. (717)

(so a veil had been woven through all the German lands, and a thread connected it to the heart of every young man. And along this thread ran the current of enthusiasm. Of course individual hearts had known of the veil or sensed it, but what was needed was for the sun to rise and reveal the cluster of precious stones and to make it plain to all that it was there – as it were a jewel for the fatherland and a shroud bringing death and destruction to the enemy.)

Natural impulses, natural beauty are, apparently, present in the adventure of love and the adventure of war. Both adventures are justified at the level of existential prompting, both are beautiful. Cöleste is beautiful when she frees herself from the matronly veil: Hugo is beautiful in the sternness that informs his face and being, and in the qualities that will make him a soldier.

Das alte Siegel is both a disturbing and, in the last analysis, a questionable story. And nowhere more so than in that uncontrolled ambivalence whereby the ethos of the old seal is both criticized and endorsed. The ambivalence is not surprising for it has its counterpart in Stifter's utterances on contemporary politics. At times peace is advocated as the supreme and only realization of God's will on earth, but on other occasions Stifter is explicit in his enthusiasm for manly virtues and, by extension, Imperial self-assertion. Similarly, *Das alte Siegel* tends, in places, to idolize the very mentality that it claims to denounce. Ultimately, Cöleste's anguish is muffled by the strange collusion between the narrator's and the protagonist's consciousness. Admittedly, the story remains a provocative and challenging work: but it does not achieve the sustained balance of a story such as *Kalkstein*, which, as we hope to show later, offers a superbly differentiated comprehension of both the process and the price of sublimation.

A similar concern with the deformation and destruction of human substance informs *Der Hagestolz*, although, as we shall see, the story does hold out a more conciliatory possibility. It recounts how Victor, an orphan, who has promised himself, out of a sense of his own vulnerability, never to marry, is sent to spend some time with his uncle who leads the life of a recluse on an island. Victor finds the uncle cold and hostile, but gradually trust and affection grow up between them. In a passionate outburst on the evening before Victor leaves, the uncle urges his nephew to marry, to break out of the isolation in which he (the uncle) has spent his life. Victor returns home to his foster mother Ludmilla (with whom the uncle had been in love in his youth), and subsequently marries Hanna, her daughter.

The text signals its structuring principle in the opening section 'Gegenbild', which establishes two contrasting images that will be sustained throughout the story.[10] There is young Victor and his friends, surrounded by the abundance of nature – 'eine glänzende Landschaft war rings um sie geworfen' (*S*, 795) (a radiant landscape surrounded them on all sides). Victor announces to his friends 'daß ich wirklich ganz und gar nicht heiraten werde, und daß ich sehr unglücklich bin' (798) (that I genuinely will not marry and that I am very unhappy). The narrator highlights the contrast between the adolescent, bombastic talk and the organic processes that occur around Victor and his friends:

Während sie so, wie sie meinten, von dem Großen redeten, geschieht um sie her, wie sie ebenfalls meinten, nur das Kleine; es grünen weiterhin die Büsche, es keimt die brütende Erde und beginnt mit ihren ersten Frühlingstierchen, wie mit Juwelen zu spielen. (796)

(As they thus talked of what in their eyes were great things, there takes place all around them what were – again in their eyes – only small things; the bushes continue to grow green, the earth, brooding over its young, begins to put forth shoots and to play with its first animals of springtime as with jewels.)

In one sense, then, the boys (and especially Victor) are out of tune with nature, they do not see the ceaseless growth that is the truth of her being. Yet, in another sense, they are not divorced from nature: their immaturity is part of the natural unfolding of their lives – 'um sie herum liegt der Frühling, der eben so unerfahren und zuversichtlich ist, wie sie' (796) (all around them there is the spring which is as inexperienced and self-confident as they are). Victor's passionate assertion that he will never marry *and* that he is not happy suggests that his pessimism goes against the grain of his emotional needs, of the promptings of his nature.

The image of burgeoning youth and nature highlights the contrast with the 'Gegenbild' – the old man sitting alone and weary on his island. For the 'Hagestolz' there is only loneliness, and fear of approaching death. There is a blight on his life, of which even his natural surroundings seem to partake:

Während die Jünglinge auf ihrem Berge emporgestrebt waren, und ein wimmelndes Leben und dichte Freude sie umgab, war er auf seiner Bank gesessen, hatte auf die an Stäbe gebundenen Frühlingsblumen geschaut, und die leere Luft und der vergebliche Sonnenschein hatten um ihn gespielt. (800)

(While the boys had pressed on up their mountain and teeming life and abundant joy surrounded them, he sat on his bench, looked at the spring flowers which were fastened to sticks, and the empty air and the sunshine played around him to no avail.)

The contrast between the two states of being, the 'wimmelndes Leben' (teeming life) and the 'Ruhe der Toten' (855) (silence of the dead) which surrounds the uncle, is further reinforced by the figure of Victor's foster-mother, Ludmilla. She is an example of old age which finds ever more urgent joy in – and surrender to – the splendour of the created world. Her affirmation is grounded in an unshakable faith in God: 'Alles, was Gott sendet, ist schön' (805), (everything that God sends is beautiful). Ludmilla is the epitome of a fulfilled and fulfilling existence – she fosters life, both literally and metaphorically.

From this realm of affirmation Victor travels to that of the 'Hagestolz', a realm whose deadness is reflected in the hammering adjectival *Leitmotiv* of 'alt'. The domestic staff are old, and –

Sogar die Hunde waren sämtlich alt; die Obstbäume, die sich vorfanden, waren alt; die steinernen Zwerge, die Bohlen im Schiffhause waren alt! (880)

(Even the dogs were old, all of them; the fruit trees that were there were old; the stone garden gnomes, the planks in the boat house were old!)

Victor's journey amounts to a 'Bildungsreise' – the sequence of the chapter headings recalls that in *Der Nachsommer*: 'Abschied', 'Wanderung', 'Aufenthalt', 'Rückkehr' (Departure, Wandering, Sojourn, Return). But the familiar *Bildungsroman* model is inverted by this journey into negativity. The uncle has surrendered to inactivity and despair because the love which he harboured as a young man has been thwarted. His anguish calls to mind Büchner's Danton: suffering has become the bedrock of atheism, whereas for Ludmilla suffering, sent by God, is but 'eine andere Art Freude' (805) (another kind of joy). The uncle's island estate is a spiritually and physically damaged world. Even his speech is blighted in the laconic hostility which reflects his profound sense of existential disgust. In a passionate outpouring, whose tenor recalls the Schopenhauerian *principium individuationis*, he asserts that there is no meaning beyond the brutal fact that 'jeder ist um sein selbst willen da' (891) (each man exists only for himself). But towards the end of this speech, the very disgust at life produces a terrible compensatory fervour as he argues that Victor must enter life, must marry and produce children. He invokes moral categories, advocates life in the service of the community, and echoes the discursive Stifter when he equates his own bachelor life with an 'einseitigen und kläglichen Verrückung' (892) (one-sided and pitiful aberration); but all moral considerations are ultimately overridden by the sheer biological imperative in the face of which personal feelings are totally irrelevant:

Wenn du schon eine Vorneigung zu einer Frauenperson hast, so tut das bei dem Heiraten gar nichts, es ist nicht hinderlich, und fördert oft nicht, nimm sie nur: hast du aber keine solche Vorneigung, so ist es auch gleichgültig. (894f.)

(If you have a predisposition towards a certain woman, that does not affect matters in marriage, it is not a hindrance, and often it is not a help either. Just take her: and if you do not have such a predisposition, that too is irrelevant.)

There is something obsessive about this advice – it echoes the uncle's insane routine of locking every door in the house in order to shut out death, the fear 'vor gewalttätiger Verkürzung seines Lebens' (800) (violent truncation of his life); however, within the overall design of the story, his speech would appear to underpin the perspective of affirmation, the 'wimmelndes Leben' as embodied in Ludmilla and enacted by the plot-line with its happy ending. This didactic strand culminates in the somewhat sententious final paragraph which dismisses the 'Hagestolz' as an aberration:

Dann scheint immer und immer die Sonne nieder, der blaue Himmel lächelt aus einem Jahrtausend in das andere, die Erde kleidet sich in ihr altes Grün, und die Geschlechter steigen an der langen Kette bis zu dem jüngsten Kinde nieder: aber er ist aus allen denselben ausgetilgt, weil sein Dasein kein Bild geprägt hat, seine Sprossen nicht mit hinunter gehen in dem Strome der Zeit. – Wenn er aber auch noch andere Spuren gegründet hat, so erlöschen diese, wie jedes Irdische erlischt – und wenn in dem Ozean der Tage endlich alles, alles untergeht, selbst das Größte und Freudigste, so geht er eher unter, weil an ihm schon alles im Sinken begriffen ist, während er noch atmet und während er noch lebt. (910)

(Always and always the sun shines down, the blue sky smiles from one millenium to the next, the earth dons her same green, and the generations descend on their long chain down to the youngest child:

89

but he is eradicated from all that, because his existence has left no image, no scions of his join those who are borne down the mighty river of time. But if he has left other traces of himself, they will fade as all earthly things fade: and when in the ocean of days finally everything, everything is swallowed up, even the greatest and most joyous of things, yet he will go under more swiftly because everything about him is sinking even as he lives and draws breath.)

It is worth mentioning that in the *Urfassung* of this story, such reflections form the opening paragraph – the tale closes with the happy ending of Victor's marriage, and with a brief final reference to the old man – 'der Oheim war nicht dabei; der Greis saß einsam und finster auf seiner Insel' (*Urf*, 375) (the uncle was not present: the old man sat lonely and dark on his island). All of which serves to make the first version more straightforward in its didacticism: Victor is taught by a terrifying negative example to put behind him his adolescent melancholy. That didactic thrust is still present in the later version: but it is subverted by the authority and pain of the uncle's grief which not even the conclusion can banish. Interestingly, Stifter seems to have felt something of this as he worked on the story. The manuscript was completed by December 1843, but it was too large for the *Iris* almanach in which it was to appear. Stifter agreed to cut the story. In the summer of 1844 he wrote to Heckenast:

Der Hagestolz selber sollte ein grandios düster prächtiger Charakter werden, aber er schwoll mir so über alles Maß der *Iris* hinaus, daß mir jetzt das Abkürzen nicht weniger Mühe machte, als früher das Concipiren. Ich freue mich nur für die Gesamtausgabe, da soll er in seiner ursprünglichen Tiefe und Gewalt auftreten können, wenn er auch einen Band füllt.[11]

(The recluse himself was to become a grandiose, gloomy, splendid character, but he grew so much beyond the proportions of the *Iris* that now the shortening is giving me as much trouble as did the initial conception of the story. I am pleased only when I think of the complete edition where he should be able to appear in his original depth and power – even if he takes up a whole volume.)

The text which is printed in Max Stefl's edition is the shortened version for publication in the *Iris*. When Stifter reworks and extends the story for the *Studien*, he produces a work in which the creative imagination is fully engaged by the experience which it is bent on repudiating. However worthy a figure Ludmilla may be, the reader is likely to remember her and the idyllic conclusion far less than the savage pathos of the old man.

One can argue that Stifter, as a Christian writer, lends creative sympathy to the figure of the 'Hagestolz' because, as his creator, he intends to show the same understanding and tolerance which the great Creator extends towards the infertile fig-tree in the biblical parable that the final section of the story invokes. But we feel that there is another sympathy at work, a deep-seated philosophical affinity between Stifter the narrator and his protagonist. As Chapters 1 and 3 of this study have pointed out, Stifter is haunted by the thought of transience, the expendability of human life within the overall design of creativity. One recalls, for example, the anguished phrase 'es wäre gräßlich absurd!' (*M*, 313) (it would be appallingly absurd!) from *Ein Gang durch die Katakomben*, or the nagging question 'why should this be?' from *Abdias* which, as we have already suggested, comes close to the questioning of a Schopenhauer or a Büchner. In *Der Hagestolz* there are indeed persistent signs that the gloomy perspective of the uncle is shared by the narrator to a considerable degree. On the second page of the story, Stifter retains a narratorial comment from the first version. Contemplating the young men with all their plans, he states:

Wir müssen hier bemerken: welch ein rätselhaftes, unbeschreibliches, geheimnisreiches, lockendes Ding ist die Zukunft, wenn wir noch nicht in ihr sind – wie schnell und unbegriffen rauscht sie als Gegenwart davon – und wie klar, verbraucht und wesenlos liegt sie dann als Vergangenheit da! (*S*, 796)

(We must comment here: what an enigmatic, indescribable, mysterious and enticing thing is the future when we have not yet reached it – how swiftly and uncomprehended it rushes past us as the present – and how transparent, exhausted and empty does it lie behind us as the past!)

Here, the narrator anticipates the uncle who insists that, however much man may strive, he is bound to experience insubstantiality: 'Denn das Leben flog, ehe es erhascht werden konnte' (894) (for life flew past before it could be grasped), and again, referring to human emotions: 'derlei Dinge sind nicht beständig, sie kommen und vergehen, wie es eben ist, ohne daß man sie lockt, und ohne daß man sie vertreibt' (895) (such things are not constant, they come and go, as is their wont, whether we beckon to them, or whether we reject them). By analogy with the narratorial comment on the second page, the overall text is so organized as to reflect both the joy in the ever regenerative energies – 'Streben', 'Jubeln', 'empor' are key terms – and the clear vision that all this is ultimately doomed. In this sense Victor's journey to the uncle's island parallels Stifter's own journey into the realm of the catacombs. Hence, the interior of the uncle's dwelling must be taken not merely as a moral indictment of his way of life: beyond the psychological and moral parameters, the dust, the shambles, 'die tote starre Fülle von Dingen und Kram, womit er sich umringte' (885) (the dead, inert mass of bits and pieces with which he surrounded himself) also function symbolically, and intimate the latent dust in all life. We may interpret them as emblems of worldly transience – there is indeed something Baroque about the description of the island estate as there is about *Ein Gang durch die Katakomben* – or we may take them to suggest the death of that vital energy in man which perceives and upholds meaning despite all the odds. Typically, Ludmilla loves even 'die ältesten unbrauchbarsten Dinge' (803) (the oldest and most useless things). She cherishes them as ciphers of future possibilities even though the narrator points out that there may be no fruition:

Da lag auf einem Schreine ein altes Kinderspielzeug, das schon lange nicht gebraucht worden war, und vielleicht nie mehr gebraucht werden wird – es war ein Pfeifchen mit einer hohlen Kugel, in der klappernde Dinge waren – sie wischte es ringsum sauber ab, und legte es wieder hin. (803)

(On a chest there lay an old toy which had not been used for a long time and which perhaps never will be used again – it was a pipe with a hollow ball with rattling things inside. She dusted all its surfaces and returned it to its place.)

For the uncle, things have lost all their potentiality and, in their dust-covered condition, they function as emblems of dead meaning. The linguistic correlative is to be found at all those points where the uncle dispenses advice, insight, yet immediately retreats into phrases which reverberate with the sense of futility: 'Aber was soll das alles? – –' (891) (But what is the point of all this? –); 'Aber du kannst übrigens tun, wie du willst' (894) (But you can of course do as you wish); 'so ist es auch gleichgültig' (895) (it comes to the same thing).

This central textual stance, which on the one hand affirms the meaning of physical and spiritual things and on the other questions it, reminds one sharply of that dual perspective in *Der Hochwald* which sees both the 'beloved objects' and the mere 'trappings' of domesticity; one also thinks of the gamble that Stifter takes in the *Mappe* with his intention to celebrate the 'poetry of clutter'; and we shall find the same syndrome in *Turmalin* where the very rooms that seem to spell a solidly settled life also exude a sense of deadness – the narration underpins this point when, later on, it describes the rooms as they lie covered in dust and devoid of life.

Victor finds his uncle's lifestyle repulsive, just as he finds 'das inhaltlose Schweigen und die tote Gleichgültigkeit an dem Manne öde und bekümmernd' (888) (the empty silence and the dead indifference of the man both barren and distressing). But the narrator is careful to point out how limited Victor's viewpoint is: the uncle has kept an old picture of his brother – it is one of those customary portraits which decorate bourgeois households as reminiscences of student days. The uncle, who typically refused to be painted, refers to the convention as a 'närrische Sitte' (870) (foolish custom). But this is not merely a moment of misanthropy, for his phrase re-

verberates with that sense of futility which the narrator
expresses and which is denied to Victor's perception:

Victor konnte sich nicht vorstellen, wie vielleicht derselbe Mann später
in dunklem einfachen Rocke und mit dem eingefallenen sorgenvollen
Angesichte vor seiner Wiege gestanden sein mag. Noch weniger
konnte er sich vorstellen, wie er dann auf dem Krankenbette gelegen
ist, und wie man ihn, da er tot und erblaßt war, in einen schmalen
Sarg getan und in das Grab gesenkt habe. (870)

(Victor was not able to imagine how it could later come about that
the same man would stand before his cradle in a simple dark coat with
hollow, careworn face, Even less could he imagine how he lay on his
sick-bed, how, when he was pale and dead, he was put into a coffin
and lowered into the grave.)

These words point back to the overwhelming sense of transience which informs the narratorial comment on the second
page. And on this level, the narrator abstains from moral
judgment and didacticism; instead, he treats Victor and his
uncle as quasi-allegorical figures who represent both the
splendour and utter meaninglessness of life, the two perspectives which are at the heart of Schopenhauer's work.

In the figure of Ludmilla, in its plot-line and in the concluding paragraph, the story would seem to assert the category
of Schopenhauer's temporal immortality ('zeitliche Unsterblichkeit'). But this assertion is relativized in so far as the
narrator shares the uncle's anguish at individuation, its curse
and its grip. The wisdom which the old man dispenses is
inseparable from his stark insight into man's expendability:

Alles zerfällt in Augenblicke, wenn man nicht ein Dasein erschaffen
hat, das über dem Sarge noch fortdauert. Um wen bei seinem Alter
Söhne, Enkel und Urenkel stehen, der wird oft tausend Jahre alt. Es
ist ein vielfältig Leben derselben Art vorhanden, und wenn er fort ist,
dauert das Leben doch noch immer als dasselbe, ja man merkt es nicht
einmal, daß ein Teilchen dieses Lebens seitwärts ging, und nicht mehr
kam. (892f.)

(Everything disintegrates at each moment if you have not created an
existence which can continue beyond the coffin. The man who in his
old age is surrounded by sons, grandchildren and great-grandchildren

often lives to be a thousand. A multiple, kindred life is still there, and when he is no more, life still continues the same and one does not even notice that one particle of this life has moved to the side, and has not continued.)

But is a human being who enters the stream of life by producing children any less individuated than one who has no children? Is human fulfilment to be measured in terms of demonstrable productivity within the grand sequence of being? 'Mit meinem Tode fällt alles dahin, was ich als Ich gewesen bin' (893) (with my death everything that I have been as an 'I' crumbles away), says the uncle. But is there any way round that being the case, always and for ever? Some sixty years later, another figure in a piece of German prose fiction will ask similar questions about individuation and its transcendence. And that figure will long for death as a release from the pain of individuation; he will also long to be represented by his perfect offspring, a son who will say 'yes' to the strain and attrition of being, who will fearlessly say 'I'. That other figure is, of course, Thomas Buddenbrook. But he can no more escape his disgust at being inalienably what he wishes he were not than can the lonely bachelor in his island fortress. Both are, quite simply, unable to free themselves from everything 'was ich als Ich gewesen bin'. The capital letter – 'Ich' – says it all. And that 'Ich' cannot be submerged in the simple integrity of that 'shining landscape' which is 'cast around it'. The human centre is irreducible: no amount of fulfilment in the frame – the splendour of nature, Victor's marriage to Ludmilla's daughter – can exorcise it.

5 · RECONCILIATIONS

In den folgenden Stunden will ich versuchen, an einzelnen Büchern, Themen und Thesen eine Ästhetik des Humanen zu behandeln – das Wohnen, die Nachbarschaft und die Heimat, das Geld und die Liebe, Religion und Mahlzeiten...

Die Abneigung der Deutschen gegen Provinzialismus, gegen das Alltägliche, das eigentlich das Soziale und Humane ist, ist eben provinzlerisch...

Man hat mich mit einiger Herablassung oft einen Autor der kleinen Leute genannt: peinlicherweise empfinde ich solche Einschränkungen immer als Schmeichelei...

Stifter, seine verzweifelte Stille, er, der die großartigste Wohnung der deutschen Literatur, den *Nachsommer* schrieb – einen Traum...

Der einzige nach Goethe, der Zusammenhänge gefunden hat, war Stifter, an dessen Werk sich, wie an Jean Pauls Werk, eine Ästhetik des Humanen darstellen ließe, die alle von mir genannten Themen einschließen würde...Ich glaube, er könnte der Vater eines neuen humanen Realismus werden, Pate stehen bei Versuchen, die Abgründe zwischen der statistischen und der in der Literatur geschilderten Wirklichkeit nicht zu schließen, auch nicht zu überbrücken, vielleicht aber langsam aufzuschütten.

Heinrich Böll (1966)

(In the following hours I want, in respect of individual books, themes, and theses, to try and discuss an aesthetic of the humane – of the domestic world, neighbourliness and home, love and money, religion and mealtimes...

The aversion of the Germans towards provincialism, towards the everyday – which is essentially the social and the humane – is, precisely, provincial...

People have often with considerable condescension called me an author of little people: embarrassingly enough, I always feel such dismissals to be flattery.

Stifter, his desperate stillness, he who wrote the greatest dwelling in German literature, *Indian Summer*, a dream...

The only person, after Goethe, who perceived connexions was Stifter, whose work – like Jean Paul's – would provide the proof of an aesthetic of the humane which would embrace all the themes I have mentioned. I believe he could be the father of a new humane realism, he could be the patron saint of attempts to take the abysses that have opened up between statistical reality and reality as portrayed in literature and not so much to close or bridge them, but rather, perhaps, slowly to fill them up.)

The works which we have examined in the previous chapter were all written in the 1840s, and there can be no doubt that Stifter's expression of Unreason is most overt in these early works. However, as has been pointed out, it would be misleading to suggest that the mature Stifter leaves this dimension behind and moves into unquestioning serenity. The problem whether, and to what degree, individuation can be reconciled with the stability and continuity vouchsafed by natural processes and moral principles persists even in his late works. But it must be stressed that from the very start of his creative career Stifter strenuously attempts to exorcise the disjunction between the human centre and the circumstances that surround it. It is in 1847 that he first formulates what was later to become the central tenet of the preface to *Bunte Steine*: 'das Große geschieht so schlicht, wie das Rieseln des Wassers, das Fließen der Luft, das Wachsen des Getreides – darum ist irgend eine Heldentat unendlich leichter und auch öfter da, als ein ganzes Leben voll Selbstbezwingung, unscheinbaren Reichtum und freudigen Sterben'[1] (greatness manifests itself as simply as the rushing of water, the flowing of the air, the growing of the corn – for that reason, any kind of heroic deed is infinitely easier and more frequently encountered than is a whole life full of self-mastery, unostentatious richness and serene dying). In this chapter we wish to examine three works which do attain this mediation between self and world, yet also intimate the cost, the heartache, that makes such reconciliation possible. We have chosen *Brigitta*, *Der Nachsommer* and *Die Mappe meines Urgroßvaters*; in terms of chronology, they cover the whole of Stifter's creative life and thus may stand as representative examples.

In *Brigitta* the narrator figure comes to stay with an old friend of his, a Major, who lives in the Hungarian steppes. Gradually the narrator discovers the profound affection which binds the Major to Brigitta, the owner of the neighbouring estate. Apparently Brigitta's husband (and father of the boy Gustav) has deserted her, but there is no official divorce, and hence she and the Major cannot marry. We learn of Brigitta's past: she was an ugly, unloved child, but was wooed by Stephan Murai, whose love brought out all the tenderness and passion of her nature. But Stephan was unfaithful to her, and the two separated. One evening, as the Major and the narrator are riding home, they come across Gustav, who has been set upon by a pack of wolves. The Major rescues him and takes the boy home to his mother. The Major weeps because he has no children, but Brigitta consoles him, and as she does so, she uses his first name. It is Stephan: the two are reunited in fully acknowledged marital love.

Brigitta anticipates to a considerable degree the central stance of the mature Stifter; in particular, it prefigures the import of *Der Nachsommer*. The bulk of its narrative concern celebrates a meaningful life beyond the ravages of subjectivity, of passion and pain. The lengthy descriptions which chronicle Brigitta's and Stephan's life on the steppes triumphantly exorcise the tensions of their past. This sense of affirmation, of a security finally achieved, is reflected in the sequence of the chapter headings which is particularly telling if we compare it, for example, with that of *Der Hochwald*. There, the final note was on 'Ruine' – here, we find: 'Steppenwanderung' (The Journey through the Steppes), 'Steppenhaus' (The House in the Steppes), 'Steppenvergangenheit' (The Past of the Steppes), 'Steppengegenwart' (The Present of the Steppes). We learn of the ways in which Stephan and Brigitta co-operate and consult in the management of their estates, drawing life and growth out of the massive indifference of the landscape. Brigitta is magnificently at home on her estate: she is a woman 'in Mitte ihrer Schöpfung' (*S*, 791), (at the heart of her creation). It is a good and strong life, whose achievement is embedded in the cyclical strength of nature's being. Over long stretches, the narration itself is as gradual as the rhythms of nature, the patient cultivation of the land which it describes. Narrative mode and subject matter merge and in the process call to mind the import of the preface to *Bunte Steine*. Furthermore, the socio-cultural and political implications are spelt out when Stephan comments 'daß man es so mit dem Boden eines Landes beginnen müsse. Unsere Verfassung, unsere Geschichte ist sehr alt, aber noch vieles ist zu tun' (757) (that we must begin thus with the earth of our country. Our constitution, our history is very old, but there is still much to be done).

The narrator experiences to the full the educative function of this way of life; his very vocabulary begins to acquire the key terms of Stifter's philosophical utterances. As he observes the daily work on the estate, he begins to understand, to gain an overview, and, persuaded by 'das gleichförmig sanfte Abfließen dieser Tage und Geschäfte' (758) (monotonously gentle sequence of these days and activities), he forgets the busy urban life 'gleichsam als wäre das ein Kleines' (758) (as though it were, so to speak, a triviality). The life on the steppes becomes for him a revelation of an ideal state of being:

Wie schön und ursprünglich ist die Bestimmung des Landmannes, wenn er sie versteht und veredelt. In ihrer Einfalt und Mannigfaltigkeit, in dem ersten Zusammenleben mit der Natur, die leidenschaftslos ist, grenzt sie zunächst an die Sage von dem Paradiese. (758)

(How beautiful and firmly rooted is the destiny of the man who works on the land – provided he understands and ennobles it. In that simplicity and variety, in that primary commerce with nature which is without passion, such a destiny approaches most nearly the story of Paradise.)

Here, then, is a Garden of Eden beyond the sin of individuation, beyond the tangle of desires that prevents man from being at one with himself, at one with the world which he inhabits. This moral, if not didactic, impetus persists; there is repeated emphasis on 'leidenschaftslos'. Thus the narrator stresses the moral force that emanates from the relationship between Stephan and Brigitta:

Mit einer Zartheit, mit einer Verehrung, die wie an die Hinneigung zu einem höheren Wesen erinnerte, behandelte der Major das alternde Weib. (784)

(The Major treated the ageing woman with a gentleness, with a respect, which almost recalled the reverence for a higher being.)

And at the end of the story, when Brigitta and Stephan are reunited, he praises her forgiveness:

Und so herrlich ist das Schönste, was der arme, fehlende Mensch hienieden vermag, das Verzeihen – daß mir ihre Züge wie in unnachahmlicher Schönheit strahlten. (789)

(And so lovely is forgiveness, the finest thing of which poor wayward man is capable on earth, that her features shone as with an incomparable beauty.)

At all such points, the text enacts the aim stated in the preface to the *Studien*, the hope that these stories will not only give pleasure, but help to further 'irgend ein sittlich Schönes' (8) (some morally beautiful aim).

But the story as a whole, and more specifically the narrator's performance, does not simply endorse this paean of praise. Alongside the emphasis on 'leidenschaftslos' we find a more complex illumination, and this strand dominates the opening sections of the work where the narrator reflects on the laws of human attraction. He insists that it is an inscrutable agency not to be equated with outward beauty. Nor is it simply to be defined in terms of our moral sense of right action and behaviour:

Eben so fühlen wir uns manchmal zu einem hingezogen, den wir eigentlich gar nicht kennen, es gefallen uns seine Bewegungen, es gefällt uns seine Art, wir trauern, wenn er uns verlassen hat, und haben eine gewisse Sehnsucht, ja eine Liebe zu ihm, wenn wir oft noch in späteren Jahren seiner gedenken: während wir mit einem andern, dessen Wert in vielen Taten vor uns liegt, nicht ins Reine kommen können, wenn wir auch Jahre lang mit ihm umgegangen sind. (735)

(So it is that we can sometimes feel drawn to somebody whom we actually do not know, his movements attract us, we like his manner, we grieve when he has left us, and we sense a certain longing, indeed a love for him, whenever in later years we think of him. While with another, whose worth is manifestly shown in all manner of deeds, we simply find that we cannot come to terms, even though we may have spent years in his company.)

The narrator speaks of a powerful force in human experience, one which seems to fly in the face of all rational or moral explanation. Almost as if to countermand the disturbing implications of this, he continues: 'daß zuletzt sittliche Gründe vorhanden sind, die das Herz heraus fühlt, ist kein Zweifel, allein wir können sie nicht immer mit der Waage des Bewußtseins und der Rechnung hervor heben und anschauen' (735) (that ultimately there are ethical reasons which the heart divines cannot be doubted, but we cannot always isolate them and explore them with the scales of consciousness and calculation). Just as in *Abdias* the assertion of certainty, of the 'heitere Blumenkette', yields to uncertainty, so here, too, the statement 'kein Zweifel' is immediately relativized. The narrator stresses that despite the efforts of science, of psychology, a great deal remains shrouded in mystery. He may assert the supremacy of moral laws, but he cannot know beyond doubt whether human attraction is based on them, and thus he is reduced to claiming that it is 'für uns noch ein heiterer unermeßlicher Abgrund, in dem Gott und die Geister wandeln' (735) (for us still a bright, unfathomable abyss in which God and the spirits move). The tensions within the extraordinary oxymoron 'heiterer Abgrund' remind us of *Abdias*.

Throughout *Brigitta*, this uncertainty is paradoxically conjoined with the commitment to reason-giving. It finds its most acute expression in the multivalency of the central term 'Schönheit'. This concept recurs, as adjective or noun, with almost obsessive regularity, yet in constantly varying significations. The account of Brigitta's past emphasizes to a considerable degree the concept of inner beauty. She grows up unlovely and unloved, but she finds strength and intensity of being in her own inner self. She is described as 'stark und keusch' (773) (strong and chaste) and, as in *Das alte Siegel*, this self-restraint constitutes a value: it is both a moral and an existential integrity, the 'Odem eines ungeschwächten Lebens' (774), (the breath of an undiminished life). The narrator states:

Wenn nur einer gewesen wäre, für die verhüllte Seele ein Auge zu haben, und ihre Schönheit zu sehen, daß sie sich nicht verachte. – (768)

(If only somebody could have been there to perceive the hidden soul and see her beauty so that she should not come to despise herself.)

It is this inner beauty which Stephan chooses in preference to the physical beauty of all the other girls; and it is this beauty which the narrator is at pains to stress at the end of the story. The reader can hardly fail to assent to this value as Brigitta is constantly correlated with the harsh, yet secretly rich, landscape in which she spends her adult life. But, as the opening page signals, the text also reaches out beyond the ethical realm and acknowledges the human need for physical beauty and passion. And this need is nowhere stronger than in Brigitta herself. Even as a baby she rejects love that stems from moral considerations: sensing the mother's 'Anwandlung verspäteter Liebe und Barmherzigkeit' (766f.) (sudden discovery of belated love and compassion), she cries and struggles free of the embracing arms. Later, when her husband shows her especial consideration and care, we read: 'Sie dachte: "Jetzt weiß er, was mir fehlt", und hielt das erstickende Herz an sich' (776) (She thought: 'Now he knows what I lack', and she pressed her hands to her choking heart). When she learns of Stephan's love-affair with Gabriele, she is not outraged, but, significantly, filled with shame. Surely, this sense of shame is not to do with offended honour, but with the realization that her inner beauty will simply not suffice:

Brigittas Herz aber ·war zu Ende. Es war ein Weltball von Scham in ihrem Busen empor gewachsen, wie sie so schwieg, und wie eine schattende Wolke in den Räumen des Hauses herum ging. Aber endlich nahm sie das aufgequollne schreiende Herz gleichsam in ihre Hand und zerdrückte es. (777)

(But Brigitta's heart was at an end. A whole world of shame had grown up in her breast as she kept silent, as she walked like a dark cloud, casting her shadow through the rooms of her house. But finally she took the swollen screaming heart, as it were, in her hand, and crushed it.)

It is the measure of the intensity of Brigitta's feeling that the image of heartbreak is given literal – and transitive – force. The need for physical beauty and attraction motivates, of course, Stephan's brief love-affair with Gabriele. With her, he experiences an overwhelming sense of freedom from the confines of morality. Significantly, the narrator partakes of this experience – his vocabulary is particularly revealing: he likens Gabriele to an 'Abgrund von Unbefangenheit' (777) (an abyss of freedom) and records that Stephan was filled by 'Übermut' (exuberance), 'ein Taumel unbeschreiblichen Entzückens' (777) (a frenzy of indescribable delight). This need for physical passion becomes a weighty stylistic register within the story and challenges categories of right and wrong, good and bad. It is there in that extraordinary moment when Stephan saves Gustav from the wolves. The narrator describes it as 'ein Schauspiel, so gräßlich und so herrlich daß noch jetzt meine Seele schaudert und jauchzt' (785) (a spectacle so terrible and splendid that my soul still shudders and rejoices). Stephan hurls himself bodily amongst the wolves:

Als ich ankam, war er schon wie ein verderblich Wunder, wie ein Meteor, mitten unter ihnen – der Mann war fast entsetzlich anzuschauen, ohne Rücksicht auf sich, fast selber wie ein Raubtier warf er sich ihnen entgegen. (785)

(When I arrived he was already in the midst of them like some miraculous destroyer, like a meteor – the man was almost terrible to look at, with no thought for himself, almost a predatory animal himself, he flung himself at them.)

Above all, the reconciliation scene between Stephan and Brigitta is only at one level a hymn in praise of holy marital love, of the sublimity of forgiveness; at another, it has totally to do with passion, which is fully acknowledged when Brigitta calls Stephan's name:

Der Major wendete sich vollends herum – beide starrten sich eine
Sekunde an – nur eine Sekunde – dann aber vorwärts tretend lag er
eines Sturzes in ihren Armen, die sich mit maßloser Heftigkeit um
ihn schlossen. (789)

(The Major turned round completely – they both started at each other
for a second – only a second – but then he stepped forward and with
one great plunge lay in her arms, which closed about him with
boundless violence.)

Indeed, throughout the story the attraction between Stephan
and Brigitta has little to do with gentleness. When he woos
her, she argues that because of her ugliness she would need a
special kind of loving, one that is 'ohne Maß und Ende' (772)
(without measure or end). And when, after years of separation,
they meet again on the steppes and decide to live as good
neighbours (very much like Risach and Mathilde in *Der Nachsommer*), it is precisely because they cannot trust themselves
and fear that 'sich wieder etwas Fürchterliches zutragen
könnte' (791) (something horrific could happen again). It is
this centre of passion which makes the reconciliation scene so
moving: in its sheer amoral intensity it totally transcends the
narrator's stress on moral achievement. The phrase one should
note is 'maßlose Heftigkeit' – 'boundless violence'. Indeed,
the fierceness of the closing scene produces some extraordinary
writing. There is, for example, the moment when Stephan and
Brigitta turn towards the wounded Gustav – 'der das Ganze
dunkel ahnte, wie eine glühende, blühende Rose lag, und
ihnen atemlos entgegen harrte' (790) (who obscurely sensed
everything, who lay like a glowing rose in bloom and breath-
lessly waited, yearned for them). The image of the rose, in
its strange fusion of beauty and vulnerability, achieves a
poignant intensity, one that has to do with Gustav's being part
of the attrition and stress of passion. (One is reminded of
Kafka's *Ein Landarzt* (A Country Doctor), of the wound that
blooms like a flower.) The reuniting of Stephan, Brigitta, and
Gustav at this moment has everything to do with passion, and
very little to do with forgiveness and gentle love. Gustav, we

recall, has 'ihn [Stephan] immer leidenschaftlich und einseitig den herrlichsten Mann dieser Erde [genannt]' (791) (always called him [Stephan] passionately and one-sidedly the most splendid man on this earth). 'Leidenschaftlich' and 'einseitig': these are key terms from Stifter's vocabulary. In many contexts they are terms of condemnation, but here they seem to constitute values in themselves. We are a long way from the preface to *Bunte Steine*. Indeed, it is noteworthy that, in the closing scene, Brigitta expresses her forgiveness of Stephan in the following words:

Ich habe gefehlt, verzeihe mir, Stephan, die Sünde des Stolzes – ich habe nicht geahnt, wie gut du seist – es war ja bloß natürlich, es ist ein sanftes Gesetz der Schönheit, das uns ziehet. (789)

(I have done wrong, forgive me, Stephan, the sin of pride – I did not sense how good you are – it was only natural, it is a gentle law of beauty that directs us.)

Here, the term 'sanftes Gesetz' appears for the first time in Stifter's creative work, and, strikingly, it does not carry the moral signification that we know from the preface to *Bunte Steine*. When Brigitta uses the term, she is referring to the irresistible pull of physical beauty; she fully acknowledges the needs of passionate, amoral man. In keeping with the dual meaning of 'Schönheit', which our analysis has highlighted, Stephan puts his hand over Brigitta's mouth and pits the concept of inner, moral, beauty against her vision. His final stance endorses the aim of the preface to the *Studien*, in particular the worship of 'ein sittlich Schönes'.

In conclusion it must be stressed that the thematic and stylistic layering of *Brigitta* acknowledges the beauty both of moral and passionate man; it aims to fuse the two in that classical union of 'Einfalt und Mannigfaltigkeit' (758) simplicity and variety) which the landscape displays. One could perhaps argue that the text does not quite attain this unity, that it oscillates within the polarity, but does not control it. Uncertainty, if not irresolution, marks the narrator's performance. This is particularly striking at the beginning of the third section 'Steppenvergangenheit'. Here he reflects on the phenomenon of beauty ('das wundervolle Ding der Schönheit'):

Es ist im Weltall, es ist in einem Auge, dann ist es wieder nicht in Zügen, die nach jeder Regel der Verständigen gebildet sind. Oft wird die Schönheit nicht gesehen, weil sie in der Wüste ist, oder weil das rechte Auge nicht gekommen ist – oft wird sie angebetet und vergöttert, und ist nicht da: aber fehlen darf sie nirgends, wo ein Herz in Inbrunst und Entzücken schlägt, oder wo zwei Seelen an einander glühen; denn sonst steht das Herz stille, und die Liebe der Seelen ist tot. (765)

(It is in the universe, it is in an eye, but then again it is missing in features which are moulded according to every rule in the canon. Often beauty is not seen because it is in the desert, or because the right eye never chanced upon it. Often it is worshipped or idolized but is not there. Yet beauty may never be absent whenever a human heart beats in intense delight or where two souls burn for each other. For otherwise the heart stands still and the love in the soul is dead.)

One notes the aim to fuse emotional needs with a higher spiritual dimension, but one feels that the passage only achieves a blurring of categories. And this is typical of the narrator as a whole. In many of his discursive comments, he tends to invoke moral values; but he also acknowledges, and gives expression to, that mysterious realm of passion beyond good and evil. In the opening lines of the story he speaks of the 'Reize des Geheimnisvollen' (735) (the charm of the mysterious); in his acquaintance with Stephan he is sensitive to the fact that 'in dem reinen beschäftigten Leben des Majors irgendein Bodensatz liege, der es nicht zur völligen Abklärung kommen ließ' (760) (that in the pure energetic life of the Major there is some kind of sediment which did not allow that life to find its clear distilled form). He also recognizes the magical charm of Gabriele, whom he likens to 'ein himmlisches tolles, glühendes Rätsel' (777) (a divine, fantastic, incandescent riddle). And yet, particularly towards the end, he takes up an increasingly moralistic stance, and when we last see him, there is a return to undifferentiated certitude: 'Im Frühjahr nahm ich wieder mein deutsches Gewand, meinen deutschen Stab, und wanderte dem deutschen Vaterlande zu' (791f.) (In the spring I once again took up my German clothes, my German stick, and turned my steps towards my German fatherland). Or could one perhaps argue that the rhetoric of the thrice repeated 'deutsch' suggests a wistfully resigned return into one-dimensionality after the complex experience and exploration of 'Einfalt und Mannigfaltigkeit' on the Hungarian steppes?

Der Nachsommer is essentially an intensified version, a 'Steigerung', of *Brigitta*: in both works, an emotional crisis lays the foundations for a particular way of life which is celebrated as morally valuable. In *Brigitta*, this process of spiritual growth culminates in the protagonists' patient cultivation of the land; in *Der Nachsommer*, it is cultivation both in a practical and in a spiritual sense. Both texts are informed by a strenuous ethical concern; and if the narrator of *Brigitta* displays at times a tendency towards a didactic one-dimensionality, then this propensity is extended to well-nigh monumental proportions in *Der Nachsommer*. But, as we shall see, even here there are points where the narrative act intimates experiences and values beyond the ethically didactic pale.

The novel tells how a young man, Heinrich Drendorf, comes one day to the house of one Herr von Risach. He is attracted to the house and the man; for he senses a unity between the man and his dwelling, an integrity and harmony that encompasses all the component circumstances – the furniture, books, paintings, flowers, the *objets d'art*, the scientific instruments. Heinrich returns frequently to the house; he meets Mathilde, a close friend of Risach's, who lives on a nearby estate, and gradually he falls in love with her daughter Nathalie. The marriage is blessed by Risach, Mathilde, and by Heinrich's parents. In the penultimate chapter of the novel, entitled 'Der Rückblick' (Retrospection), Heinrich learns of Risach's past: how he came as a young tutor into the house of Mathilde's parents, how he fell in love with Mathilde, how her parents urged them to wait, to devote themselves to their education and careers. In this, young Risach who has no family, sees a sacred obligation. He accepts the parental decision, but Mathilde bitterly resents his acquiescence. They part; both subsequently to enter into loveless marriages. But when they are both widowed, they come together again. Mathilde apologizes for – and retracts – her former harsh judgment of Risach, and they live as friends and neighbours in the peace and harmony of their Indian Summer. And into that world of the Indian Summer, Heinrich is initiated. If Risach and Mathilde inhabit this 'Nachsommer ohne vorher-gegangenen Sommer' (*N*, 682) (Indian Summer without a preceding summer) so Heinrich Drendorf learns to convert his summer into an Indian Summer.

The novel signals its centre of gravity in its title: it is about the Indian Summer, it is the circumstantial and loving description of a life lived in harmony both with the daily tasks of running an estate and with the patient labours of spiritual cultivation, of *Bildung*. And, as in *Brigitta*, subject matter and narrative mode are at one: just as Risach's world exists in willed isolation from the common affairs of men, so the novel is removed from the common world of reader expectations. It is, in this sense, deeply symptomatic that we learn the name of the young protagonist only very late in the novel. Such interest as might be engendered by outward action and complex characterization is reduced to a minimum; instead, the novel cherishes the world of the Indian Summer, upholds the things and circumstances of the contained life. And this cherishing gives symbolic density to the novel: the objects and facts of Risach's world become suffused with a meaning and significance which, so it is implied, are all too rarely vouchsafed to man.

This nineteenth-century Indian Summer reinstates and celebrates the values of the eighteenth-century classical legacy: the ravages of individuality are overcome, healed by an all-embracing moral and aesthetic education. As Risach makes clear, this way of being is not a second best:

Es gibt eine eheliche Liebe,...die vielleicht das Spiegelklarste ist, was menschliche Verhältnisse aufzuweisen haben. Diese Liebe trat ein. Sie ist innig ohne Selbstsucht, freut sich, mit dem andern zusammen zu sein, sucht seine Tage zu schmücken und zu verlängern, ist zart, und hat gleichsam keinen irdischen Ursprung an sich. Mathilde nimmt Anteil an jeder meiner Bestrebungen. Sie geht mit mir in den Räumen meines Hauses herum, ist mit mir in dem Garten, betrachtet die Blumen oder Gemüse, ist in dem Meierhofe, und schaut seine Erträgnisse an, geht in das Schreinerhaus und betrachtet, was wir machen, und sie beteiligt sich an unserer Kunst und selbst an unsern wissenschaftlichen Bestrebungen. Ich sehe in ihrem Hause nach, betrachte die Dinge im Schlosse im Meierhofe auf den Feldern...(681f.)

(There is a marital love...which perhaps, of all human relationships, comes closest to mirror-like clarity. This love came about. It is intense, but without self-seeking, takes pleasure in being with the other person, seeks to adorn his days and to prolong them, is tender and has as it were no earthly source to it. Mathilde shares in all my projects. She walks with me round the rooms of my house, she is with me in the garden, looks at the flowers or the vegetables, is in the dairy farm and watches its yield, goes into the carpentry workshop and observes what we are doing, and she takes part in our arts and even in our scholarly undertakings. I see that all is in order in her house, I look at the things in the castle, in the dairy farm, in the fields...)

In Goethean terms, *Entsagung* (renunciation) has led Risach and Mathilde into a purer state of being. The original intensity of feeling has been transmuted into the intensity of a way of life in which the *vita contemplativa* and *vita activa* are supremely fused. At one point Risach states that the happiness which he and Mathilde experienced as young lovers is not lost: 'Es ist nicht abgeblüht, es hat nur eine andere Gestalt' (367) (it has not faded, it has merely acquired a different form). This 'andere Gestalt' is the reverent absorption of the self into the tasks and objects of man's practical and spiritual estate. And in order that the reader may partake in this way of being, Risach's voice is widened into the very voice of the novel: as a narrative text, *Der Nachsommer* embodies quite radically 'eine andere Gestalt'. For some seven hundred pages, incantatory cadences of pure registering aim to persuade the reader into that selfless seeing and perceiving which are the basis of a morally anchored life. Style, narrative structure and plot-line all serve this one aim. Just as Heinrich essentially enacts 'Gehorsam' (obedience) by listening to Risach and following his example, so the reader is encouraged to listen to the narrative voice and to find that sense of stability which it advocates. At the end of the novel, this stability is concretized in the three estates which all embody Risach's way of life: there is Risach in the 'Aspernhof', Heinrich's parents and sister in the 'Gusterhof', Mathilde, Natalie and Heinrich in the 'Sternenhof'. It is a three-cornered bastion against the disintegrative forces of the times as Stifter explicitly stated: 'Ich habe eine große einfache sittliche Kraft der elenden Verkommenheit gegenüber stellen wollen'[2] (I wanted to confront the most wretched depravity with a great, simple, ethical force). The thematic aim and the aesthetic organization which it entails are most strikingly crystallized at one point where Risach reflects on the function of art. We read:

'Es wäre des höchsten Wunsches würdig, wenn nach Abschluß des Menschlichen ein Geist die gesamte Kunst des menschlichen Geschlechtes von ihrem Entstehen bis zu ihrem Vergehen zusammenfassen und überschauen dürfte.'

Mathilde antwortete hierauf mit Lächeln: 'Das wäre ja im Großen, was du jetzt im Kleinen tust.' (388)

('It would be the most worthy object of the highest wish if, on the conclusion of all human things, one spirit could survey and summarize the whole art of the human race from its beginnings to its end.'

Mathilde answered with a smile: 'That would be a larger version of what you are doing within a small compass.')

'Nach Abschluß des Menschlichen' signifies indeed the place where Risach's mode of being, and more importantly the novel as a whole, is situated. It is thus no surprise that the work has divided critics ever since its publication. Typically, Nietzsche admired its willed transcendence of the common realm of man, whereas a modern critic, Horst Glaser, denounces the work as being deeply implicated in the efforts of mid-nineteenth-century Restoration.[3]

We do not wish here to trace the manifold symbolic representations of the novel's import; the reader may find the studies by Amann, Lindau, and Sjögren[4] particularly helpful in this respect. Our concern is to suggest that even in this monument to man's spiritual potential, to the perfect relatedness of human centre and the frame of circumstances, there are fissures and gaps. And these gaps yield room for critical reflections, particularly on whether individuality can and should be so transcended, whether the transmutation of 'Verhältnis', human relationship, into 'Verhältnisse', circumstances, is ultimately valid. The novel, of course, does its utmost to stifle such questions: it is highly significant that the fissures which are suggested by Mathilde's melancholy are only acknowledged toward the end of the novel, in the chapter 'Rückblick' (Retrospection). And even this section, the potentially crucial stock-taking of a life, is rendered in monologue form: it is Risach who recounts the past. Mathilde's voice is hardly heard, although her perspective, we sense, may be far less serene. Earlier in the novel, Heinrich overhears by chance a conversation between Risach and Mathilde. She laments: 'Wie diese Rosen abgeblüht sind, ist unser Glück abgeblüht'. Typically, the narrative only registers Risach's conciliatory reply that it has not faded, but taken on 'eine andere Gestalt' (a different form). Heinrich moves away from the window, quite explicitly 'um von dem weiteren Verlaufe des Gespräches nicht mehr zu vernehmen' (367) (in order to hear no more of the further course of the conversation). But, despite this narrative refusal to pursue a potentially critical analysis, the 'Rückblick' chapter offers us a chance to glimpse beneath the tranquil surface. The key term 'Verhältnis' occurs at the end of the chapter. Heinrich Drendorf asks why Risach and Mathilde have not married. The old man replies: 'Die Zeit war vorüber,...das Verhältnis wäre nicht mehr so schön gewesen, und Mathilde hat es auch wohl nie gewünscht' (685) (the time had passed,...the relationship would no longer have been so beautiful, and Mathilde also did not wish it).

Here there sounds a note of regret, of loss, of something forfeited that can never be recaptured. Perhaps the Indian Summer of the good life is not the only value that this extraordinary novel expresses. Perhaps it also intimates a price paid that is intolerably high – as in the bittersweet symbol of the rose that recurs throughout the book.

Risach recounts how he came into the house of Mathilde's parents as a teacher and, more importantly, as an educative presence in the eighteenth-century sense. As the mother says: 'zur Erziehung muß man etwas sein' (633) (to educate you have to be something). Tutor and pupil fall in love, and both experience for the first time (and, as it turns out, for the only time) a totally new dimension, a magical intensity of being. As in *Brigitta*, in the description of Stephan's relationship with Gabriele, so here, too, the central term is 'Zauber'. Risach remembers their first embrace: 'War ich wie bezaubert' (650) (I was as though enchanted). In the face of this 'zaubervoll anmutsvoll unbegreiflich' (653) (magical, lovely, incomprehensible) experience, the significance of all else pales. With Mathilde's agreement Risach approaches her parents. The reply is negative – they are urged to wait until they are more mature. Risach has such reverence for Mathilde's parents, and for the love Mathilde feels for them, that he, as it were, becomes their advocate: he returns to Mathilde and tries to persuade her of the necessity that they break off their relationship.

In other words, Risach modifies the claims of feeling in the name of moral considerations – he acknowledges the 'Widerstand' (661) (resistance) of practical reality and responsibility. But as the mother foresees when she defines such an acknowledgement as 'Untreue an Mathilden' (661) (infidelity to Mathilde), Mathilde rejects, even denounces, his stance as a betrayal of the very 'Zauber' that has bound them together:

Er macht es unmöglich für alle Zeiten, daß ich ihm noch angehören kann, weil er den Zauber zerstört hat, der alles band, den Zauber, der ein unzerreißbares Aneinanderhalten in die Jahre der Zukunft und in die Ewigkeit malte. (667)

(He makes it impossible for all time that I should belong to him, because he has destroyed the magic that bound everything together, the magic that promised an inseparable union for future years and for all eternity.)

Risach argues that these ties will remain, that it is only a matter of the 'Aufhebung des Äußerlichen unseres Bundes auf eine Zeit' (668) (suspension of the externals of our relationship for a time). But for Mathilde, there can be no such temporary non-realization of feeling: she insists that, in following the voice of reason and reasonability, Risach has betrayed not only their love, but himself, his very being and selfhood:[5]

'Kannst du eine Zeit nicht mehr du sein? Kannst du eine Zeit dein Herz nicht schlagen lassen? Äußeres, Inneres, das ist alles eins, und alles ist die Liebe. Du hast nie geliebt, weil du es nicht weißt.' (668)

('Can you for a time cease to be what you are? Can you for a time cause your heart to stop beating? Outer and inner, it is all one, and all of it is love. You have never loved if you do not know that.')

This crisis does not simply record the breakdown of one specific human relationship. The four pages reverberate with the issues that were at stake in the eighteenth-century transition from the ethos of the *Sturm und Drang* to that of Classicism, and in Stifter's own development from what is commonly called his early subjectivism to mature objectivity. And the questions entailed still preoccupy present-day moral philosophy. The problem whether, and to what degree, the acknowledgement of *Widerstand*, as represented by the outer world, involves a loss of selfhood informs, for example, the work of Bernard Williams.[6]

In *Der Nachsommer*, there are a number of hints that Risach, with his morally informed decision, forfeits human substance and becomes the shell of a man who follows the dictates of *Widerstand* and pays the price. This much emerges from his account of the marriage which he subsequently contracts: he obeys the social voice that pronounces it to be a duty to marry and produce children: 'Es sei auch Pflicht gegen die Menschheit und den Staat' (674) (it is a duty toward humanity and the state). Here one is reminded of Corona's argument in *Der Waldgänger*, of the uncle's advice in *Der Hagestolz*. And here, too, the verdict is devastating: Risach states that this marriage 'mir ein Vorwurf bis zu meinem Lebensende sein wird, weil es nicht nach den reinen Gesetzen der Natur ist, obwohl es tausend Mal und tausend Mal in der Welt geschieht' (674) (will remain a reproach to me till the end of my days, because it is not according to the pure laws of nature, although it happens thousands and thousands of times in the world). The anguish of one caught in the crossfire between the voice of duty and the demands of inclination strikes mercilessly home as Risach remembers:

Wir lebten in Eintracht, wir lebten in hoher Verehrung der gegenseitigen guten Eigenschaften, wir lebten in wechselweisem Vertrauen und in wechselweiser Aufmerksamkeit, man nannte unsere Ehe musterhaft; aber wir lebten bloß ohne Unglück. (675)

(We lived in harmony, we lived with the highest regard for each other's good qualities, we lived in mutual trust and in mutual attentiveness, people called our marriage exemplary; but we simply lived without unhappiness.)

This is the famous Stifterian rhetoric of evenness – but the solid presence of the thrice repeated 'wir lebten' highlights only the absence of fulfilment.

This one passage may be taken as a crucially important example: in so far as it is stylistically of a piece with the general speech rhythms of Risach, it suggests that the incantatory rhetoric, the stately order of his discourse throughout the work may promise more than it can achieve. The reader is not likely to forget the sting of Mathilde's accusation. And he may well look back on *Der Nachsommer* as a text whose efforts at stability (the stylistic tranquillity, the countless descriptions and discursive passages) are interrupted by points of stark discontinuity. This is particularly true of the late but powerful sting of the 'Rückblick' chapter, containing, as it does, that unforgettable incident in which, literally, Risach's life-blood flows, betokening the sacrifice made to moral obligation:

Ich griff mit der bloßen Hand in die Zweige der Rosen, drückte, daß mir leichter würde, die Dornen derselben in die Hand, und ließ das Blut an ihr nieder rinnen. (669)

(I plunged my bare hand into the branches of the roses, pressed the thorns into my hand until I felt calmer, and let the blood trickle down.)

Once the reader is alerted to such points he may well begin to adopt a critical distance toward Risach's, and the novel's, discourse throughout and react in a manner not dissimilar to that of Mathilde when she rejects Risach's moral postulations: ' "Ja, ja, das sind die Worte", sagte sie' (668) ('yes, yes, those are the words', she said). We may then question whether the novel, despite its heavy didactic presence, in fact resolves the problem of selfhood. We begin to notice a number of passages which suggest that this is not the case. One may, for example, consider Risach's sceptical attitude towards the value of 'Amt', public office, and, more crucially, the value of serving mankind:

Es wäre die schwerste Sünde, seinen Weg nur ausschließlich dazu zu wählen, wie man sich so oft ausdrückt, der Menschheit nützlich zu werden. Man gäbe sich selber auf, und müßte in den meisten Fällen im eigentlichen Sinn sein Pfund vergraben. (616)

(It would be the gravest sin to choose one's path exclusively in order, as is so often said, to serve humanity. One would be abandoning oneself, in most cases one would necessarily be burying one's talents.)

In the course of repeated reading, one becomes aware of an unsettling irresolution in Risach's self-portrait. He asserts that from childhood onward he had the urge to be 'Herr meiner Handlungen' (609) (master of my actions), and yet that self-assertion did not prevent him from assenting to, even passionately engaging with, alien things: 'wo mir ein Fremdes durch Gründe und hohe Triebfedern unterstützt gegeben wurde' (609) (where something foreign was presented to me as sustained by reasons and high motives). However, as we have seen, the two occasions on which he follows the voice of 'ein Fremdes' (the separation from Mathilde, and his subsequent marriage) prove to be profoundly problematical. Chapter 3 of volume III ends with Risach reflecting on the choices that are open to young people, and the didactic voice comes to the fore again: 'Es ist schwierig, und mögen, die beteiligt sind, darüber wachen, daß weniger leichtsinnig verfahren werde' (617) (it is difficult and may those who are involved keep watch that less carelessness prevails). But one cannot help feeling that the choice may ultimately be located beyond safe moral parameters, and it is perhaps telling that Risach at this point suddenly states: 'Lasset uns über diesen Gegenstand abbrechen' (617) (let us break off our discussion at this point).

In conclusion, we would suggest that *Der Nachsommer* is a determined exorcism of individuation, but that, within this portrayal of a cherished and cherishing life, there are persistent hints of a blighted centre. The work reverberates with the haunting possibility that to fill one's life with both practically and morally valuable 'Verhältnisse' may not be enough. The novel spends some seven hundred pages on the anchored life. Of these a mere sixty evoke the past, a past which in so many ways would seem to function merely as the necessary dark relief to the exhaustive catalogue of a harmonious existence. The 'Rückblick', at one level, stands as a didactically conceived element: within the overall work it may be taken to represent the central argument in Herder's essay *Übers Erkennen und Empfinden in der menschlichen Seele* (On Knowledge and Feeling in the Human Soul), in particular the assertion that the turmoil of 'Empfindung' is a necessary phase on the path to ever higher 'Erkenntnis'. Yet, on closer examination, this is not the case: in so far as the 'Rückblick' chapter is allowed to reverberate, it lends critical differentiation to the onslaught on subjectivity which is there in every line of the book. Stifter tended to refer to his novels as 'Erzählungen', which would make *Der Nachsommer* a *Rahmenerzählung* (tale with a frame). The proportions are extraordinary – seven hundred pages of frame to sixty of *Binnenerzählung*, inset story. But that inset story exists beyond the reach of the frame. Only just. The gaps do not quite close, and therein resides the energy and fascination of the novel.[7]

Perhaps one can best sum up the critical interaction of forces in *Der Nachsommer* by interpreting two passages as self-reflective statements on the thematic and narrative structure of this text. When Heinrich finds himself for the first time in Risach's house, he states:

In dem Zimmer, in welchem ich mich befand, hörte man nicht den geringsten Laut eines bewohnten Hauses, den man doch sonst, es mag im Hause noch so ruhig sein, mehr oder weniger in Zwischenräumen vernimmt. (48)

(In the room in which I found myself one could not hear the slightest sound of an inhabited house which one normally – however quiet the house may be – hears more or less at intervals.)

In a fundamental sense, this statement applies to the novel itself in so far as it is essentially concerned with the realm 'nach Abschluß des Menschlichen', a territory largely un-inhabited by individuality. However, within the 'Rückblick' chapter we find a poignant counterpart to this statement; in an unforgettable formulation Risach reflects on his life:

So lange alle die Verhältnisse, welche in meinen Amtsgeschäften vorkamen, in meinem Haupte waren, war nichts anderes darin. Schmerzvoll waren nur die Zwischenräume. (673)

(As long as all the circumstances which occurred in my administrative affairs filled my head, there was nothing else in it. Only the gaps were painful.)

Precisely this phenomenon of painful 'Zwischenräume' marks Stifter's most persistent narrative endeavour, *Die Mappe meines Urgroßvaters*. The novel exists in three main versions: the *Urmappe* (1841), the *Studienmappe* (1844) and the final *Romanmappe* (1867) (a fourth version, which marks the transition from *Studienmappe* to the *Romanmappe* can be left out of the reckoning). The *Mappe* is, then, a key work because it spans the whole of Stifter's creative life. In our discussion we shall concern ourselves with the last version.

The narrator discovers in an old chest papers belonging to his great grandfather, a doctor named Augustinus. We are given reminiscences of his student days, we learn of his close friendship with Eustachius, who one day suddenly disappears. The doctor is haunted by the desperate need to find Eustachius again. When he takes up a career as general practitioner, Augustinus gets to know Margarita, the daughter of the 'Obrist' (colonel) who lives nearby. He falls in love with her, but one day, on seeing her in conversation with a relative, he becomes convinced that she no longer loves him. He reproaches Margarita, who is profoundly offended by his inability to trust her, and says that, while she will continue to love him, marriage is out of the question. Augustinus leaves in anguish, but he is comforted by the gentle Obrist, who tells him his life story. It is the story of a passionate youth, of gradually ripening wisdom and maturity, of the profound love for his wife who dies in an accident in the forest. The Obrist teaches Augustinus by his example, and Augustinus is reclaimed from his despair and reunited with the world. We are given many illustrations of his skill as a doctor, and we see him gradually winning the trust and affection of the local community. One day he comes to the estate of a nobleman and is shown some drawings. He is convinced that these are by none other than Eustachius, and he is very much confirmed in this by Isabella, the daughter of the 'Freiherr', who has had an unhappy relationship with the artist.

The *Mappe* would seem to be the perfect test-case for Stifter's literary evolution. Kunisch sees in the three versions the gradual unfolding of Stifter's classical style, a dimming down of passion, an ever more urgent sense that, in spite of individual heartache, the world abundantly and rightly *is*.[8] This view has, in one form or another, been advanced by those critics who have undertaken detailed comparisons of the early and late versions of Stifter's works in order to document his progress toward the overwhelming serenity of his mature style. Yet, in our view, the rewriting and recasting of the *Mappe* does not work in quite the way that Kunisch maintains. The *Romanmappe* ought, on Kunisch's terms to be more complete, more rounded off than the earlier versions. But it is not. It remains curiously sketchy – and this is not just because it is incomplete: it has an internal fragmentariness and discontinuity. The reworking does not entail a simple process of transfiguration: rather, it involves a reshaping of the uncertainty within the narrative. The description of Augustinus's emotional turmoil is strongest in the *Urmappe*, the suicidal mood that follows the quarrel with Margarita is most vividly handled in the *Studienmappe*. In contrast, the *Romanmappe* brings a diminution of passion – the stylistic and structural affinity with *Der Nachsommer* and even *Witiko* is clear, but, paradoxically, this mutedness and the sheer weight and space given to the chronicling of a solid life only throw into greater relief the pain of those moments when fissures appear in the texture of that life. The theme of waiting, waiting to be made whole, runs through the two earlier versions, and this tension remains in the *Romanmappe*: there is the precarious balance between an anchored life and the irruptions of the incalculable ('das Unbegreifliche'). Fissures and cracks threaten all the lovingly evoked circumstances that surround, but do not banish, the possibility of radical disturbance. In this sense, the *Romanmappe* is critically suspended between a *Lebensskizze*, a mere sketch of a life, and the determination to join up the discrete strokes of the pen into a solid image of integrity and wholeness. The loss of Eustachius, which figures in the *Urmappe*, disappears from the *Studienmappe*, but only to reappear with greater urgency in the *Romanmappe* and, with it, the sense of deprivation, of waiting for fulfilment. The rewriting, then, involves a redistribution of emphases: but common to all versions is the tension between the continuity of an ordered life and the irruption of passion, heartbreak, loss. When Stifter, in his letter to Heckenast, repudiated the *Studienmappe*, he referred to it as 'eine heillose Geschichte' – a hopeless story, one lacking in wholeness. He wanted, he tells his publisher, to portray three characters 'in denen sich die Einfachheit, Größe und Güte der menschlichen Seele spiegelt'[9] (in which the simplicity, greatness and goodness of the human soul would be mirrored). Yet the story, apparently, turned out to be 'heillos'.

The aim to find and to convey wholeness informs above all that strand within the novel which records Augustinus's life as a country doctor. Many pages chronicle his struggles to establish himself, his daily rounds, his plans for improving the community. Within this morally grounded strand, the loss of Margarita has a crucial function: the crisis serves to further moral growth. Again, Stifter follows Herder by making the turmoil of 'Empfinden' a decisive element with the progress of 'Erkennen'. On this level, the Obrist plays a vital role. As Augustinus leaves Margarita, he follows him and says: 'habt Ihr denn im Heraufgehen nicht auch bemerkt, Herr Doktor, wie heuer das liebe Korn so schön steht' (*M*, 161) (have you, on the way up, not also noticed, doctor, how this year the lovely corn is standing so gloriously). The words are not, in any immediate sense, words of comfort: they remind Augustinus of what is *also* there – of the undivided continuity and splendour of the given world. Cold comfort, perhaps: but his words have their effect: 'Ich sah das Korn des Friedmeier an, von dem der Obrist gesagt hatte. Es war sehr schön, und seine Bärte glühten in dem Abendsonnenschein' (162) (I looked at Friedmeier's corn of which the Obrist had spoken. It was very beautiful, and the husks were glowing in the evening sunshine). The language could not be simpler. If the individuated being of man has played him false, this sentence, in all its simplicity, registers an undivided being that cannot play false, that simply is.

This lesson in 'Erkennen', the gaining of a greater overview, is reinforced in the next chapter where the 'gentle Obrist' tells his story: it is a story in which pain and deprivation are shown to be the foundation of a fully rooted life, a life which registers the splendidly objective, indifferent glory of the surrounding corn. The Obrist was, we learn, a gambler and a wastrel, but he comes gradually to cherish the stable and lasting things in life. His moral growth is crowned when he retires from the army and marries. But in a tragic accident in the mountains, he loses his wife. They are coming down on a high log slide, the Obrist in front, the wife carrying the dog in the middle, and a workman bringing up the rear. The wife suddenly becomes dizzy and falls, but she forbears to cry out because she does not want to endanger her husband. Only when he has completed the perilous descent does he realize the enormity that has occurred. It is one of Stifter's supremely laconic stabs of pathos – 'sie lag unten zerschmettert' (she lay there broken). The workman had realized that the wife was losing her balance –

Da habe er ihr den Rat gegeben, sich nieder zu setzen. Aber es sei wie ein weißes Tuch bei seinen Augen vorbeigegangen, und dann habe er nur mich allein gesehen. (176)

(So he advised her to sit down. But it was like white cloth floating past his eyes, and then he only saw me.)

That is all. There is no more to the scene than this. A brutal fact, a strange unreality about the fall – a curiously disembodied beauty ('*es* sei wie ein weißes Tuch'). There is an unsettling modesty to the irruption of tragedy here. They find the body next day – 'ein Häufchen lichter Kleider, und darunter die zerschmetterten Glieder' (177) (a heap of light clothes and under them the broken limbs). And there is also the almost magical – yet macabre – incident: the wife's body took the full weight of the fall, and the dog is unharmed. But the dog goes mad during the night it spends alone with its dead mistress; it tries to bite the Obrist, and the workman is forced to shoot it. The Obrist's account, in its measured tones, rises to a climax of heartbreak as he presses home (in the present tense) the urgency of the grief:

O Herr, das könnt Ihr nicht ermessen, nein Ihr wisset es jetzt noch nicht, wie es ist, wenn das Weib Eures Herzens noch die Kleider anhat, die Ihr am Morgen selber darreichen halfet, und jetzt tot ist, und nichts mehr kann, als in Unschuld bitten, daß Ihr sie begrabet. (177)

(Oh sir, you cannot fathom, you cannot yet know, how it is when the wife of your heart is still wearing the clothes which you that very morning helped her choose and is now dead and can do nothing more than simply, in all innocence, ask you to bury her.)

Normally, the Obrist addresses Augustinus as 'Herr Doktor' – here it is the simple 'Herr'. And the present tense is used, we feel, not just as a historic present, but in its full temporal force. The Obrist is doing more than reliving the scene: the wife is dead now, every day of his life, as the bedrock of deprivation on which his life is grounded. The austerity to the grief makes it not so much a feeling as a condition. And alongside that condition there runs the continuity of life – the world goes on 'als ob nichts geschehen wäre' (179) (as though nothing had happened). The numbing cruelty of nature is the only comfort – 'die Sonne stand am Himmel, die Getreide wuchsen, die Bäche rauschten, nur daß sie dahin war, und daß es war wie der Verlust einer goldenen Mücke' (180) (the sun stood in the sky, the crops grew, the streams rushed, except she was no more, and it was like the loss of a golden gnat). If the undisturbed totality of matter is irrelevant to the death of the wife, so the death of the wife is irrelevant to that totality. This is the centre of the Obrist's story. And it is the perception of that totality, of continuity beyond the catastrophic, that makes the good life possible: indeed, suffering so destroys the individual that it produces that disinterestedness, that patient service of being which the gentle Obrist embodies. Nowhere else does the reticence of Stifter's prose so poignantly intimate the price that is paid in and for that service, a service which has to do with *also* noticing the corn. Augustinus begins to learn the lesson which the Obrist has to convey, and in his turn passes on what he has learnt. In his profession as a doctor, he contributes toward the continuity of being, and his service has an inherently ethical dimension, the alleviation of human suffering. Moreover, he can help Isabella, the psychologically threatened daughter of the 'Freiherr'. He shows her how to overcome melancholy, to find a relatedness to the world around her, to walk through the landscape with him and to say 'wie doch alles schön ist, Herr Doktor' (266) (how beautiful everything is, doctor).

This stance of affirmation beyond anguish and pain is the central moral concern of the novel, and it is underpinned by a perfectly corresponding structural organization: Stifter highlights the issue of continuity and moral growth by making an ever expanding chain of recollections the central narrative device. At the start of the novel, the narrator describes his family home and focuses on the possessions left by his great-grandfather. Amongst the doctor's things, amongst the 'Gewirre von Papieren, Schriften, Päckchen, Rollen, Bindzeugen, Lappen, Handgeräten und anderem Wust' (18) (tangle of papers, writings, packets, rolls, bandages, cloths, tools and other jumble), the narrator finds the volumes in which the great-grandfather has chronicled his life story. These recollections are the story which Stifter's novel tells. As we have seen, at a critical point in his life, the great-grandfather is helped by the Obrist telling a story. And in that story, the Obrist recounts how, at a crisis in *his* life, he benefited from something he heard from an old 'Kriegsobrist'. The Kriegsobrist had once advised a girl who wanted to die because of an unhappy love affair to write down her experiences and feelings 'wie sie eben in der Zeit sind' (169) (just as they are at that time). She should then seal the diary and only open it some three or four years later: 'da sei alles anders, und man lerne erst, wie man gewesen' (170) (then everything would be different, and one would then learn what one had been). The diary, then, will be the precipitate of a life at a point of crisis, and, when one looks back on it, one will be able to judge the extent to which one has grown over the years. The Obrist himself, Augustinus's friend, has apparently done this. Once when he was lying wounded in hospital, he opened his diary of some five years previously:

alles war anders geworden, als ich einst gedacht hatte, ich erkannte, daß ich erst jetzt die rechten Ansichten habe, und brannte vor Begierde, sie gleich nieder zu schreiben. (170)

(Everything had turned out differently from what I had once assumed, I realized that only now had I acquired the right views, and I was consumed with the desire to commit them to paper.)

So he writes:

Weil es das erste Päckchen war, das ich geöffnet hatte, wußte ich noch nicht, daß es mir bei einem jeden so ergehen werde, auch bei dem, das ich jetzt mit solcher Inbrunst nieder geschrieben hatte. Die rechten Ansichten waren beim Öffnen eines Päckchens oft nicht mehr die rechten, und es wurden die neuen nieder geschrieben. Und so ging es fort. Ich habe mir durch diese Beschäftigung erst eine Redeweise und Handlungsweise zugebildet. (170)

(Because it was the first packet which I had opened, I did not yet know that it would be the same with each packet, even with the one which I had just written with such fervour. The right views were, when I opened the packet, often no longer right, and new ones were written down. And so it went on. By this means I acquired a way of talking and behaving.)

In writing and rewriting his life, the individual experiences to the full his 'Zeitlichkeit', his temporality and transitoriness. With each new context he may judge his accumulated experiences differently.[10] It is potentially an open-ended process for even 'die rechten Ansichten' can only be provisional. Yet it is suggested that this continuous re-evaluation serves not so much to highlight the absurdity of the quest for certainty, but rather furthers moral growth in that it leads towards a stoically distanced perception of ever-unfolding life, the 'Überblick über ein Größeres'. The Obrist has kept the various versions of his selfhood, and invites Augustinus to read them whenever he wants to. The latter, too, begins to write at a point of crisis when he is forced to ask himself what his existence is achieving: 'Ich finde eine Ruhe meines Herzens in den Einschreibungen, und habe eine Befriedigung in denselben' (202) (I find my heart growing calmer as I put pen to paper, and I derive fulfilment from these writings). Moreover, he also learns from reading the Obrist's papers: 'ich lerne aus diesen Schriften, und werde sie alle lesen' (209) (I learn from these writings, and I shall read them all).

The narrator, in his turn, passes the great-grandfather's writings on to us, the readers. So the process of growth through writing and reading continues: we may even conjecture that it was Stifter's own as he moved from *Urmappe* to *Studienmappe* to *Romanmappe*. It is tempting to follow the orthodox view and to impute a teleological consistency to this process. No doubt, the *Mappe* aims to convey the sense of harmonious continuity; we are asked, as so often in Stifter, to perceive the healing powers of both Nature and Reason. But it is more a matter of hope than of certitude – Augustinus pronounces at one point: 'Hoffen wir auch auf das Wachsen der Vernunft' (85) (let us hope in the growth of reason). And as the Obrist's reflections make clear, the flux of human life is such that growth must be precarious, that it cannot be subsumed under the simple category of linear cohesiveness. In this sense, it may strike us as appropriate that the *Mappe* remained a fragment and, above all, that its genesis is not one of linear progression: the *Romanmappe* returns to the story 'Von den zwei Bettlern', which is omitted from the *Studienmappe*. We do not know, we can only conjecture from the plot-line and from the persistent *Leitmotif* of 'Es wird gut sein' (94) (it will be good) that it was Stifter's aim to reunite Augustinus with his long lost friend Eustachius. But as the final text stands, the *Romanmappe* ends with Eustachius not found, with Augustinus and Margarita not reunited, and we would argue that the reader, while fully bearing in mind Stifter's integrative efforts, must also live with this central experience of discontinuity. In this context, the figure of Eustachius plays a vital role.

The doctor's student days are very much dominated by his

affection for Eustachius. The latter is a young man of artistic, even somewhat fantastic temperament, who stands security for a friend and who disappears when he is required to pay the sum agreed. Augustinus clears Eustachius's debt, and unceasingly inquires into his whereabouts – but to no avail. The link with Eustachius is never sundered: when Augustinus meets Margarita, she reminds him of Eustachius's beloved Christine, just as Innozenz, who becomes engaged to the doctor's sister, is somehow very like Eustachius. Continually there vibrates this need to find Eustachius. At one point (in words that recall Stifter's rejection of the *Studienmappe*) Augustinus reflects: 'so ist denn das die heilloseste Geschichte, die ich wie einen bösen Schaden nicht von mir bringe' (74) (so this is then the most unholy story which, like some evil defect, I cannot shed). In one sense, Eustachius and Augustinus function as contrastive figures who enact the conflicting demands of unbounded subjectivity and social morality. From what we see and hear of Eustachius we may conclude that he represents essentially what his clothes signal: with his red stockings, grey trousers, yellow waistcoat and green coat he is likened to a siskin, a *Zeisig*, the bird which in German has come to stand as a metaphor for the irresponsible human being. Throughout he functions largely as a creature free from the constraints of reality. He stands, of course, in a long line of characters in Stifter's oeuvre who, in one form or another, embody that kind of freedom and are most typically referred to as 'Narren', fools. The colourful clothes of Eustachius are in sharp contrast to those of Augustinus, the keen pupil of social reality: he first appears dressed in black and white, the combination of the contemporary *élégant*, but on his return to the country, the realm of his future responsibilities, he dresses in coarse grey cloth, wears heavy boots, carries a stout black-thorn stick, and only his green waistcoat and cap afford some colourful relief. The symbolic intimation is beautifully sustained: Eustachius indulges in fantasies, in painting and poetry, while Augustinus is determined to acknowledge reality both in a practical and moral sense. He dresses properly in order to find approval – one notes the modal verb in his phrase 'man muß ihnen gefallen' (34) (one has to please them); he becomes a tutor and a vet in order to earn money, and he looks forward to the time when he will return home and 'allen helfen, die es bedürfen und mich achten' (39) (help all those who need it and who respect me).

At first it would appear that these two modes of being, the poetic and the prosaic, can enjoy a state of synthesis: the two friends interact without losing their inherent identity. Eustachius begins to dress in black and white, but does not abandon his imaginative life – he paints and writes for pleasure, but also manages to sell some of his products; and, conversely, Augustinus pursues his career as a devoted student and yet is free enough to be 'übermütig', to cherish the life of the 'lustigen Bettler' (43) (carefree beggars). But this state of balance ends abruptly when Eustachius disappears. Augustinus is shattered and the urge to find Eustachius never ceases to haunt him. However, this is not simply a personal obsession: the private need is widened into a general imperative in so far as Christine and above all Cäcilia, the landlady of their student days, partake of this desire to find Eustachius again. Cäcilia states throughout, and quite categorically, that Eustachius must be found at all costs, that it is 'gottvergessen', blasphemous treachery, not to search for him (193). More and more the text suggests that the loss of Eustachius is not only the loss of a friend, but of that whole existential dimension which the twentieth century has subsumed under the category of the pleasure principle. It can only be found at the cost of practical living, as Augustinus realizes:

Ich dachte nun daran, was Cäcilia von Eustachius gesagt hatte. Wenn es wahr ist, und ich selber glaubte, daß es wahr sein könnte, so würde ich ihn, wenn ich alle meine Zeit und alle meine Bemühungen diesem Zwecke widmete, vielleicht finden; aber dann müßte ich meinen Beruf aufgeben. Oder ich muß bei meinem Berufe bleiben, und Eustachius lassen. Ein Schwanken zwischen diesen zwei Dingen fand bei mir jetzt keinen Augenblick statt. Ich muß in meinem Amte bleiben, er hat sich in seine Lage begeben, und muß sie haben. (194f.)

(I now thought of what Cäcilia had said about Eustachius. If it is true, and I myself believed that it could be true, then, were I to devote all my time and all my energies to this end, I would perhaps find him. But then, I would have to give up my profession. Or I must stay with my profession and leave Eustachius. Not for a moment did I hesitate between these two alternatives. I must stay in my job, he has chosen his situation and must be left in it.)

This is the typical choice of the determined realist who acknowledges the 'muß' both of practicality and morality. But he cannot shed the memory of Eustachius and what he stands for. And this memory begins to generate a sense of critical, if not ironic, distance towards his own orderly life. Many years later he reflects 'Augustinus sitzt im Hause seiner Väter' (53) (Augustinus sits in the house of his fathers) surrounded by the belongings of Eustachius. This self-critical stance is most explicit at the end of Part I when Augustinus accuses himself of having neglected everything that Eustachius represented:

Als mir einmal Eustachius aus den Chören Aeschylos vorlas...hat mir die Sache nicht sehr gefallen? Habe ich aber dann den ganzen Aeschylos für mich gelesen? Nein. Ich habe es dem Eustachius überlassen, der seine Worte oft allein in seiner Kammer rief, daß Cäcilia meinte, er sei doch nicht bei Sinnen. (197f.)

(When on one occasion, Eustachius read to me from the choruses of Aeschylus, did it not give me the keenest pleasure? But did I then read the whole of Aeschylus on my own? No. I left it up to Eustachius, who often declaimed the words alone in his room with the result that Cäcilia thought he was probably out of his mind.)

Throughout, the strand which is concerned with the relationship between Augustinus and Eustachius offers a great deal of material for a socio-psychological interpretation. The upshot of that analysis must be that Augustinus's gain in social reality and morality entails a blighting loss of imaginative energy. (One is at times reminded of Gottfried Keller, and of Musil's remark – which could so well apply to Augustinus – 'Man hat Wirklichkeit gewonnen und Traum verloren' – 'one has gained reality and lost the dream'.)[11] This theme is subtly prefigured in the opening pages of the *Mappe*: the narrator recalls his grandmother saying that in her and in Augustinus's experience, life increasingly forfeits its magic:

Alles nimmt auf der Welt ab, der Vogel in der Luft und der Fisch im Wasser. Und so nimmt auch das Seltsame im Leben ab. (13)

(Everything in the world is declining, the bird in the air, the fish in the water. And so, too, does the strangeness in life decline.)

These words not only anticipate the restricted existence that Augustinus is forced to lead after the separation from his friend; they also bear on Stifter's persistent preoccupation with, and conflicting reactions to, the incomprehensible, the magical. We shall have occasion to return to this point when we examine *Bergkristall* and *Katzensilber*.

There can be no doubt that a socio-psychological evaluation of the function of Eustachius serves to throw the dutiful life of Augustinus into critical relief and lends resonance to his own recurrent questioning whether his way of life is ultimately valid. When he starts his activity as a country doctor he wonders: 'Wird sie zu dem Heile derer sein, die dir vertrauen, und zu deinem Heile?' (56) (Will it be for the well-being of those who trust you and for your own well-being?). And at the end of Part I he agonizes: 'Bin ich ein rechter Mensch gewesen oder ein rechter Arzt? Wer bin ich als Mensch gewesen?' (196) (Have I been a decent human being or a decent doctor? What have I been as a person?).

But it is surely also valid to take the figure of Eustachius in a wider sense, to read his disappearance as a metaphor which intimates those gaps within a life that no amount of effort can fill. His absence is the most powerful presence, and Augustinus experiences this, quite literally, as a curse on his life. He first laments 'O du verruchter Freund, O du verruchter Freund' (45) (oh you cursed friend, oh you cursed friend). Amidst his achievements as a country doctor he cannot find wholeness: 'Nur Eines war böse in meinem Herzen. Zuweilen

saß ich auf einem Steine, und seufzte: "O du schrecklicher
Eustachius! o du schrecklicher Eustachius!" ' (65) (There was
only one sorrow in my heart. Sometimes I would sit on a
stone and sigh: 'Oh you terrible Eustachius! oh you terrible
Eustachius!'). On this level, the need is never explained, never
psychologized: it simply remains a central element in Augustinus's being, a part of him that is irremediably waiting for
Eustachius. This 'heilloseste Geschichte', the fruitless search
for Eustachius, strikes one in many ways as a nineteenth-
century prefiguration of *Waiting for Godot*, and we would
argue that it functions as the crystallization of all those other
strands in the novel which suggest that the world is perversely
resistant, beyond the grasp of Reason – in other words, strands
which reach out beyond the confines of the novel's moral
concerns.

The central example is the breakdown of the relationship
between Augustinus and Margarita. Of course, there is an
explicable centre to this crisis: when Augustinus sees Margarita
kissing her cousin Rudolph, he suddenly doubts her. Margarita
feels that with this doubt her whole integrity has been called
into question, and she declares that she now cannot marry
him: 'Ihr habt mir nicht geglaubt. Wenn ich den Glauben
nicht finde, bleibe ich bei meinem geliebten Vater' (157) (You
have not believed me. If I cannot be believed, I shall stay with
my beloved father). Clearly, this suggests that the fault in
Augustinus is excessive emotion, unreflective, and hence destructive, passion. Yet this decisive scene ultimately goes
beyond the morally or psychologically interpretable and intimates a sense of radical, inexplicable disturbance. Paradoxically,
the muted, heavily stylized register of the *Romanmappe* highlights this. At the moment of crisis, Margarita's language is
as stately as ever; it is informed by those measured rhythms,
those slow cadences which epitomize Stifterian gradualness.
But in this scene, the linguistic control and order highlight the
void at the centre, the fact that she cannot marry Augustinus.
The more one reads these pages, the more one is disturbed

by Margarita's language. At issue is not the fact that, as so often in Stifter, common expectations of mimesis are ignored; the crucial point is that on close examination her words withhold all meaning. Take the following passage:

'Sprecht, lieber Freund', antwortete sie, 'setzet Euch zu mir auf diesen kleinen Stuhl, und sprecht alle Worte, die Euch gut dünken, und die Euerm Herzen zu einer Erleichterung sein können.'
'Wie kann ich sprechen, wenn das Ziel des Gespräches weggenommen ist', entgegnete ich.
'Sprecht außerhalb dieses Zieles', sagte sie.
'Gibt es da etwas?' fragte ich.
'Ich fühle, daß es noch sehr viel gibt', antwortete sie.
'Ihr fühlt das?' fragte ich.
'Ja', entgegnete sie, 'Liebe, Freundschaft, Hochachtung.' (156)

('Speak, dear friend', she answered, 'sit next to me on this little chair and speak all the words that seem right to you and that can bring relief to your heart.'
'How can I speak if the goal of this conversation is taken away', I replied.
'Speak outside that goal', she said.
'Is there anything there?' I asked.
'I feel that there is still a great deal there', she answered.
'You feel that?' I asked.
'Yes', she replied, 'love, friendship, respect.')

One might decode this passage along the lines of the familiar motif of *Entsagung*, but this would be to ignore the sting of Augustinus's question whether there can be language 'außerhalb dieses Zieles'. He demands that the traffic of words be underwritten by the traffic of facts, he asks for referentiality; but that referentiality is not given despite the insistent tenor of Margarita's statements: she employs terms of certitude, 'wissen', 'entscheiden', 'klar und deutlich', she refers to such categories as 'lieben', 'achten', 'verehren'; but this very clarity functions as a *reductio ad absurdum*: it is content-free and does not assist us in defining the essence (if there is any) of her proposition. Where and how are we to locate the logic of Margarita's reasonings and feelings? If Augustinus has offended her with his lack of faith how can she promise to love and respect him? And how can this love be an inalienable imperative, as she suggests, when it is robbed of its very status as an imperative: 'diese Pflicht löse ich nicht auf; ich lasse nur jetzt aus ihr nicht folgen, was sonst gefolgt wäre' (158) (I am not dissolving this obligation; I am simply not allowing the consequences to ensue now which otherwise would have ensued).

These examples must suffice, but throughout the scene one gains the impression that Margarita's statements enact the semantics of the phrase 'words to no avail': they are finely controlled motions of reasoning, but only motions, and thus highlight the unfathomable nature of the breakdown, a flow located beyond all explication. Taken as a whole, the dialogue of these three pages is very close to that passage where Augustinus encounters the obstinacy of the villagers who refuse to see a doctor:

'Aber einen Grund müßt ihr doch haben', sagte ich.
'Der Grund ist, daß wir nicht zu dem Doktor gehen', sagte er.
'Nun, so geht nicht zum Doktor', sprach ich.
'Ja, ja, da habt ihr recht', antwortete er, 'wir gehen nicht zum Doktor.' (67)

('But you must have a reason', I said.
'The reason is that we don't go to the doctor', he said.
'In that case, don't go to the doctor', I said.
'Yes, you're right there', he answered, 'we will not go to the doctor.')

At such moments – and these are not isolated cases – the very style that we have come to associate with Stifter ceases to be the organ of Reason and instead articulates an absurd, inconsequential world. As a final example one thinks of the moment when Augustinus's sister, Anna, declares that she cannot yet marry Innozenz. She loves him, she comforts him 'Es wird schon gut werden' (214) (it will be all right), but, without giving any reason, immovably insists: 'jetzt noch nicht' – 'not now'. And again, the laconic control makes the scene all the more unsettling.

If one links all such points of sudden discontinuity – one

would also include the story of the Obrist, the abrupt sequence of deaths towards the end of the novel – then the tensions at the heart of the *Mappe* become manifest: throughout, there are moments when the narrative act ceases to suggest 'das Licht der Vernunft' (the light of Reason) – and they do not simply function as momentary glimpses which will ultimately vindicate the light. No doubt, the aim is there. In the *Studienmappe*, Augustinus and Margarita get married in the end, and Stifter's overall plan must have been to endorse the words of the Obrist: 'Durch den Segen, der aus dem Schmerze in die Taten fließt, kommt die Erwartung eines Heils, und das Heil erscheint in der Empfindung der Taten' (239) (through the blessing that flows from pain into action comes the expectation of salvation, and the salvation appears in the sensation of the actions). But despite this didactic function, the discontinuities are simply there, utterly resistant to the teleological impulse of the novel.

They are the cracks in a text whose structural and thematic aim is solidity. And once these cracks begin to appear, the reader will become aware that the novel as a whole is precariously poised. The architecture of the narration is most typically reflected in those litanesque sequences which chronicle the doctor's life in the country, the patient pursuit of meaning. The paratactic principle dominates and is epitomized in those page-long cascades of paragraphs starting with 'dann' (then). And throughout, there is the discreetly placed *Leitmotif* 'es wird gut sein', the teleological promise that these are not random sequences, but lead forward towards fulfilment. However, if one loses sight of that promise, then Stifter's 'classical' style, as it is commonly called, the pure constatation of being, the reverent 'ontic' mode, can turn in on itself and take on that deadening effect which we associate with the works of Thomas Bernhard. Take the following examples:

Dann sind rauschende Wasser und graue Steine. Dann sind hellgrüne Wiesenflächen und verschiedenfarbige Felder. Dann sind braune Holzhäuser mit Steinen auf dem Dache. (85f.)

(Then there are roaring waters and grey stones. Then there are light green patches of meadows and many-coloured fields. Then there are brown wooden houses with stone roofs.)

and:

Dann fuhren wir zu dem Mörichbauer, den ein Pferd geschlagen hatte. Dann zu dem Knechte des Bauers Fehn, der sich durch einen Stein die kleine Zehe zerquetscht hatte. Beide waren besser. (189)

(Then we went to the Mörich farmer who had been struck by a horse. Then we went to the labourer of Fehn, the farmer whose little toe had been crushed by a stone. Both were better.)

Such passages are a challenge to the reader. They require an act of faith on his part if the registration of creation's plenitude and meaningful living is not to collapse into a catalogue of unregenerate phenomena. It is the faith that Stifter relied upon when he set out to create the 'poetry of clutter', the same faith that, in terms of *Der Nachsommer*, will leap from the dreary 'Einerlei' of nature and daily human life into the sublime 'Einerlei', the cipher of divine cohesion.

How problematic this gamble is emerges perhaps most acutely at the end of Part I where Augustinus agonizes whether his way of life is valid. There follow some four pages of self-denunciation, pages that list experiences, people, places, activities of which he has taken too little notice. And Part I ends with the following passage:

Das Geschick fährt in einem goldenen Wagen. Was durch die Räder nieder gedrückt wird, daran liegt nichts. Wenn auf einen Mann ein Felsen fällt oder der Blitz ihn tötet, und wenn er nun das alles nicht mehr wirken kann, was er sonst gewirket hätte, so wird es ein anderer tun. Wenn ein Volk dahin geht, und zerstreut wird, und das nicht erreichen kann, was es sonst erreicht hätte, so wird ein anderes Volk ein Mehreres erreichen. Und wenn ganze Ströme von Völkern dahin gegangen sind, die Unsägliches und Unzähliges getragen haben, so werden wieder neue Ströme kommen, und Unsägliches und Unzähliges tragen, und wieder neue, und kein sterblicher Mensch kann sagen, wann das enden wird. Und wenn du deinem Herzen wehe getan hast, daß es zucket und vergehen will, oder daß es sich ermannt und größer wird, so kümmert sich die Allheit nicht darum, und dränget ihrem

Ziele zu, das die Herrlichkeit ist. Du aber hättest es vermeiden können, oder kannst es ändern, und die Änderung wird dir vergolten; denn es entsteht nun das Außerordentliche daraus. (203)

(Fate travels in a golden chariot. What is crushed by the wheels is of no importance. If a rock falls on a man or the lightning kills him, and if he therefore can no longer achieve all those things which he otherwise would have achieved, somebody else will do it. If a people declines and is scattered, and cannot accomplish what it otherwise would have accomplished, another people will accomplish it even more abundantly. And if whole streams of people have come and gone, who have borne unsayable and innumerable things, so new streams will come and will bear unsayable and innumerable things, and after them new streams and still other new streams, and no mortal man can say when it will end. And if you have bruised your heart so that it twitches and threatens to break – or so that it takes courage and grows stronger, the totality is not concerned, and presses on towards its goal which is splendour. But you could have avoided it, or you can change it, and the change will be credited to you; for what emerges in the process is something remarkable.)

This is a classic example of what one might call the perspective of the greater overview (to borrow again that phrase from the preface to *Bunte Steine*, the 'Überblick über ein Größeres'). It is a perspective which perceives the totality of life of which individual man is but a tiny fragment, it sees the ultimate meaning, the 'Herrlichkeit'. But the gloomy perspective of *Ein Gang durch die Katakomben* is also powerfully at work. The opening sentence articulates a total ruthlessness: the law of the continuity of matter is the law of individual expendability. And the continuity of matter is indifferent to the individual's cognitive and affective life, to his need to judge with categories of human achievement or failure. Yet, as in *Ein Gang durch die Katakomben*, the passage finally leaps into the assertion of meaning. The last sentence of the passage attempts to assimilate man's capacity for choice, his *können*, to this totality. It seeks to forge a seamless unity between the laws of being and the moral sphere of human choice. And in our view, it does not work. We are told that if man can choose to avoid it (what is the 'it' referred to?), if he can change for the better (better by what criteria?), then that change will be rewarded (by what? by whom?). Why should being care? Why should it notice a man leading the good life? The passage does not say. It can only *believe*. And it is this embattled faith that lies at the heart of the *Mappe*, of its stylistic and thematic tensions.

6 · NARRATIVE AND STYLE

[Kafkas Dichtungen] sind erfüllt von einer vernünftigen, wenn auch ironisch–, ja satirisch-vernünftigen, verzweifelt vernünftigen, nach bester Kraft auf das Gute, Rechte und Gottgewollte gerichteten Sittlichkeit, welche sich schon in ihrem gewissenhaft-sachlichen, sonderbar ausführlichen, korrekten und klaren, durch einen genauen und beinahe amtlichen Konservatismus oft geradezu an Adalbert Stifter erinnernden Vortragsstil malt.

Thomas Mann (1941)

([Kafka's writings] are replete with a rational – if, admittedly, ironically and satirically rational – a desperately rational morality, one which with might and main directs all its energy towards what is good and right and godly; a morality which is echoed in a conscientiously dispassionate, strangely exhaustive, correct and clear expository style which, in its precise and almost bureaucratic conservatism, positively recalls Adalbert Stifter.)

Stifter hat sehr wohl gewußt oder zumindest gespürt, wie dünn das logische, sprachliche Parkett war, auf dem er sich bewegte...An zahlreichen Stellen sucht er den vorhergegangenen Satz durch den nachfolgenden geradezu zu bestätigen. Die Angst, und es ist keine andere als die alte Angst seines Lebens, zwingt ihn dazu, die Sprache bis auf ihr Skelett abzumagern, die Phantasie bis auf ein Minimum zurückzunehmen und nichts mehr dem 'Zufall' zu überlassen.

Peter Rosei (1976)

(Stifter knew very well – or at least he sensed – how thin was the logical, linguistic parquet flooring on which he moved...At frequent points he seeks literally to confirm the previous sentence by the succeeding one. The fear – and it is none other than the perennial fear of his life – obliges him to starve language until only the skeleton remains, to hold back the imagination to a minimum so that nothing remains that is left to 'Chance'.)

In the previous two chapters we have been particularly concerned to establish the thematic range of Stifter's art, one that extends from stark tragedy to the celebration of lives anchored beyond the stresses and strains of individuation. In this chapter we wish to examine texts that cover the whole range of Stifter's themes, but we wish to concentrate particularly on the style and narrative mode which Stifter employs. It is our belief that, in technical terms, Stifter is one of the supreme practitioners of prose writing in the nineteenth century. Only when one realizes the full measure of his linguistic achievement can one situate him justly within the European context.

By way of prelude to this chapter of stylistic analysis we wish to quote one of the most remarkable pieces of prose that ever came from his (or, one is tempted to add, anybody else's) pen. It is a passage in which, late in life, he tries to set down his earliest recollections. He reaches back into experiences that occurred before he was conscious of his own individuated selfhood. He writes what is, in effect, a primal psychic drama: the experiences are not decoded into individuated particulars. There is no perspective of assured hindsight, of the adult self which knows better. Rather, we are made to eavesdrop on a consciousness that only registers primary experiences of hot and cold, above and below, nearness and distance, security and threat. And at the centre of what would seem to be purely a set of sense impressions there unfolds a quite specific drama: that process of individuation which is both the precondition of self-knowledge and the wound that separates the human self irrevocably from simple, integral existence. To this drama, as we have endeavoured to show in the previous chapters, Stifter bends his finest creative energies. The upshot is a narrative performance that is, like this piece of prose, largely descriptive: but at the heart of this descriptive writing we sense the unmistakable undertow of individuated experience:

Ich bin oft vor den Erscheinungen meines Lebens, das einfach war, wie ein Halm wächst, in Verwunderung geraten. Dies ist der Grund und die Entschuldigung, daß ich die folgenden Worte aufschreibe. Sie sind zunächst für mich allein. Finden sie eine weitere Verbreitung, so mögen Gattin, Geschwister, Freunde, Bekannte einen zarten Gruß darin erkennen und Fremde nicht etwas Unwürdiges aus ihnen entnehmen.

Weit zurück in dem leeren Nichts ist etwas wie Wonne und Entzücken, das gewaltig fassend, fast vernichtend in mein Wesen drang und dem nichts mehr in meinem künftigen Leben glich. Die Merkmale, die fest gehalten wurden, sind: es war Glanz, es war Gefühl, es war unten. Dies muß sehr früh gewesen sein, denn mir ist, als liege eine hohe, weite Finsternis des Nichts um das Ding herum.

Dann war etwas anderes, das sanft und lindernd durch mein Inneres ging. Das Merkmal ist: Es waren Klänge.

Dann schwamm ich in etwas Fächelndem, ich schwamm hin und wieder, es wurde immer weicher und weicher in mir, dann wurde ich wie trunken, dann war nichts mehr.

Diese drei Inseln liegen wie feen – und sagenhaft in dem Schleiermeere der Vergangenheit, wie Urerinnerungen eines Volkes.

Die folgenden Spitzen werden immer bestimmter, Klingen von Glocken, ein breiter Schein, eine rote Dämmerung.

Ganz klar war etwas, das sich immer wiederholte. Eine Stimme, die zu mir sprach, Augen, die mich anschauten und Arme, die alles milderten. Ich schrie nach diesen Dingen.

Dann war Jammervolles, Unleidliches, dann Süßes, Stillendes. Ich erinnere mich an Strebungen, die nichts erreichten, und das Aufhören von Entsetzlichem und zu Grunderichtendem. Ich erinnere mich an Glanz und Farben, die in meinen Augen, an Töne, die in meinen Ohren, und an Holdseligkeiten, die in meinem Wesen waren.

Immer mehr fühlte ich die Augen, die mich anschauten, die Stimme, die zu mir sprach, und die Arme, die alles milderten. Ich erinnere mich, daß ich das 'Mam' nannte.

Diese Arme fühlte ich mich einmal tragen. Es waren dunkle Flecken in mir. Die Erinnerung sagte mir später, daß es Wälder gewesen sind, die außerhalb mir waren. Dann war eine Empfindung, wie die erste meines Lebens, Glanz und Gewühl, dann war nichts mehr.

Nach dieser Empfindung ist wieder eine große Lücke. Zustände, die gewesen sind, mußten vergessen worden sein.

Hierauf erhob sich die Außenwelt vor mir, da bisher nur Empfindungen wahrgenommen worden waren. Selbst Mam, Augen, Stimme, Arme waren nur als Empfindung in mir gewesen, sogar auch Wälder, wie ich eben gesagt habe. Merkwürdig ist es, daß in der allererersten Empfindung meines Lebens etwas Äußerliches war, und zwar etwas, das meist schwierig und sehr spät in das Vorstellungsvermögen gelangt, etwas Räumliches, ein Unten. Das ist ein Zeichen, wie gewaltig die Einwirkung gewesen sein muß, die jene Empfindung hervorgebracht hat. Mam, was ich jetzt Mutter nannte, stand nun als Gestalt vor mir auf und ich unterschied ihre Bewegungen, dann der Vater, der Großvater, die Großmutter, die Tante. Ich hieß sie mit diesen Namen, empfand Holdes von ihnen, erinnere mich aber keines Unterschiedes

ihrer Gestalten. Selbst andere Dinge mußte ich schon haben unter-
scheiden können, ohne daß ich mich später einer Gestalt oder eines
Unterschiedes erinnern konnte. Dies beweist eine Begebenheit, die in
jene Zeit gefallen sein mußte. Ich fand mich einmal wieder in dem
Entsetzlichen, Zugrunderichtenden, von dem ich oben gesagt habe.
Dann war Klingen, Verwirrung, Schmerz in meinen Händen und Blut
daran, die Mutter verband mich, und dann war ein Bild, das so klar
vor mir jetzt dasteht, als wäre es in reinlichen Farben auf Porzellan
gemalt. Ich stand in dem Garten, der von damals zuerst in meiner
Einbildungskraft ist, die Mutter war da, dann die andere Großmutter,
deren Gestalt in jenem Augenblicke auch zum ersten Male in mein
Gedächtnis kam, in mir war die Erleichterung, die alle Male auf
das Weichen des Entsetzlichen und Zugrunderichtenden folgte, und
ich sagte: 'Mutter, da wächst ein Kornhalm'.

Die Großmutter antwortete darauf: 'Mit einem Knaben, der die
Fenster zerschlagen hat, redet man nicht'. Ich verstand zwar den
Zusammenhang nicht, aber das Außerordentliche, das eben von mir
gewichen war, kam sogleich wieder; die Mutter sprach wirklich kein
Wort, und ich erinnere mich, daß ein ganz Ungeheures auf meiner
Seele lag, das mag der Grund sein, daß jener Vorgang noch jetzt in
meinem Innern lebt. Ich sehe den hohen schlanken Kornhalm so
deutlich, als ob er neben meinem Schreibtische stünde; ich sehe die
Gestalten der Großmutter und Mutter, wie sie in dem Garten herum-
arbeiteten, die Gewächse des Gartens sehe ich nur als unbestimmten
grünen Schmelz vor mir; aber der Sonnenschein, der uns umfloß, ist
jetzt ganz klar da.

Nach dieser Begebenheit ist abermals Dunkel. (*M*, 602–4)

(I have often succumbed to wonderment at the phenomena of my life,
which has been as simple as the growing of a blade of grass. This is
the reason and excuse for my writing the following words. Primarily
they are for me alone. But should they find broader circulation, may
my wife, my brothers and sisters, my friends and acquaintances receive
them as a gentle greeting, and may strangers find nothing unworthy
in them.

Far back in the empty void is something akin to joy and bliss,
which penetrated my being, seizing it powerfully, almost destroying
it, and which nothing in my future life ever quite resembled. The
characteristics which have remained with me are: it was radiance, it
was feeling, it was below. It must have been very early, for I have
the feeling that the high, broad blackness of a void lies around it.

Then there was something else, which moved gently and soothingly
through my being: the characteristics are: they were sounds.

Then I was swimming in something fan-like, I swam this way and that, it grew softer and softer in me, and then I became as though drunk, then there was nothing more.

These three islands lie like pieces of fairy-tale and legend in the veiled sea of the past, like primeval memories of a people.

The following peaks emerge ever more sharply from the sea; the ringing of bells, a broad gleaming, a red twilight.

One thing which recurred time and time again was utterly clear. A voice which spoke to me, eyes which looked at me, and arms which soothed everything. I screamed for these things.

Then there were grievous things, intolerable, then sweet and satisfying things. I remember efforts which achieved nothing, and the cessation of the terrible and the destructive. I remember light and colours which were in my eyes, I remember sounds which were in my ears, I remember ecstasies that were in my being.

More and more I felt the eyes which looked at me, the voice which spoke to me, and the arms which soothed everything. I remember that I called this 'Mam'.

I once felt these arms carry me. There were dark patches in me. Memory later told me that they were forests which were outside me. Then there was sensation, like the first one of my life, radiance and tumult, then there was nothing more.

After these sensations there is again a large gap. Situations that occurred must have been forgotten.

Then the external world rose before me whereas hitherto only sensations had been registered. Even Mam, eyes, voice, arms had only been as sensations in me, even forests, as I have just mentioned. It is strange that there was something external in the very first sensation of my life, and in fact it was something that only penetrates the imaginative capacity very late and with great difficulty, something spatial, a below. That is an indication of how powerful the impact must have been which that sensation caused. Mam, which by now I called mother, stood as a figure before me and I could distinguish her movements, then father, grandfather, grandmother, aunt. I called them by these names, experienced good things from them, but can recall no difference between their figures. I must have been able to distinguish other things at the time, but without my being able later to recall a figure or a difference. This is proved by an event that must have occurred in that time. I found myself once again in the realm of the terrible and destructive of which I have spoken above. Then there was a ringing sound, confusion, pain in my hands and blood on them, mother was bandaging me, and then there was an image which stands so clearly before me now as though it were painted in pure colours on porcelain. I stood in the garden, within me there was a sense of relief which always followed the fading of the terrible and the destructive, and I said: 'Mother, over there a stalk of corn is growing.'

My grandmother then answered: 'One does not talk to a boy who has broken the windows.' I did not, admittedly, understand the connection, but the exceptional that had retreated from me came back immediately: my mother did not, in fact, speak a word, and I remember that something quite monstrous lay on my soul: which may be the reason why that experience is still alive within me. I can see the tall, slender stalk of corn as clearly as though it were standing by my writing desk; I can see the figures of the grandmother and mother, as they worked in the garden. I can only see the plants in the garden as an indefinite green softness before me; but the sunshine, which flooded around us, is now quite clearly present.

After this event there is darkness again.)

The incident of the broken windows could well stand as the motto for Stifter's whole creative endeavour. There is the inalienable experience of sudden, unmediated destruction and horror; there is the comfort found in the tender ministrations of the mother. Above all, there is the security that comes from noticing the intact, simple world beyond and outside the vulnerable self – the growing of the corn. Yet the comfort, too, is threatened: the grandmother is angry, the mother is silent, the horror returns. But so too does the stalk of corn.

From these impulses, from this commingling of the reassuring and the catastrophic, Stifter derives the thematic eloquence of his art. To its specifically stylistic energy we wish now to turn.

i. *The integrative text*

In this section, we shall examine a number of works in which the accommodation of the individual within the world around him is both achieved and celebrated. It is no accident that *Granit*, in which the reconciliation of centre and frame is aesthetically so satisfying and convincing, has a child for its protagonist: with the narrative interest focusing on a child, the whole drama of individuation is, by definition, shorn of many problematic aspects to do with adult choice and responsibility. In other works, as we shall see, that same reconciliation strikes one as highly problematic – not least because adult life is portrayed with a radical diminution, even denial, of its whole affective and psychological complexity.

Granit is a *Rahmenerzählung*. In the frame-narration a little boy is the object of a practical joke played by an old man who sells pitch and cart grease. The boy is persuaded to allow his feet to be annointed with pitch: and when he runs into the house to show his mother, he leaves a trail of pitch marks all over the freshly scrubbed floors. The mother loses her temper, beats him, and the boy is heartbroken at the turmoil he has created. But his grandfather is on hand to console him: he cleans the boy's feet and then takes him for a walk, in the course of which he tells a story about the plague that suddenly broke out many generations before, in this same landscape through which they are passing. The grandfather depicts the social and moral chaos which the plague brings with it. We learn of a pitchburner's family who take to the woods to escape infection; but their precautions are in vain. All are stricken and die – with the exception of their young son who manages to nourish himself on berries and wild fruit. He finds a girl who is gravely ill, and, with no thought for his security, he tends her and nurses her back to health. A peasant hears the magic song of a bird which gives the recipe for an antidote against the plague. Gradually, the threat fades and life returns to normal. Years later, the boy and the girl marry, becoming prosperous and respected members of the community. At the end of the grandfather's account we return to the present time of his narrative performance: when he and his grandson arrive home, the tranquillity of the familial order has reasserted itself. As the boy is about to fall asleep, the mother comes in to bless him, and the following morning he has forgotten all his sorrow.

Even a mere summary suggests that everything in this story is so organized as to intimate continuity beyond the catastrophic, stability beyond the destructive moment. In this sense, the block of granite named in the title is only in the first instance a realistic detail; ultimately, it functions symbolically. At the beginning of the story we read: 'Der Stein ist sehr alt, und niemand erinnert sich, von einer Zeit gehört zu haben, wann er gelegt worden sei' (*BSt*, 19) (the stone is very old and nobody remembers hearing of a time when it might have been laid). And at the end of the story, the narrator reflects: 'Seitdem sind viele Jahre vergangen, der Stein liegt noch vor dem Vaterhause, aber jetzt spielen die Kinder der Schwester darauf' (51) (Since then many years have passed, the stone still lies before my father's house, but now my sister's children play on it). Thus, stretching from infinite past into infinite future, the block of granite stands as the emblem of 'rock-solidity' enshrining the continuity of both the natural and the social realm.

The thematic concern of *Granit* is clearly the 'Überblick über ein Größeres', as postulated in the preface to *Bunte Steine*, that perspective within which the seemingly momentous emerges as insignificant ('klein') and the inconspicuous, world-sustaining laws emerge as truly great ('groß'). This concern is above all reflected by the form of the story, and the device of the *Rahmenerzählung* plays a crucial role. Narratively, we are never allowed to forget the present context within which the grandfather tells his tale. We are constantly aware of his vantage point as narrator: his account of the plague asserts both closeness to those events and detachment from them. The links are made in a number of ways. The grandfather heard the story from his grandfather who was alive at the time; the 'Schmiermann' (pitchburner) who plays the practical joke on the little boy is descended from the family in the plague story; despite the disasters, the continuity of family, community and landscape has been maintained. And thus all the landmarks which the grandfather points out stand as emblems of the strength and solidity of a world which has been neither invalidated nor destroyed by the terrifying events of so many years ago. The insistent presence of the frame – on frequent occasions it usurps the centre of narrative interest – is a constant reminder that the freak occurrence of the plague does not have the last word. The landscape enshrines the continuity of being in which the recurring triumphs over the exceptional, the eternal over the temporal.[1]

In many ways, then, *Granit* is more frame than story: its centre of gravity, both thematically and stylistically, is the frame, the circumstances that surround individuated existence. The individual finds strength and significance in so far as he is – and knows himself to be – part of the continuity of the living process. Time and again, the narrative frame brings the rhetoric of affirmation to bear on the catastrophes of the plague story. Before he launches on his account, the grandfather says to the little boy: 'Ich habe dir darum die Wälder gezeigt und die Ortschaften, weil sich in ihnen die Geschichte zugetragen hat, welche ich dir im Heraufgehen zu erzählen versprochen habe' (30) (I have shown you the forests and the villages because in them the story occurred which I promised to tell you as we walked up here). In other words, the showing ('zeigen') of the panorama of abundant life pre-empts the telling ('erzählen') of the forces of death. Just as the destruction wrought by the plague is securely encapsulated in the continuity of nature, so the horror is cocooned in the circumstantial weight and strength of the narrative frame. And similarly, the freak disturbance of the sacred order of family life is exorcised by the even flow of time. The reconciliation of the family conflict is accomplished without reference to moral values: neither the boy nor the mother apologize for what occurred a few hours previously. The passage of time – rather than the learning of moral lessons – is the healing power. One might argue, then, that time functions as the agent of Reason. The grandfather comforts the boy: 'Aber lasse nur Zeit, sie [die Mutter] wird schon zur Einsicht kommen, sie wird alles verstehen, und alles wird gut werden' (26) (But be patient, your mother will come to see and understand everything, and everything will turn out well). And in the end his words are, by implication, vindicated. *Granit*, like so many of Stifter's works to which the theme of waiting is central, can be seen as a modest rural version of theodicy in the wake of eighteenth- and nineteenth-century idealistic philosophy of history.

One might argue, of course, that this security of thematic purpose and narrative mode is threatened, that the constellation of continuity versus destruction can work both ways: just as the solid frame of the landscape exorcises the terror of the plague, so the notion of that sudden destruction may haunt the security of that frame. *Granit* leaves some leeway for such a reading: the terror of the plague certainly strikes home. One thinks of those moments when the grandfather's simple speech patterns cease to be comforting assurance and suddenly modulate into a ritual of horror. He says of the plague: 'aber niemand hatte geglaubt, daß sie in unsere Wälder herein kommen werde, weil nie etwas Fremdes zu uns herein kömmt, bis sie kam' (31) (but nobody had believed that it would come into our forests, because no foreign elements ever do reach us – until it came). The laconism, limiting itself to the brute fact of 'kommen', exposes us mercilessly to the 'Fremdes' as it invades and destroys the familiar, the norm. There are many moments when the stark stylization of the fairy-tale mode captures a world beyond all reason and reason-giving. There is, for example, the description of the desperately sick girl: 'es hatte wirre Haare und lag so ungefügig in dem Gestrippe, als wenn es hineingeworfen worden' (44) (she had tangled hair and lay so awkwardly in the undergrowth as though she had been flung there). The brutal factuality captures the literal and metaphorical dislocation of horror. Or one thinks of the stark simplicity of moments such as the following:

Die Menschen erschraken, und rannten gegeneinander...Die Kinder liebten ihre Eltern nicht mehr und die Eltern die Kinder nicht, man warf nur die Toten in die Grube, und ging davon. (31f.)

(People took fright and ran into each other...Children no longer loved their parents, parents no longer loved their children, they threw the dead bodies into the pit and went away.)

Er ging auf eine freie Stelle des Waldes, und da war jetzt überall niemand, niemand als der Tod. (43)

(He went into an open space in the forest, and everywhere that he looked there was nobody to be seen, nobody but death.)

This last example recalls the shattering fairy-tale told by the grandmother in Büchner's *Woyzeck*. These are important moments, and they weigh heavy in the grandfather's narration. Moreover, the threat of Unreason is reinforced in so far as the destructive irruption of Mother Nature links with the sudden disruption of familial peace in the frame, the mother furiously beating her little son. The story suggests that family bliss is not as unproblematic as the preface to *Bunte Steine*, with its emphasis on love and respect, leads us to believe. We are reminded that familial order entails parental authority which may be given to questionable exercises of power.

There is, then, a layer in *Granit* which recalls the gloomy perspective of *Abdias*. But ultimately the story sails home into security. The elements of threat are, at every turn, countermanded by stylistic stratagems of comfort and faith. There is first the geometrical figure of the circle, the *Rundgang*: grandfather and the boy leave the turmoil at home behind, walk through the tranquillity of the landscape and finally return to the house where peace has been restored. And the import of this movement is complemented by the imaginative *Rundgang* of the grandfather's tale which moves in a circle from original stability through horror back to harmony. Furthermore, there are the exchanges between grandfather and boy such as the following:

'Und was ist das, das sich weiter vorwärts von der Alpe befindet?' fragte er wieder.
'Das ist der Hüttenwald', antwortete ich.
'Und rechts von der Alpe und dem Hüttenwalde?'
'Das ist der Philippgeorgsberg.'
'Und rechts von dem Philippgeorgsberge?'
'Das ist der Seewald, in welchem sich das dunkle und tiefe Seewasser befindet.'
'Und wieder rechts von dem Seewalde?'
'Das ist der Blockenstein und der Sesselwald.'
'Und wieder rechts?'
'Das ist der Tussetwald.' (28)

('And what is that which stands in front of the alp?' he asked again.
'That is the Hütten forest', I answered.
'And to the right of the alp and the Hütten forest?'
'That is the Philippgeorgsberg.'
'And to the right of the Philippgeorgsberg?'
'That is the Seewald, the forest with the dark, deep lake.'
'And further to the right of the Seewald?'
'That is the Blockenstein and the Sesselwald.'
'And further to the right?'
'That is the Tussetwald.')

This stately exchange of question and answer is utterly characteristic of what passes between the boy and his grandfather on their walk. Such passages have little to do with the realist's employment of 'local colour': rather, the stylization suggests quite specifically the rhythm of a litany. The little boy is, as it were, saying an article of faith, and the object of that faith is the landscape which, by its very presence, answers the threat of the plague and the disruption of family peace. The naming of the landscape evokes the very act and meaning of Christening: to bestow in the name of God that name by which He calls and holds His creation.

This import is strengthened by the emphasis on reverent perception – one thinks of the grandfather's constantly repeated injunction 'Siehe' (behold), of the boy's receptiveness as epitomized in his trusting refrain 'Ja, Großvater' (Yes, grandfather), or a passage such as the following:

Ich hatte Gelegenheit, als wir weiter gingen, die Wahrheit dessen zu beobachten, was der Großvater gesagt hatte. Ich sah eine Menge der weißgelben Blümlein auf dem Boden, ich sah den grauen Rasen, ich sah auf manchem Stamme das Pech wie goldene Tropfen stehen, ich sah die unzähligen Nadelbüschel auf den unzähligen Zweigen gleichsam aus winzigen dunkeln Stiefelchen heraus ragen, und ich hörte, obgleich kaum ein Lüftchen zu verspüren war, das ruhige Säuseln in den Nadeln. (28)

(As we walked on, I had occasion to notice the truth of what my grandfather had said. I saw a host of whitish-yellow flowers on the ground, I saw the grey grass, I saw on many trunks the pitch standing like drops of gold. I saw the innumerable clumps of needles on innumerable branches, projecting as it were out of tiny dark boots, and I heard, although there was scarcely a breath of wind, the quiet rustling in the needles.)

And, running alongside this rhetoric of reverent, precise perception, we have a rhetoric of being. There is the grandfather's set-piece description of the people whose fires produce the columns of smoke that constantly appear in the landscape:

Da sind zuerst die Holzknechte, die...Dann sind die Kohlenbrenner, ...Dann sind die Heusucher, die...Dann sind die Sammler, welche ...Endlich sind die Pechbrenner, die...(29)

(First there are the woodsmen who...then there are the charcoal burners who...then there are the haymakers who...then there are the pitch burners who...).

This is again that typical non-predicative use of the verb 'sein' which vibrates with the sense of plenitude – the 'ontic style'.[2] At one point we read: 'ich rastete, betrachtete die Dinge, die da waren, als: die Wägen...die Pflüge und Eggen...die Knechte und Mägde...und die Dinge gesellten sich zu denen, mit denen mein Haupt ohnehin angefüllt war' (37) (I rested, and looked at the things that were there, for example: the carts...the ploughs and harrows...the farmhands and maids ...and the things joined those which already filled my head). In this telling example we note that 'die Dinge, die da waren' include both objects and people. All are part of the sacred continuity of being. The danger that this cataloguing could lose its life-affirming effect is kept fully at bay by the all-embracing function of the frame narration and the figure of the grandfather. While other figures of authority come in for implicit or explicit criticism, the grandfather stands as the very embodiment of benign, wise authority. It is not surprising that critics have pointed out echoes of the figure of Christ – one thinks of the moment when the grandfather washes the boy's feet which recalls Christ washing the feet of his disciples. Such interpretations may be suggestive, but one must emphasize that the story manages to stay this side of the purely allegorical. Within the typical Stifterian stylization, the text succeeds in fusing realistic detail and metaphorical significance. Take the following example: in the course of their walk, the boy begins to lose his footing. The grandfather then teaches him to step firmly:

'Siehst du, alles muß man lernen, selbst das Gehen. Aber komme, reiche mir die Hand, ich werde dich führen, daß du ohne Mühsal fort kömmst.'
Er reichte mir die Hand, ich faßte sie, und ging nun gestützt und gesicherter weiter. (35)

('Do you see? We have to learn everything, even how to walk. But come, give me your hand, I will lead you so that you can move forward without difficulty.'
He gave me his hand, I took hold of it and walked on, supported and feeling more secure.)

On one level, this is a finely observed realistic detail; but on another level, the passage attains figurative meaning: it suggests that man, guided by reason, can learn a way of being and proceeding which holds teleological promise. Again one is reminded of the eighteenth-century legacy, and in particular of Herder, who, in delineating his view of history, writes: 'As our walk is a continual falling to the right and left, and yet we advance at every step, so is the progress of culture in races of men and in whole nations.'[3]

The grandfather stands unquestioned. His perception is precisely that 'Überblick über ein Größeres', and from this perspective there emanates faith in the world. Stifter makes sure that this guide and interpreter of the world is not doubted: the boy, the immediate recipient of the grandfather's words, is totally naive. He does not ask probing questions, he does not argue. Another recipient might have exposed the fragility of the grandfather's tale; he might have argued that the account of how the people are cured of the plague is very much couched in Christian legendary terms, that in reality the plague may simply have run its course; he might also have queried the didactic function of the fairy-tale: does the pursuit of the 'sanftes Gesetz', the moral law, necessarily entail reward, let alone social reward in the shape of a wealthy girl and a castle? *Granit* closes the door firmly on such questioning. The little boy is the very embodiment of innocent obedience, who accepts both the punishment by the mother and the comfort from the grandfather unquestioningly.

There are instances in Stifter's work where the functions of authority and obedience are critically illuminated (*Das alte Siegel* comes to mind, for example), but in *Granit* this is not the case – or rather: no longer the case, for the first version, *Die Pechbrenner* (The Pitch Burners), differs in this respect quite radically. In the first version, the whole story of the pitch burner's family is told with an urgency and specificity that is totally lacking in *Granit*. The members of the family are named: there is a daughter, Martha, and the little boy is called Joseph. The father orders his family to shun all contact with other people; and when a foreign family appears and requests shelter, he drives them away with a burning brand. But the little boy, Joseph, disobeys: he gives the family shelter and brings them food. When the father discovers what has happened, he blames Joseph for the fact that the plague has spread to their family. And with the terrifying words 'Ich habe dein Urteil beschlossen' (*Urf*, 292) (I have decided your sentence) he takes the little boy and forces him to climb up by ladder on to a huge, sheer rock. He leaves him there with a pitcher of water and half a loaf of bread. His parting words, before he disappears with the ladder, are: 'Hier hast du Wasser und Brod, es reicht auf zwei Tage, wenn diese vorüber sind, so magst du auf diesem Felsen verhungern, oder hin-abspringen' (293) (Here are water and bread, there is enough for two days, and when they have passed, you can either die of hunger on this rock, or jump down). Time passes: father and mother are stricken with the plague, and the boy is left alone. The passage that follows is the most horrific that ever came from Stifter's pen:

Der Knabe hatte in der Nacht auf dem Felsen vor Frost gezittert, aber er hatte nichts gesagt. Siehst du, Kind, wie es sein muß, wenn er die ganze Nacht auf der Höhe des Steines saß und nichts um sich hatte, als den Himmel und die finstern Tannen. Aber es ist der Morgen gekommen, es hat die Sonne gescheint, zuerst von der einen Seite, dann von oben, dann von der andern Seite. Der Knabe hat von seinem Brote gegessen, von seinem Wasser getrunken und ist ruhig geblieben. Als es aber wieder Abend geworden war, als die Tannen in Dunkelheit versunken waren, als der Mond an dem Himmel stand und seine schrecklichen Strahlen in die Zacken der Waldbäume hing, rief der Knabe leise: 'Vater!' Als er nicht gehört wurde, rief er noch einmal: 'Vater!' Da es aber immer finsterer wurde, da es stille war und die Kälte der Nacht auf die Gräser und Gesteine hernieder kam, rief er so laut er nur konnte: 'Vater, lieber Vater, lasse mich nicht mehr in der Nacht auf dem Felsen, ich habe gefehlt, züchtige mich, wie du willst, ich will es nicht mehr tun, Vater, Vater, lasse mich von dem Steine hinunter.' (295)

(In the night the boy had trembled with cold on the rock, but he had said nothing. Do you see, child, how it must be, when he sat all night on top of the rock with nothing around him but the sky and the dark pine trees. But the morning came, the sun shone, first from one side, then from above, then from the other side. The boy ate from his bread, drank from his water, and remained calm. But when evening came again, when the pines disappeared in the darkness, when the moon rose in the sky and sent her terrible rays into the jagged shapes of the trees of the forest, the boy called out quietly: 'Father!' But as no one heard, he called again: 'Father!' As it grew more and more dark, as it was quiet and the coldness of night descended on the grasses and stones, he called out as loudly as he could: 'Father, dear father, do not leave me any longer to spend the night on the rock,

I have done wrong, punish me as you will, I will not do it any more. Father, father, let me come down from the rock.')

No answering voice is heard. It is the following morning before help appears in the shape of the little girl whose family Joseph has succoured. The remainder of the story is as we know it in the *Bunte Steine* version. Yet in *Die Pechbrenner* the happy ending to both the inset story and the frame narrative does not manage to draw the sting from that terrible account of the boy's punishment. For that scene leaves undiminished in the reader's mind the possibility that the order of family life may be anything but sacred. The disproportion between punishment and crime, the ominous cruelty of a father saying to his son 'I have decided your sentence' – all this reminds us of Kafka. Quite specifically of that incident recounted in the *Brief an den Vater* (Letter to the Father) which becomes the very symbol of the father's capricious, but unshakable, authority – 'pawlatsche'.[4] 'Pawlatsche' is the Czech name for a balcony, and Kafka recalls how his father punished him for a minor piece of naughtiness by locking him out on the balcony one winter night. Not, of course, that either *Die Pechbrenner* or Kafka's *Brief an den Vater* are texts of overt revolt against the authority of the father: but the implied criticism is devastating.

There is one revealing moment in the text of *Die Pechbrenner* where the divergence of ontological and moral concerns becomes manifest. The grandfather says: 'Siehst du, Kind, wie es sein muß, wenn er die ganze Nacht auf der Höhe des Steines saß'. At first sight, one tends to misread the sentence as 'siehst du... wie es gewesen sein muß' – 'do you see how it must have been': the implication being that the hearer is asked to imagine how Joseph must have felt, abandoned on the rock at night. But, in fact, the grandfather uses the modal verb with the present infinitive of the verb 'to be' – he asks for our assent to the fact that such things *must be*. But the rhetoric of ontological necessity simply breaks down here; because the punishment of Joseph is decreed not by the laws of nature, but by decisions taken by another human being. And in this way, the moral issue which *Granit* suppresses reverberates powerfully in *Die Pechbrenner*. Indeed, in the first version, there is a very particular stylistic echo which amplifies the moral issue by transferring it from the inset story to the frame. Joseph cries out: 'züchtige mich, wie du willst, ich will es nicht mehr tun, Vater, Vater, lasse mich von dem Steine herunter'. But the parent does not come, does not liberate the child from the rock. And in the frame narrative, too, we have a little boy's fear that adults will 'mich weiter *züchtigen*' (267) (*punish* me further). Help arrives with the appearance of the grandfather: but not before the boy has been left to suffer *on the stone* – 'dann ließ sie mich los, und ließ mich auf dem Steine des Vorhauses, der zum Klopfen des Garnes dastand, weinend und schluchzend sitzen' (266) (then she let go of me and left me sitting, weeping and sobbing, on the stone in the porch which was there for the beating of darning thread). The echo of Joseph's suffering on the rock is manifest.

Clearly, the story of *Die Pechbrenner* undermines the very foundation on which the second version rests and which it reinforces: the validity of authority, the ethos of obedience. It is no wonder, therefore, that in 1852 Stifter made drastic changes. He comments that his intention is to keep the story more in line with the character and views of the grandfather, and he hopes to give the work a 'Hauch der Innigkeit und Reinheit' (aura of tranquillity and purity).[5] No doubt, the revision has artistic merit – the inset story is considerably tightened up – but the conservative intention, both philosophically and politically, is obvious. Stifter removes almost all traces of parental cruelty; he renames his story *Granit*: the title refers to the stone in front of the parental home, the guarantor of solidity. Were one to give *Die Pechbrenner* the title 'Granit', the stone would symbolize not only the strength and permanence of natural and social processes – but also the unforgettable horror of what one human being can do to another. Thus if it is true that the second version is artistically more of a piece, it is also true to say that, intellectually, it may be too much of a piece. In its determination to exorcise brittleness it runs the risk of being too rock-solid.

This reservation apart, *Granit* is ultimately persuasive because of the particular intensity with which a child's reverent and vulnerable closeness to the circumstances of its existence is rendered. Difficulties arise, however, when the human centre is not the child, but an adult, where questions of moral choice, of sexual relationship are involved. Stifter can pen cautionary tales in which the recalcitrant individual is educated to an acceptance of the right relatedness to the world of which he is part. The danger is that simple moralizing is the result, a narrative which validates foregone conclusions. Stifter does not altogether avoid this danger in such stories as *Die drei Schmiede ihres Schicksals, Die Narrenburg, Der Waldbrunnen, Zwei Schwestern, Das Haidedorf, Der Waldsteig, Der beschriebene Tännling, Nachkommenschaften*. There are, of course, fine things in these stories, but the fine things are often at odds with the didactic purpose: and the contradiction produces dislocation rather than an enrichment of theme and import.

In typological terms, however, there is a group of works which heighten the integrative aim of *Granit* to an extraordinary degree and strive at all costs to reconcile individuated man with the circumstances that surround him. This is the late prose which one may regard as the very hypostatization of the fusion of frame and centre. Here, the most famous – and notorious – text is *Witiko*. This enormous historical novel is totally sustained by that weighty stylization which the works discussed so far all display in varying degrees; both in thematic and structural terms, the concept of theodicy is here developed into monumental proportions.

Witiko, the last male of a distinguished family, leaves his estate in order to serve the cause of virtue, decency, rightness in the world of practical politics. On his journey he meets a girl, Bertha, whose image and presence will not thereafter leave him. Witiko is sent by the gravely ill Duke Sobeslav to

Prague to observe the choice of a successor to the dukedom. The nephew, Wladislaw, is chosen by the princes who hope that the new leader will be putty in their hands. Witiko declines to serve the new Duke and returns to his estates. But rebellion troubles the country, and Witiko determines to discover the nature of the political situation. The new Duke is, in fact, not the plaything of the princes, indeed, he is attempting to curb the power of the aristocracy. But he is prepared to capitulate before the rebels if thereby peace can be achieved. Witiko realizes that the Duke is the right ruler of Bohemia, and he supports him in this and in three other campaigns. Witiko and the Duke become close allies and friends: men of decision, of firmness of action and will, yet men of scruple and compassion who can pardon and rehabilitate their opponents. Witiko marries Bertha and is revered as a true and faithful servant of Bohemia.

In 1861 Stifter writes a most revealing letter about the artistic intentions behind *Witiko*:

Ich bin durch die Natur der Sache von der gebräuchlichen Art des historischen Romanes abgelenkt worden. Man erzählt gewöhnlich bei geschichtlichem Hintergrunde Gefahren, Abenteuer und Liebesweh eines Menschen oder einiger Menschen. Mir ist das nie recht zu Sinne gegangen. Mir haben unter Walter Scotts Romanen die am besten gefallen, in denen das Völkerleben in breiteren Massen auftritt...In ihren Schicksalen zeigt sich die Abwicklung eines riesigen Gesetzes auf, das wir in Bezug auf uns das Sittengesetz nennen, und die Umwälzungen des Völkerlebens sind Verklärungen dieses Gesetzes...Es erscheint mir daher in historischen Romanen die Geschichte die Hauptsache und die einzelnen Menschen die Nebensache.[6]

(It lay in the nature of the material that I deviated from the traditional species of the historical novel. Normally one recounts the dangers, adventures and unhappy love affairs of one person or several people against an historical background. That never seemed right to me. Of Walter Scott's novels the ones I liked best were those in which the life of whole peoples is represented in terms of the broad mass...In such destinies we can follow the progression of a mighty law which, when we apply it to ourselves, we call the moral law; and the upheavals in the life of a people are transfigured expressions of this law...It seems to me therefore that in historical novels history is the main thing – and individual people are secondary.)

Stifter rejects the notion that the historical novel focuses on individuals whose destiny is the exceptional embodiment of the corporate pressures of an historical situation. Instead, he seeks to create a text which will focus on the course of historical processes, a course which is to reflect, indeed to enact, the moral law. In other words, a Hegelian conception of history lies at the centre of *Witiko* and determines the aesthetic organization of the novel. Hegel's *Philosophie der Geschichte* ends as follows: 'Daß die Weltgeschichte dieser Entwicklungsgang und das wirkliche Werden des Geistes ist, unter dem wechselnden Schauspiele ihrer Geschichten – dies ist die wahre Theodizee, die Rechtfertigung Gottes in der Geschichte'[7] (that world history is this sequence of development and the true growth of the spirit behind the changing spectacle of its stories – this is true theodicy, the justification of God in the workings of history). *Witiko* is the narrative version of this philosophy: it is the massive attempt to document the things and circumstances of the historical world, and yet to say them not as part of an intractable tangle, but as a sequence which harbours the logic of Reason. The aesthetic principle of order is to intimate the supreme ordering principle of Reason. Accordingly, the action unfolds in fiercely patterned sequences. The device of repetition attains crucial importance: it makes every paragraph, every sentence function as magic formulae which, from the very start, conjure up the sense that the events, historical substance, are suffused with the redeeming power of the sublime Law. This is, for example, the essence of the cascading 'da' clauses when we are introduced to Witiko:

Zur Zeit, da in Deutschland der dritte Konrad, der erste aus dem Geschlecht der Hohenstaufen, herrschte, da Bayern der stolze Heinrich inne hatte, da Leopold der Freigebige Markgraf in Österreich war, da Sobeslaw der Erste auf dem Herzogstuhle der Böhmen saß, und da man das Jahre des Heiles 1138 schrieb, ritt...(*W*, 13)

(At the time when in Germany the third Konrad, the first of the house of Hohenstaufen, ruled, when proud Heinrich possessed Bavaria, when Leopold the Generous was Margrave in Austria, when Sobeslaw the First sat on the dukely throne in Bohemia, when it was the year of grace 1138, there rode...)

Patterning dominates the dialogue both in the grand public scenes of political debate and the private exchanges between Witiko and his neighbours. In these ritualistic exchanges, a single voice is echoed to the point where it expresses a corporate will – and, again, that voice points ultimately to the will of Reason:

'Dieser Jüngling ist Witiko unser Nachbar im Walde, und, so lange es ihm genehm ist, unser Gast.'
'Er ist willkommen', rief einer der Männer.
'Er ist willkommen', rief ein anderer.
Und: 'Er ist willkommen' riefen alle. (188)

('This young man is Witiko our neighbour in the forest and, as long as it may please him, our guest.'
'He is welcome', cried one of the men.
'He is welcome', cried another.
And: 'He is welcome' they all cried.)

If history were pure idea, if political debate could yield values and facts proof against the reductive questioning that we know as psychology and sociology, then *Witiko* would be the supreme historical novel. But in the face of historical reality, Stifter's novel can only strike us as a utopian dream in which the temporal and contingent is elevated into timeless patterns of cognitive and ethical truth. Again, Hegel's lectures on the philosophy of history come to mind, above all the critical point near the beginning where he states: 'Wenn man nämlich nicht den Gedanken, die Erkenntnis der Vernunft, schon mit zur Weltgeschichte bringt, so sollte man wenigstens den festen, unüberwindlichen Glauben haben, daß Vernunft in derselben ist'[8] (if one does not bring the thought, the cognition of reason to bear on world history, then one should at least have the firm, unshakable belief that reason is present in world history). This faith, rather than cognition, informs the novel in so far as, time and again, it has the stylistic feel of the fairy-tale or legend. Here is the first exchange between Witiko and Bertha:

'Was stehst du mit deinen Rosen hier da?'
'Ich stehe in meiner Heimat da', antwortete das Mädchen; 'stehst du auch in derselben, daß du frägst, oder kamst du wo anders her?' 'Ich komme anders woher', sagte der Reiter. 'Wie kannst du dann fragen?' entgegnete das Mädchen.
'Weil ich es wissen möchte', antwortete der Reiter. (27)

('Why are you standing here as you do with your roses?'
'I am standing here in my home', the girl replied; 'are you also standing in your home that you ask such questions, or did you come from somewhere else?' 'I come from somewhere else', the rider replied. 'How can you then ask such questions?' the girl said.
'Because I want to know', answered the rider.)

The dialogue is well-nigh untranslatable: there is a weightiness assigned to simple verbs such as 'dastehen', 'fragen', 'wissen', to simple adverbs of place 'da', 'hier', 'woher', that immediately slithers into banality when translated. Yet to normalize the statements is to lose that characteristic flavour of a ritualized *Märchen*. And this is the register which dominates this enormous novel. When Witiko sets off on his travels he comes into contact with the 'scarlet riders', and among them is the nephew of Duke Sobeslaw, the man who will succeed his uncle. From him Witiko hears of the appalling feuds that threaten to tear Bohemia asunder; later he will witness the meeting which decides Sobeslaw's successor, a meeting full of tension and disagreement. Yet such experiences, which invoke the common world of history with its quarrels and frictions, do not have the last word. What prevails is that legendary tone, part fairy-tale, part *Heilsgeschichte*, sacred narrative, in which secular events become the outward and visible signs of a divine pattern, and that pattern is the alpha and omega of the novel.[9] Just as the narration is perfectly joined – *gefügt* is the appropriate German term – so, too, the powerfully dominating *Leitmotif* 'Es wird sich fügen' (it will come about as decreed) spells the faith in the all-cohesive design of history.

In terms of the theory and history of narrative forms, *Witiko* represents an attempt on Stifter's part to create a fiction in which the subjectivity of the modern epic (in the Hegelian sense) is reversed: a world in which events and values can be in accord, in which scruple, thought, and inwardness do not lead to inactivity, irresolution.[10] At one point, late in the novel, Witiko is praised for his right actions, and he replies that he only did what circumstances required. The Cardinal answers: 'So wäre gut, wenn alle wüßten, was die Dinge fordern, und wenn alle täten, was die Dinge fordern; denn dann täten sie den Willen Gottes' (724) (it would be good if everybody knew what things demand from us and if everybody did what things demand; for then they would do the will of God). Thus, in *Witiko*, values and circumstances go hand in hand. If, for the German novel of the first few decades of the nineteenth century, as Heinz Schlaffer suggests,[11] Hamlet becomes the prototypical novel hero in all his vacillation and uncertainty, *Witiko* is the attempt to write a novel in which the curse of irresolution is lifted from the protagonist and the epic form.

How valid is this exorcism, the redemption from any kind of psychological and social realism? One thinks of Thomas Mann's admiration of the work:

Auch ich habe den *Witiko* lange gemieden, weil ich ihn für langweilig hielt. Und dabei wußte ich doch, daß es höchst abenteuerliche Arten des Langweiligen gibt und daß der Langweiligkeit nur ein wenig Genie beigemischt zu sein braucht, um in eine Sphäre zu versetzen, worin von langer und kurzer Weile all-überall nicht mehr die Rede sein kann. *Witiko* ist ein solches Traum-Abenteuer einer Langweiligkeit höchster Art.[12]

(I too long avoided *Witiko* because I regarded it as boring. And yet I knew that there are highly adventurous kinds of boredom, and that boredom needs only to be tinged with genius for us to be transported into realms where questions of interest and boredom can simply not arise – never and nowhere. *Witiko* is such a dream adventure in a boringness of the very highest kind.)

But does *Witiko* really move in that highest sphere of timelessness? In so far as the novel makes absolutely no concessions to common reader expectations, it would seem to attain to the total autonomy of the aesthetic phenomenon. But this is only part of the truth. *Witiko* is no Flaubertian 'livre sur rien', no book about nothing. Its subject matter, the triumph over Bohemian unrest, particularizes the concept of Reason, politicizes it into the reason of the unitary Habsburg empire. Moreover, the very pursuit of 'Langeweile' partakes of Stifter's contemporary historical context. As the semantics suggest, 'Langeweile' is the attempt to prolong the moment as much as possible, to stem the flux of time. In terms of the preface to *Bunte Steine*, to give in to the pressures of time is to lose moderation and reason – to move slowly, if not to stand still, is, by implication, to be wise. In this sense, *Witiko*, the very pinnacle of slow motion, links with the wisdom of 'weises Zögern' (wise hesitation) which marks Austrian rule in the nineteenth century, the determination to halt the flux of time for fear that change may entail dissolution. Stifter's affinity with the stance of Grillparzer is evident: Witiko is a figure akin to the Rudolf of *König Ottokar*, whose one aim it is to guarantee the stability of the empire against all threats. Grillparzer, however, in sharp contrast to Stifter, wrote an epitaph to that ideal in the figure of that other Rudolf in *Ein Bruderzwist in Habsburg*. This play acknowledges that the policy of 'weises Zögern' must be doomed: the play ends with the Thirty Years War looming on the horizon. Grillparzer displays a critical distance toward his own cherished ideals which the (historically) determined monumentalism of *Witiko* will not admit.

The problems of a narrative theodicy become particularly acute in the late novellas which attempt to heighten a specific personal story into a generalized *Heilsgeschichte*. In both *Der Kuß von Sentze* and *Der fromme Spruch*, Stifter strives to make a love story, with its tensions and reconciliations, intimate the theme of peace among men, among nations. *Bergmilch*, the last story in *Bunte Steine*, to which we shall return later, is clearly a forerunner of these texts. In these works, as in *Witiko*, we have a stylization of human experience to the point where every dialogue, every action, every meeting between people is drained of its individual, affective colour. Ritualization reigns supreme. The intimation of conflict is located within such an overtly sacramental world that frame and centre blend in a seamless union. Sacred gradualness so informs both the manner and the matter of the works that the upshot is an extraordinary act of exorcism which, if it is to work, has to overcome the reader's disbelief that a whole story can be written like this.

Der Kuß von Sentze concerns a family in which there is a particular tradition of a formally exchanged kiss of peace which entails a contract that there shall be no enmity, no evil doing between the two members who exchange that kiss. In the history of the family this kiss has, on occasion, been more than the emblem of a truce: it has become a kiss of love. Our story concerns two fathers who arrange for their children, Rupert and Hiltiburg, to meet in order to discover if they can love one another. The meeting is polite but cool. One night, as Rupert is due to leave Hiltiburg's home, he is embraced by a shadowy figure who plants a passionate kiss on his lips. Some time later, Rupert and Hiltiburg are reunited; it is suggested that, as they cannot love one another, they should at least exchange the kiss of peace. They do so: and it is a repeat of that fleeting kiss at night, a kiss of love and passion.

By any standards, this is an extraordinary story: its narrative and stylistic ponderousness is of a piece with the family's ponderous attempts to legislate for the kiss of love. In the Sentze family we witness the determination to treat emotionally loaded relationships, between siblings, between male and female members, by keeping passion, destructiveness at bay and by legislating for continuity, i.e. marriage. Rupert announces his visit to Hiltiburg as follows:

Unsere Väter wünschen, daß wir eine Neigung zu einander fassen, aus welcher eine Eheverbindung wird. Wenn ich die Neigung fassen

kann, wenn Du auch zu mir diese Neigung zu fassen vermagst, so
werde ich sehr erfreut sein. (*BSt,* 633)

(Our fathers wish that we should conceive a fondness for each other
out of which a marital relationship could emerge. If I can conceive
this fondness, if you too can conceive this fondness for me, I shall
be very pleased.)

This, then, is the strenuously resolute attempt to exorcize
passion and conflict by incorporating them into familial continuity. Initially, it does not work: there is a whiff of caprice,
tension, dislike. There are other hints which disturb the placid
surface, hints at a past that was not always manageable. There
is, for example, Walchon, Rupert's uncle, a somewhat laconic,
isolated figure who devoted his life to collecting mosses. His
credo seems as joyless as it is orderly:

Alle Dinge, die ich seit meiner Jugend zu Gutem und Großem
unternommen hatte, sind nicht in Erfüllung gegangen. Ich habe mich
gefügt und habe abermals in die Zeit hinübergelebt. Nur die Naturdinge
sind ganz wahr. Um was man sie vernünftig fragt, das beantworten
sie vernünftig. (649)

(All the things which, since my youth, I have undertaken in the
service of greatness and goodness have not come to fruition. I accepted
this and once again I went on living out my time. Only the things of
nature are true. If you ask sensible questions of them, they will answer
sensibly.)

Man, it would appear, is an aberration, and to contain that
aberration to a minimum the family attempts to legislate for
the kiss, to make sure that the kiss at all costs prevents hatred
and strife. Moreover, even the kiss of passion is converted into
an institutional thing:

Weil nun der Kuß nicht bloß den Streit verhindern, sondern auch
Liebe erzeugen konnte, so teilten ihn die Sentze in zwei Arten ein.
Den Liebeskuß nannten sie den Kuß der ersten Art, oder schlechtweg
den ersten Kuß, den Friedenskuß nannten sie den Kuß der zweiten
Art oder schlechtweg den zweiten Kuß. (630)

(But because the kiss was able not simply to prevent strife, but also to
produce love, so the Sentze family divided the kiss into two types: they
called the kiss of love the kiss of the first type – or simply the first

kiss; they called the kiss of peace the kiss of the second type – or simply the second kiss.)

The leaden, stately prose is of a piece with the Sentze ethos, the pedantic regulation of the emotional life. What in *Das alte Siegel* was the object of critique is here raised to the level of an unequivocal value.

Of course, there *is* a spontaneous kiss of passion: the one Hiltiburg gives Rupert on the night he leaves to join the army. It is repeated when they meet again: the kiss of peace turns out to be the kiss of love. Thus passion merges with contractual austerity, with the demands of family continuity. It all amounts to a piece of rigidly controlled, almost bureaucratic, wishful thinking. Energy and emotion are made to fuse with the endless reiterations of normative behaviour. And if passion will not obey the demands of orderliness, then presumably one should do without it and live by the rules, as the two fathers have done. Rupert's father evokes the past in a sequence of clauses which strikes one as the monotonous drum-beat of orderliness:

Seit Walchon und ich das nämliche, schöne Fräulein zu ehelichen gewünscht, seit wir uns den Friedenskuß gegeben und ihn so gehalten haben, daß keiner mehr das schöne Fräulein begehrte, seit wir unsere Gattinnen in das Grab gelegt haben...(632)

(Since the time that Walchon and I wished to marry the same beautiful girl, since we exchanged the kiss of peace and have kept our vow such that neither of us continued to desire the beautiful girl, since we buried our wives...)

No doubt there is a human heart somewhere that knew anguish, but it is not allowed to ruffle the imperturbable progression of temporal clauses. We must presume that there is such a centre, that it can come alive again – the story closes with the two brothers, like Rupert and Hiltiburg, exchanging the kiss of love. But no narrative time or energy is devoted to that centre, the story is all about the framework that houses the morally and narratively admissible. This is the pinnacle of Stifter's exorcism of individuation: *Der Kuß von Sentze* resolutely presses beyond all traditional categories of narrative and human interest.

The same is true of *Der fromme Spruch*. Dietwin and Gerlint are brother and sister. They have a nephew and niece respectively, also called Dietwin and Gerlint, to whom they stand *in loco parentis*. Both young people are to inherit from their uncle and aunt. The uncle and aunt feel that the inheritance of the estates could well be crowned if they were to marry. The only problem is that, when they were young, they quarrelled constantly, and, while the disposition of estates can be planned, marriages, according to the old 'pious saying', are made in heaven. However, the uncertainty is happily resolved, and the story ends with the marriage of Dietwin and Gerlint.

Der fromme Spruch unfolds with relentless symmetry. None of the characters are individuated – whether in action or in speech habits. All their affective life is subsumed in the stately progress of question and answer. Marriages may be made in heaven, but this one is given in the sameness of identical lives. Relationships – 'Verhältnisse' – become indistinguishable from the circumstances – 'Verhältnisse' – which house them. Nothing, one feels, is left to chance, although the possibility is raised that the nephew and niece might kick over the traces. But disorder is securely exorcised, conflict evaporates before the stylization which makes the characters interchangeable. This is being beyond individuation, a sublime tediousness which legislates as surely for the holiness of the heart's affections as it does for the disposition of assets, clothing, gardens.

There is a wonderful set piece in Ionesco's *The Bald Prima Donna* where Mr and Mrs Smith find themselves discussing a family of which every member is called Bobby Watson. The comic impetus derives from the discrepancy between the sheer unmemorableness of the family and Mr and Mrs Smith's desperate attempt to individuate the members, to tell one from another. In Ionesco human substance evaporates before the schemata of interchangeable existence, whereas in Stifter's story the very schematism is infused with the pathos of wish-fulfilment.

Der fromme Spruch begins with the crucial notion of custom, recurrence, sameness:

Dietwin von der Wieden hatte die Gepflogenheit, an jedem vier-undzwanzigsten Tage des Monates April gegen den Abend in das Gut seiner Schwester einzufahren. (*BSt*, 665)

(Dietwin von der Wieden was in the habit, on every twenty-fourth day of the month of April, of arriving towards evening at the estate of his sister.)

The horses are quartered 'gehörig' – 'fittingly' – in the stable, and Dietwin goes to change his clothes. And, once his servant has assured him that his dress is impeccable, he calls on his sister. What results is less a conversation than a ritualized audience. They inquire after each other's well-being, they assure themselves that there has been no intrusion into their ordered existence by irritants from the day-to-day business of estate management, and the dialogue closes as follows – Gerlint is speaking:

'Bei mir ist nichts vorgekommen.'
'So stehen die Sachen vortrefflich', antwortete er.
'Es geht so gut, wie alles nur immer gehen kann', sagte sie, 'und so sei noch einmal gegrüßt, Dietwin.'
'Sei gegrüßt, Gerlint', erwiderte er. (666)

('And with me nothing has happened.'
'So everything is in excellent order', he answered.
'Everything is going as well as it could possibly be', she said,
'and so I greet you once again, Dietwin.'
'I greet you, Gerlint', he replied.)

And so the first meeting concludes: things are apparently in order. Nothing has happened – which is equated with the highest happiness.

They meet the following day: Dietwin goes to the great hall of his sister's castle – 'In dem Saale war ein kostbarer Teppich auf den Marmorboden gebreitet, auf dem Teppiche stand ein sehr geräumiger rotseidener Armstuhl, und in dem Armstuhle saß in ihrem aschgrauen Seidenkleide Gerlint' (667) (in the hall a precious carpet had been spread on the marble floor, on the carpet stood a capacious red silk armchair, and in the armchair sat Gerlint in her ash-grey silk dress). The very rhythm of the sentence enshrines the priorities: first the things, the circumstances and finally the person as part of an unbroken hierarchy. It is hierarchy that is underpinned by narrative validation: whereas, as we shall see, in *Turmalin* that same descriptive mode is made to vibrate with unease at the stultification of human substance.

There follows a lengthy review of their estates, their hopes that the nephew and niece (together with their estates) could be joined in marriage. The augury would seem good: nephew and niece have the same names as their guardians; like their guardians they are separated by some six years. As Gerlint puts it:

Wunderbar sind die Namen der Kinder, wunderbar ihr gleicher Altersunterschied, wunderbar die Verhältnisse, die sie zu uns gebracht haben, wunderbar ihre Ähnlichkeit mit uns, und am wunderbarsten, daß wir beide unabhängig von einander den Gedanken ihrer Verehelichung faßten. (677)

(Wondrous are the names of the children, wondrous the identical difference in years, wondrous the circumstances that brought them to us, wondrous their physical similarity to us, and most wondrous of all, that we both – each independently of the other – should conceive the idea of their marrying.)

There is such a symmetry at work here that it would seem wondrous if the pattern were suddenly broken. Somewhere, in the background, there is the hint of passion – in Gerlint's love for her husband, in the nephew's and niece's battles when they were children, in the fact that Dietwin (the younger) has apparently fought a duel with a man who showed interest in Gerlint. But we are asked to take this on trust as a concession to certain areas of common experience which are firmly transcended in the higher purpose and dignity of these charmed, encapsulated lives. Here is the climatic moment of passion when nephew and niece speak of their love for each other:

'Gerlint', rief Dietwin, 'ich kann es nicht ertragen, wenn dein Auge auf irgendeinen Mann blickt.'
Gerlint wendete sich um, und rief: 'Dietwin, ich kann es nicht ertragen, wenn dein Auge auf ein Weib blickt.'
'Gerlint', rief Dietwin.
'Dietwin', rief Gerlint. (727)

('Gerlint', cried Dietwin, 'I cannot bear the thought that your eye should rest on any other man.'
Gerlint turned round, and cried: 'Dietwin, I cannot bear the thought that your eye should rest on another woman.'
'Gerlint', cried Dietwin.
'Dietwin', cried Gerlint.)

If, as Mallarmé said, everything in the world exists to achieve the status of a book, then Stifter's *Der fromme Spruch* is a story which fulfils that precept, for nothing is ultimately resistant to the rage for order. But this order is questionable, both aesthetically and philosophically: the emphasis on firmly founded and ever recurring customs, 'Sitten', clearly aims to intimate the binding force of morality, 'Sittlichkeit'. But repetition does not in itself confer moral value, and by the same token the linguistic repetitions in Stifter's story cannot establish philosophical validity. The attempt to bridge the gap between the common 'Einerlei', to recall *Der Nachsommer*, and the sublime 'Einerlei' is, to say the least, dubious.

Some critics (for example, Arts, Seidler and Wildbolz)[13] have tried to defend these stories by seeing them as ironic, as calling into question the human rigidity that sustains them; and they have invoked Bergson's definition of the comic impetus – 'du mécanique plaqué sur du vivant' (something mechanical imposed on something living). But it is difficult to trace or prove such irony, and we would do well to recall the exchange of letters between Stifter and Leo Tepe that took place in 1867. Stifter had submitted *Der fromme Spruch* to the journal *Die katholische Welt*. Leo Tepe refused to accept the story, and wrote to Stifter giving the reasons which led his editorial committee to this decision:

Die Erzählung ist unnatürlich; solche steife Personen gibt es nicht, ihre Reden sind alle wie auf Schrauben gestellt; die alltäglichen Dinge sind in endloser Breitspurigkeit vorgeführt; die Handlung ist fast null; der Stil ist gezwungen und voll Wiederholungen; man glaubt kaum, daß es dem Verfasser ernst ist, und man ist manchmal geneigt, das Ganze für eine Karikatur der aristokratischen Familien zu halten.[14]

(The story is unnatural; such stiff persons do not exist, their speeches are all as though mounted on stilts; everyday things are paraded before us with endless expansiveness; the action is almost nil; the style is forced and full of repetitions; one can hardly believe that the author is serious, one is sometimes tempted to regard the whole piece as a caricature of aristocratic families.)

The criticism is not only devastating, but highly perceptive. It is noteworthy that the editorial board only raises the question of a possible ironic intention because of their sheer disbelief that anybody can intend such a piece of prose to be taken straight. In his reply, Stifter seizes the lifeline that Tepe's letter throws him, and attempts to justify the story in terms of a comic intention:

Es sollte allerdings die Lächerlichkeit nicht des hohen Adels, dessen Benehmen bei uns durchgänging leicht und fein ist, sondern gewisser Leute auf dem Lande mit veralteten Formen nicht gerade satirisch sondern scherzend dargestellt werden, diese Leute sollten aber doch gut und ehrenwert sein.[15]

(Admittedly, the ridiculousness, not of the higher aristocracy whose behaviour in our country is consistently gracious and fine, but of certain country people with outdated forms of behaviour was to be treated not exactly satirically, but in a joking spirit – but these people should nevertheless be good and honourable.)

One notes Stifter's reluctance here: it is difficult not to feel that the defence he puts up is a halfhearted concession to a point of view that is ultimately poles apart from his own. We find it impossible to perceive any traces of irony in the stories – any hint of an implicit authorial presence that operates with different values from those that sustain the narrative viewpoint or the characters' behaviour. Perhaps one should borrow two terms from Ian Watt, and suggest that *Der Kuß von Sentze* and *Der fromme Spruch* are not 'works of irony': but that for us, the readers, they function as 'ironic objects'.[16] In other words, the irony derives not so much from the text as from the critic's disbelief that Stifter, who incidentally regarded *Der fromme Spruch* as one of his 'edelsten und lebensvollsten Dichtungen'[17] (noblest writings, full of life), can have meant such petrification to constitute a value.

In our view, this petrification is the extreme product of Stifter's ideology of Reason, his unceasing and ever-increasing determination to build texts which would stand as unshakable houses of meaning. In this context, one must remember the motif of 'bauen', building, which is so central to Stifter's works. It may be pertinent to recall that in the *Mappe* the Obrist calls it an obsession: 'allein das wird wohl mein letzter Bau sein, obwohl man das Bauen, wie andere Leute das Trinken, nicht aufgeben kann' (116) (but this will probably be my last building, although one cannot give up building – just as other people cannot give up drink). He goes on to add 'daß man die Sache sollte zweimal verrichten können' (116) (one ought to be able to do the thing twice). Stifter himself did build most of his texts at least twice, and Adorno makes the perceptive comment: 'Die letzten Novellen Stifters geben vom Übergang der gegenständlichen Treue in die manische Obsession die deutlichste Kunde, und keine Erzählung hat je Teil an der Wahrheit gehabt, die nicht in den Abgrund hinabgeblickt hätte, in welchen die Sprache einstürzt, die sich selbst aufheben möchte in Namen und Bild'[18] (Stifter's last *Novellen* are the clearest evidence of the transition from objective fidelity to manic obsession, and no story partakes of the truth unless it has perceived the abyss into which language plunges when it tries to cancel itself out in becoming pure name and picture).

There are signs in Stifter's oeuvre which suggest that he was aware that the creation of a narrative still-life, as emblem of Reason, is problematic, that the still-life may turn out to be merely dead nature. One may think of his splendidly comic story *Nachkommenschaften*. It starts with the agony of a landscape painter who, for three pages, ponders on the absurdity of creating pictures. He figures out that, given the longevity of his family, he may be doomed to live another seventy years and produce so many pictures that it would take at least fifteen wagons to transport them. And this at a time when the world threatens to drown in a flood of landscape paintings. Here, then, is a Stifter reflecting in the comic mode on the deadening compulsion of art. But such scruples are not only to do with the inherent absurdity of the aesthetic act: they are also linked with Stifter's ambivalence toward his own cherished concern to uphold the values of bourgeois humanism. The didactic strain of so many of his works would suggest that, having shed the exuberance of his youthful subjectivism, he consistently espouses the views expressed in the preface to *Bunte Steine*. This is largely the case, but time and again there are signs of unease. The previously quoted reply to Tepe is very revealing in this respect: it asserts that *Der Kuß von Sentze* ironizes the outdated forms of behaviour of the rural aristocracy, yet it also suggests that these people are to be respected as honourable beings.

This double focus can also be detected in as early a text as *Zuversicht*. Here, a group of upright citizens listens to a story dealing with the horrors of the French Revolution, with patricide and suicide. The didactic aim would seem to be clear: the story shows that all men have in part a 'tigerartige Anlage' (*BSt*, 350) (tigerish disposition), but it is in the power of man to resist that tiger, the excess of passion. However, the closing lines of *Zuversicht* are informed by an unmistakable ironic distance:

Da die Stunde der Trennung gekommen, sagten sie sich schöne Dinge, gingen nach Hause, lagen in ihren Betten und waren froh, daß sie keine schweren Sünden auf dem Gewissen hätten. (354)

(As the time had come for them to separate, they said beautiful things to one another, went home, lay in their beds and were glad that they had no weighty sins on their consciences.)

Here, the style suggests a distancing from bourgeois stability and righteousness which is unmistakably critical. One is reminded of Gottfried Keller, of his 'three upright combmakers', lying in their beds like herrings or matches, of Frau Regel Amrain, that epitome of bourgeois virtue, lying proudly in her enormous coffin. There is, then, a latent tendency in Stifter to write against the grain of the didactic intention.

This ambivalence can create dislocations which we may not be able to redeem by applying Raymond Williams's notion of 'creative disturbance' to which we have already referred.[19] *Bergmilch* is a case in point. Here, too, the aim is to make conflict and its resolution within the life of a family intimate the ideal of peace among nations. But there is one fundamental problem which is not solved even by such a painstaking critic as Himmel:[20] in the first half of the story we learn how the bachelor Schloßherr strives to surround himself with a congenial surrogate family. He employs a warden and eventually a teacher for the warden's children. The three men are so similar that they merge into one, and the boundaries of personal property and individual life are erased. The teacher, we are told, 'sagte nach kurzer Zeit gleichfalls wie die zwei andern Männer: "Mein Hauswesen, meine Kinder"' (*BSt*, 286) (after a short time said, like the two other men, 'my goods and chattels, my children'). This harmonious trio could be regarded as emblematic of total unison, the undivided family of man. But the narrator repeatedly describes the three men as strange, 'wunderlich' and 'sonderbar', and thus distances himself from them. And yet the same narrator relies on structural and stylistic principles which spell exactly this kind of unison. This is particularly the case towards the end of the story. Lulu – even her name is a tautological structure – marries her beloved. He is not individualized, he has no name, but is simply called the stranger and is identified by the white coat which he wore when he first appeared on the scene as a

French soldier. They end up by having two children, who are promptly named after their two uncles, Alfred and Julius, and we last see these four figures wearing white coats which have been made out of the original white coat. Symmetry of costume, symmetry of character, all in celebration, one presumes, of the story's allegorical centre, the vision of a morally rejuvenated future society. Yet earlier in the text, this very symmetry is judged to be quirky – 'wunderlich'. What is the critic to do? We do not think that one can speak here of conscious irony on the part of Stifter; but in the light of this central disjunction one may argue that the text of *Bergmilch* calls its own solidity into question.

It is this phenomenon which we want to examine in the following section, with special reference to two stories from *Bunte Steine*: *Turmalin* and *Katzensilber*.

ii. *The unstable text*

Turmalin first records how the peaceful life of the Rentherr and his family is shattered when his best friend, the actor Dall, seduces his wife. The wife tells her husband, but then disappears, suddenly and without any explanation. The Rentherr desperately tries to find her, but in vain. Finally, he also disappears, together with the baby, and the contents of the flat are auctioned off. In the second half, the woman from whom the narrator has heard the account of the Rentherr's marriage takes over the story. Many years ago, her routine suburban life was interrupted by a series of strange events. There was the haunting sound of a flute one night, there was the intriguing sight of an old man wandering through the streets, accompanied by a young girl with an abnormally large head, and there was the grand, but derelict 'Perronsche Haus' in the neighbourhood. One day, the woman hears that apparently the doorkeeper of the 'Perronsche Haus' has killed himself in his basement flat. She rushes to the scene. It turns out that the doorkeeper is the old man whom she had noticed before, and the girl, passively sitting there with her flute and a jackdaw, is his daughter. Appalled by the desolate scene, the woman takes the girl with her. Gradually it is revealed that the old man was the Rentherr. The woman and her husband do all they can to educate the girl. Gradually, the enlargement of her head recedes; she learns to sew and so is able to earn a living. Thus, in the end she has become a modestly viable member of society.

Most critics regard *Turmalin* with misgivings – the story is felt to be irredeemably fragmented. But recently, Eve Mason has shown[21] how the tale is totally informed by Stifter's moral point of view. There can be no doubt that *Turmalin* is intended to function as a moral tale. The opening paragraph of the story signals this with the utmost clarity:

Es ist darin wie in einem traurigen Briefe zu entnehmen, wie weit der Mensch kömmt, wenn er das Licht seiner Vernunft trübt, die Dinge nicht mehr versteht, von dem inneren Gesetze, das ihn unabwendbar zu dem Rechten führt, läßt, sich unbedingt der Innigkeit seiner Freuden und Schmerzen hingibt, den Halt verliert, und in Zustände gerät, die wir uns kaum zu enträtseln wissen. (*BSt*, 119)

(From it one can conclude, as from a sad letter, how far man can go when he darkens the light of his reason, when he no longer understands things, when he abandons his allegiance to the inner law which leads him unswervingly towards what is right and good, when he surrenders totally to the intensity of his joys and sorrows, when he loses all hold and becomes involved in situations which we can scarcely disentangle.)

In accordance with the tenets of the preface to *Bunte Steine*, passion emerges as a destructive power: sudden sexual attraction, jealousy, the inability to come to terms with the one disruptive incident and to regain equilibrium – this whole chain leads to the catastrophe. What was once a stable family life ends in a state of total dissolution: of the mother there is no trace, and the Rentherr and his daughter lead a radically diminished life, at the very periphery of social and emotional normality. Virtually imprisoned in the basement, the girl is made to write every day an imagined description of the death of her father, of the lonely, hopeless existence of her mother:

Wenn ich dann mit der Aufgabe, wie der Vater tot auf der Bahre liegt, und wie die Mutter in der Welt umher irrt, und in der Verzweiflung ihrem Leben ein Ende macht, fertig war, stieg ich auf die Leiter und schaute durch die Drahtlöcher des Fensters hinaus. Da sah ich die Säume von Frauenkleidern vorbei gehen, sah die Stiefel von Männern, sah schöne Spitzen von Röcken oder die vier Füße eines Hundes. Was an den jenseitigen Häusern vorging, war nicht deutlich. (152f.)

(When I had finished with the task [of describing] how father was lying dead on the bier and how mother was wandering through the world and in despair took her own life, then I would climb up the ladder and look through the holes of the wire mesh at the window. Then I saw the seams of women's dresses, men's boots pass the window, I saw pretty lace on skirts or the four feet of a dog. What was happening in the houses on the other side was not clear.)

Deprived of a balanced life, the girl also suffers physically – a glandular condition is the cause of her enlarged head.

This, then, is the terrifying eclipse of the sun, but one can argue that in typical Stifterian manner the eclipse vindicates the light of reason. The inner law which 'unabwendbar zu dem Rechten führt' is not only mirrored in the moral law which inspires the woman narrator and her husband to help the girl: it is also embodied in the narrative law of the story which so organizes its plot-line as to suggest that familiar circular movement from stability through disaster back into stability. Of course, there may be but small comfort – in the end, the girl only makes a modest living as a seamstress – nevertheless, the horrific negativity is countermanded by restorative efforts. In this sense, the care bestowed upon the girl points to the tenets of the preface, the gentle law and its sustaining ('menschenerhaltend') function.

Yet, as suggested above, critics have balked at this story, and this is not surprising for there is an undeniable disjunction between the clear signal of the first paragraph and the actual narrative performance: neither the narrator nor the woman who recounts the second half of the story invokes the moral criteria of the opening section. Indeed, the act of narration is innocent of moral judgement, and the emphasis falls on the sheer strangeness, the disturbingly dislocated quality of what is before us. This becomes especially clear if we compare *Turmalin* with its original version *Der Pförtner im Herren-hause*. The contrasts are as striking as they are important: for in the early version the authorial narrator is explicit in blaming Dall for thoughtlessly destroying a happy marriage – with terrible consequences for the well-being of husband, wife, and child. In the rewriting process Stifter heightens the strangeness of his subject matter (in the first version there is no mention of the oppressive, petrified quality of the Rentherr's married life), and the narration registers – rather than interprets – that very strangeness.[22] The category of the incomprehensible ('das Unbegreifliche'), which we have so frequently encountered in this study, is again hauntingly present. Thus already in the first version we read: 'Lassen wir die Sache stehen, wie sie steht, wenn wir sie auch nicht begreifen können' (*Urf*, 307) (let us leave the matter as it stands even though we cannot understand it). By contrast, as we have seen, the second version opens with didactic determination; but we would argue that the original 'nicht begreifen können' reverberates within *Turmalin*, indeed even within the first paragraph. One may ascribe a dual meaning to the phrase 'was da erzählt wird, ist sehr dunkel' (*BSt*, 119) (what is here told is very dark). On one level, the statement partakes of the didactic strain by suggesting that it is a sombre tale about the loss of reason; at another level, the phrase intimates that the story is 'dunkel' in the sense of opaque, resistant to interpretation.

Given this dual interpretative possibility, one can argue that *Turmalin* provides us with two narrative strands: one which presents events in such a manner that the skilled Stifter reader will be able to decipher the events and find moral meaning – and the other which moves beyond moral illumination and exposes us to the experience of the inexplicable. And the two strands are quite unnervingly interwoven. To take a few examples: alerted by the forthright tenor of the opening paragraph, the reader will look eagerly for signs which would announce the loss of reason. And as the camera, for some six pages, registers the details of the Rentherr's life, we are given much opportunity. We are told that the Rentherr is 'ein wunderlicher Mensch' (119) (a strange person). The walls of his room are totally covered with pictures of famous people; there are movable ladders which enable him to reach the higher pictures, and the couches and chairs have castors on them so that every inch of this extraordinary portrait gallery can be enjoyed. The collection strikes one as a dead thing, animated only by an almost fetishist concern for *possession*:

In Hinsicht des Ruhmes der Männer war es dem Besitzer einerlei, welcher Lebensbeschäftigung sie angehört hatten, und durch welche ihnen der Ruhm zu Teil geworden war, er hatte sie wo möglich alle. (120)

(In respect of the fame of these men, it was a matter of indifference to the owner which activity they had pursued and thereby risen to fame: as far as possible, he had collected all of them.)

The Rentherr is so much at one with the circumstances that surround his existence that he becomes an object amongst other objects. We could be in the world of Flaubert's *Bouvard et Pécuchet*, of Keller's Züs Bünzlin (in *Die drei gerechten Kammacher*). The rooms of the Rentherr's wife give a similar impression: they are full of beautiful things, *objets d'art*, and, as part of the list, another beautiful object, we have the child:

Unter diesem Zelte stand auf einem Tische ein feiner Korb, in dem Korbe war ein weißes Bettchen, und in dem Bettchen war das Kind der beiden Eheleute, das Mädchen, bei dem sie öfter standen und die winzigen roten Lippen und die rosigen Wangen und die geschlossenen Äuglein betrachteten. (122)

(Below this tent there stood on a table a fine basket, in the basket there was a small white bed, and in the bed was the child of the two married people, the girl next to whom they often stood observing the tiny red lips and the rosy cheeks and the closed eyes.)

The very inertness of the syntax here suggests something life-less, more a museum piece than a palpable human reality.

Taking their cue from the opening paragraph of the story, critics have decoded this lengthy description of the flat into a moral diagnosis. Steffen suggests that the castors on the furniture symbolize the Rentherr's lack of inner stability,[23] Mason regards the rooms as emblems of a stifled and stifling life,[24] and she traces the lack of 'Maß' which then accounts for the catastrophic eruption. Given the opening paragraph, such tracing of cause and effect is perfectly legitimate. And yet this Stifterian reasoning on the part of the critic goes against the very behaviour of the text which does not explicate, but rather contrives to shock in a manner not unreminiscent of Kleist: after some six pages, the epic code of leisurely description is suddenly abandoned and the next paragraph bluntly states: 'Endlich fing Dall ein Liebesverhältnis mit der Frau des Rentherrn an, und setzte es eine Weile fort' (125) (finally Dall began a love affair with the wife of the Rentherr and continued it for a while). The stylistic shock is such that no matter how much explication the critic brings to bear, its brutal force remains unabated. As in *Abdias*, where we have pointed out the disjunction between the opening section and the actual narrative, one is forced to live with that compression of the laconic and catastrophic.

Stifter retains the category of the incomprehensible through-out. After the wife's confession, order seems to re-establish itself: the Rentherr sits 'ruhig und sinnend' (126) (calm and thought-ful), and tells his wife that he understands. But at this very point, the reader is to experience another shock – we read:

Eines Tages verschwand die Frau des Rentherrn. Sie war ausgegangen, wie sie gewöhnlich auszugehen pflegte, und war nicht wieder gekom-men. (126)

(One day the wife of the Rentherr disappeared. She had gone out as she was accustomed to do, and she never returned.)

The slow deliberate style with its repetitions highlights the empty centre, the absence of reason-giving. The same applies on the next page: the Rentherr goes four times to Dall, convinced that the actor knows the whereabouts of his wife, but Dall does not know. Finally we read:

Der Rentherr kam nach einigen Tagen noch einmal, tat dasselbe, und bekam dieselbe Antwort. Dann kam er nicht mehr. Er verabschiedete seine Magd, er nahm das kleine Kindlein aus dem Bette, er nahm es auf den Arm, ging aus seiner Wohnung, sperrte hinter sich zu, und ging fort. (127)

(The Rentherr came again after some days, did the same, and received the same answer. Then he came no more. He dismissed his maid, he took the small child from the bed, he took her in his arm, left his home, locked the door behind him, and went away.)

Again, the ritualistic code with its finely controlled repetitions leads precisely into nowhere. Even in the second half of the story where the didactic impulse prevails, stressing as it does the manifestations of the 'gentle law', the category of the incomprehensible is not relinquished. Some three pages tell us of strenuously repeated attempts to trace the course of events since the collapse of the Rentherr's family – but all such efforts to piece things together are in vain.

These examples will have to suffice: they show that the solid arch of *Turmalin* as a moral tale is quite strikingly shot through with gaps, points of discontinuity. Stifter is clearly determined to write a stable moral tale, and yet he builds in motifs and structures which point to a realm beyond the reach of moral or psychological explication. In part we do get, of course, the promised moral tale, but our reading memory is far more likely to retain the laconic constatation of uninterpretable events.

Once one focuses on this aspect of *Turmalin*, then whole sections of the text begin to take on an unsettling self-reflective function. Indeed, one might even argue that the opening paragraph tells us not only that the story is about characters who lose the light of reason, but that the narration itself will reach points where it will deviate from the stable course of the moral tale, from its 'inneres Gesetz', and will become 'involved in situations which we can scarcely disentangle'. Take the following examples. The woman recalls the girl's flute playing:

was die Aufmerksamkeit so erregte, war, daß es von allem abwich, was man gewöhnlich Musik nennt, und wie man sie lernt. (134)

(What so aroused attention was that it deviated from everything that one normally calls music and learns as music.)

Does this not apply to the narrative act in *Turmalin?* It sets out to be, as it were, 'programme music', yet time and again it deviates from the category of the 'gewöhnlich' which is so central to the preface of *Bunte Steine*, deviates from the Stifterian edifying text which was then, and perhaps still is, music to the public ear. The woman goes on to comment on the compelling charm of the flute playing:

Was am meisten reizte war, daß, wenn er [der Spieler] einen Gang angenommen und das Ohr verleitet hatte, mit zu gehen, immer etwas anderes kam, als was man erwartete, und das Recht hatte, zu erwarten, so daß man stets von vorne anfangen und mitgehen mußte, und endlich in eine Verwirrung geriet, die man beinahe irrsinnig hätte nennen können. (134)

(The most enticing thing was that when the player had established a certain direction and had induced the ear to follow, something different always occurred, different from what one had expected and one had the right to expect, so that one always had to start from the beginning, to try and follow – only to end in a confusion that could almost have been described as mad.)

This surely summarizes our reading experience with *Turmalin*. We follow the promise of a firmly directed tale, but the narrative constantly plays havoc with these expectations: un-explicated turning points challenge our interpretative efforts, and again one is reminded, as in *Abdias*, of the Kleistian games with the expectant reader. Finally the woman comments on the girl's writings: 'Der Ausdruck war klar und bündig, der Satzbau richtig und gut' (155) (the expression was clear and to the point, the syntax correct and good), yet they do not reveal 'Grund, Ursprung und Verlauf des Ausgesprochenen' (155) (the basis, the origin, the precise course of the events described). Again, does this not apply to *Turmalin* as a whole? Stifter does create the didactic arch, does compose sentences which are as firmly controlled as the most typical examples that we have encountered in this study – and yet: he does not tell us why the protected wife suddenly gives in to Dall, why, to quote the Rentherr, 'sie habe an Dall fallen müssen' (126) (she had to succumb to Dall). Why does she leave? Why does the Rentherr leave? Where has he been all these years and what has become of his wife? We shall never know. Of course, the critic will interpret, will take up the invitation of the opening paragraph and explicate the story in moral terms, thus giving it a cohesive meaning. This procedure parallels the efforts of the woman who seeks to tame the girl's language, 'jene wilde und zerrissene ja fast unheimliche Unterweisung' (157) (that wild and disjointed, indeed, almost uncanny disquisition) and transmute it into 'einfache übereinstimmende und verstandene Gedanken' (157) (simple, coherent, and comprehensible thoughts). The implications are obvious: if we, the critics, try to integrate the text of *Turmalin* at all costs, we run the risk of ending up with a neat moral tale that resembles those modest carpets which the girl, normalized and weaned of her weird commerce with the flute and the jackdaw, produces and sells at the end of the story. Thus, in our view, any interpretation of *Turmalin* must acknowledge Stifter's aim to write a gloomy moral tale in order to celebrate the light of reason – but it must also acknowledge the sheer creative energy that goes into the rendering of 'das Unbegreifliche'.

One can, of course, account for the duality of *Turmalin* by suggesting that it reflects once again Stifter's deep-seated uncertainty, that tightrope between Reason and Unreason. But, recalling our comments on *Zuversicht* and *Bergmilch*, we would be more specific here and view this syndrome in terms of literary sociology. *Bunte Steine*, as indeed the whole of

Stifter's work, is written for a bourgeois public, the *Bürgertum*. And *Turmalin* is the only *Bunte Steine* story which deals exclusively with *Bürger*. On the level of moral tale, the text shows and underwrites the bourgeois aim to maintain stability, order – one thinks of the room of the Rentherr's wife, the woman's efforts to reintegrate the abnormal girl, the neat order of her suburban household. But, at all its points of dislocation, the text suggests that this very order is somehow not enough, that underneath the stable surface, the *Bürger* longs for other, unfamiliar realms of experience. One remembers that both the woman and her husband are drawn to the flute playing which does not follow the laws of regularity, and to the girl's writings which are not subordinated to meaning – 'ich würde sie Dichtungen nennen, wenn Gedanken in ihnen gewesen wären' (155) (I would call them poetry if there was any thought in them). Although, of course, this bourgeois couple will do their utmost to bring about normality, there is the definite sense that the very order of their life generates a fascination with the extraordinary.

This thematic strand is epitomized in the figure of the Rentherr. His room is full of objects which allow the *Bürger* to play intermittently the roles of the painter, poet, musician. Furthermore, his collection of portraits show no criterion of selection – his only aim is to be surrounded by images of greater lives. In order to enter that world fully he avails himself of all those couches and ladders of varying heights. If the neat rooms of his wife reflect firmly established order (the kind of order that we have seen in *Der Hochwald*, *Der Nachsommer*, *Die Mappe*), then the Rentherr's room suggests the urge to break out, to change perspectives. The text is quite explicit here. There are the ladders which 'man in jede Gegend rollen und von deren Stufen aus man verschiedene Standpunkte gewinnen konnte' (120) (one could move into any area and from whose rungs one could gain a variety of viewpoints). Not only the ladders, but all the furniture, the very emblem of bourgeois stability, is fitted with castors. It is in this context that the figure of Dall, the actor, makes supreme sense. His brilliant performances allow the spectator to experience other states of being – and even in his private function he refuses to be tied down to the laws of stability. 'Er lebte daher in Zuständen, und verließ sie, wie es ihm beliebte' (124) (he lived therefore in states of being which he left as it suited him). It is precisely this sense of freedom which makes him the darling of society – 'er belebte sie, und gab ihr Empfindungen' (124) (he enlivened them and gave them feelings). His function, then, parallels that of the images on the walls of the Rentherr's room, and the link is linguistically reinforced by the *Leitmotif* of 'Rollen': the 'Rollen' (roles) of the actor, like the 'Rollen' (castors) on the furniture (at one point the word is repeated five times within nine lines) carry the *Bürger* into other, wider realities. In this sense, Dall's seduction of the wife is but the sexual version of a much more fundamental seduction: his art and way of being threaten society by luring it away from the singularity of one state of being ('Zustand') into the plurality of 'Zustände'. We remember Plato's *The Republic* where the art of acting is denounced as deeply subversive: because the actor plays all sorts of roles, he threatens the stability of the state which rests on the postulate: one man, one role. *Turmalin* illuminates the tensions within the *Bürgertum* – its aim to maintain stability, 'Zustand', its urge to break out into 'Zustände'.

In conclusion, we would suggest that, paralleling the tensions within the characters, the text itself follows both impulses. On the didactic level, it obeys the 'inner law' of the moral tale. But at all those points where it deviates from the firm direction signalled by the opening paragraph it takes on other roles, moves into 'Zustände', and thus undermines its own status as a stable bourgeois tale.

A similar impulse is at work in *Katzensilber*. Stifter saw the story as a tale in the Romantic mode, celebrating the mysteries of nature. Louise von Eichendorff was moved by the poetic power of the story and Stifter, deeply gratified, responded:

'Ich hielt das *Katzensilber* für das beste und zarteste Stück'[25]
(I felt *Katzensilber* to be the best and most delicate piece). But
the text confronts one with considerable problems. In our
analysis we have been greatly assisted by Mason's recently
published article on the story.[26]

Katzensilber tells how the very epitome of the bourgeois
family, father, mother, and their three children, regularly join
grandmother in the country and spend several months in a
peaceful secluded valley. It is an idyllic life: the children enjoy
walking up to the Nußberg while grandmother tells them
fairy-tales. On these excursions, they are gradually joined by a
mysterious 'braunes Mädchen' (brown girl). One day, they
are overtaken by a violent hailstorm. But the 'braunes
Mädchen' quickly builds a shelter of branches and later leads
the grandmother and the children back home, over the
dangerously swollen river. The grateful parents attempt to find
out more about the girl, but in vain. Gradually, however, she
grows closer to the family. Years later, the girl plays again
the role of rescuing agent: the house is on fire, and the girl
manages to rescue the boy Sigismund from certain death. The
house is rebuilt and the girl is now fully part of the family.
But at the very height of this harmony, she suddenly departs,
lamenting 'Sture Mure ist tot, und der hohe Felsen ist tot'
(*BSt*, 274) (Sture Mure is dead, and the high rock is dead).
Over the years, the family gradually forgets that painful
separation, but Sigismund, even as an adult, remembers the
girl with nostalgic affection.

Katzensilber combines a realistic tale about a bourgeois
family with a strong fairy-tale element. To take the portrayal
of the family first: as in *Turmalin*, there is a dual perspective.
On the one hand there is a sustained register of assent. The
very opening lines underwrite stylistically a peaceful, stable
world. There is the farm:

ein stattlicher Hof. Er steht auf einem kleinen Hügel, und ist auf
einer Seite von seinen Feldern und seinen Wiesen und auf der andern
von seinem kleinen Walde umgeben. (213)

(an imposing farm. It stands on a little hill, and is surrounded on one side by its fields and meadows and on the other by its small forest.)

Clearly, the repetition of the adjective 'klein' and the possessive pronoun 'sein' underpins the sense of order and idyllic intactness. And the ethos of solidity acquires concrete form in the familiar motif of 'bauen' which recurs throughout the story. Furthermore, the narration painstakingly records the family's yearly arrivals and departures, sixteen times the expeditions to the 'Nußberg' are chronicled. The repetition principle attains metaphorical meaning: the sheer regularity of the narrative suggests the essential regularity of this bourgeois existence. The formal, structural category reflects the socio-moral category of sustained order. Thus, all those walks with the grandmother function as emblematic scenes of togetherness and Stifter highlights the idyllic quality by piling diminutive on diminutive. Throughout such passages, the regularity of the bourgeois way of life is underwritten by an overtly patterned narrative which is the stylistic correlative of the loving, minute strokes of the brush that we associate with nineteenth-century genre painting.

But there is also a diametrically opposed perspective at work. As Mason points out,[27] the repetitive rhythm of this family life takes on a deadening effect. Her remarks support our previous observations that Stifter's reliance on the repetition principle is fraught with risks; it is precariously poised between the 'Einerlei' of mere repetitive factuality and the sublime 'Einerlei' of a divinely underwritten order. As the story progresses, there are increasingly moments of critical distance, passages which suggest that in all this solidity there is a disturbing strand of self-satisfaction, even insensitivity. The grandmother, for example, lies about the crucial help of the 'braunes Mädchen' during the hailstorm, the rejoicing family tends to ignore the girl – gratitude is not freely and spontaneously given. And yet, in the end, the family does respond in the only way that is open to their bourgeois nature: their gratitude towards the girl takes the form of material presents and of teaching her the ways of the social world: proper dress, speech, reading. Overall examination of the story would suggest that Stifter does not resolve the issue of bourgeois orderliness. Just as in *Zuversicht* or *Turmalin* he assents to, yet also questions, the pursuit of the solid life, so, too, in *Katzensilber* he views this way of life as questionable in its materialistic encapsulation, yet also as intrinsically valuable. Thus after the fire we read 'als der Herbst gekommen war, stand das Haus schöner und stattlicher da, als es je gewesen war' (272) (when autumn came the house stood more beautiful and imposing than ever). And when the narration records how the children have grown up, Stifter's style generates solidly framed family pictures:

Emma war eine schöne Jungfrau geworden, die ernsthaft blickte, blaue Augen im stillen Haupte trug, die Fülle der blonden Haare auf den Nacken gehen ließ, und wie ein altdeutsches Bild war. (274)

(Emma had become a lovely young woman, whose blue eyes gazed earnestly from her gentle head and whose blond hair hung abundantly around her neck. She was like an old German picture.)

The passage continues in this vein. It sounds like a parody of nineteenth-century medievalism, but there is no internal support for an ironic reading, and one cannot help recalling Droste's wry comment on *Der beschriebene Tännling:* 'soso! frommdeutschtümlich, etwas à la Motte-Fouqué'[28] (dear me! old German piety, something à la Motte-Fouqué).

The tensions which mark Stifter's portrayal of the bourgeois world have serious ramifications, particularly when one examines the fairy-tale strand. Mason shows how *Katzensilber* persistently invokes the fairy-tale tradition, and there is no need for us to elaborate on this point. Suffice it to say that the text speedily moves in the direction of the fairy-tale by abandoning the real names of the children: we find the stylized trio of 'Blondköpfchen', 'Schwarzköpfchen', 'Braunköpfchen', and of course we are reminded of, for example, Grimm's *Schnee-weißchen und Rosenrot* (Snow White and Rose Red). The fairy-tale impulse culminates in the figure of the 'braunes Mädchen'. She has some realistic roots in so far as it is suggested that she is a gipsy girl. But, in the main, she takes on the function of a benevolent nature spirit. On three occasions she acts as a rescuing force. Her function as providential agent is mythically reinforced in that the hailstorm, the swollen river and the burning house evoke the archetypal patterns of trial by ice, water and fire. In keeping with the fairy-tale tradition, it is typically the children who are closest to the 'braunes Mädchen' and bring about communication between her and the adult world.

All this suggests that Stifter aims to write a modern fairy-tale in which the realms of social man and nature, the world of everyday prose and the mystery of poetry are fused. He takes up the Romantic fairy-tale tradition and reworks traits of all those stories which he heard as a child from his grandmother. Yet, in the act of reading, one becomes more and more aware of underlying frictions. In particular the critical perspective on the bourgeois life does not tally with the poeticizing aim of the story. One feels that this family is so steeped in material reality that it cannot be lifted from its solid, prosperous existence into the poetic realm of the fairy-tale. Stifter is, of course, not the first to encounter this problem. One thinks of E. T. A. Hoffmann, whose influence on Stifter is indisputable. But Hoffmann tackles the problem, the antinomy of social reality and poetic dream, by building into his stories a strand of consciously sustained irony. Thus the text enacts the Romantic dream, but consistently signals that it is a mere dream. As we shall see later, Stifter achieves a similar balance in *Bergkristall*: there, we find on the opening pages the conscious juxtaposition of the poetic dream and the dreary prose of reality.

But in *Katzensilber*, Stifter does not comment on the organization of the text. At first sight it strikes one as an intact, delicately wrought artefact, and Stifter must have viewed it as such when he called it 'das beste und zarteste Stück'. Yet on close examination, the text emerges as a conceptual, and hence stylistic, battlefield: pitted against the poeticizing aim there is a powerful realistic strand; and this applies not only to the portrayal of the family, but to nature itself. On the one hand, the landscape is seen in terms of peacefully poetic pictures. Concrete details and such stylistic elements as diminutives are all arranged so as to create animated idylls. There is the 'Bächlein', the little brook, with its 'grauen flinken Fischlein' (219) (grey, nimble fish), there are the 'Mäuslein' (little mice), and 'Eichhörnchen' (squirrels) skipping through the bushes. This stylistic principle of naive animation culminates of course in the elf-like figure and function of the 'braunes Mädchen'. On the other hand, however, we find a register of stark constatation: here, the style is devoid of animating, poeticizing devices; instead, language relies entirely on the laconic force of elementary linguistic structures, of grammar and syntax. Take the description of the hailstorm: 'Es schlug auf das Laub, es schlug gegen das Holz, es schlug gegen die Erde' (231f.) (it beat against the foliage, it beat against the wood, it beat against the earth).

Such passages highlight the central friction in *Katzensilber*: the text operates with two kinds of 'es', two kinds of 'it'. One is the Romantic personification principle, the 'es' as embodied in the 'braunes Mädchen' – the other is the impersonal pronoun 'es', the indifferent 'it' of the natural laws. And in sharp contrast to the 'braunes Mädchen', the workings of this natural law do not relate to man, but are radically alien. This point is stylistically driven home by a sequence of verbs in the passive which all convey the sense of anonymous destruction:

Das Laub wurde herab geschlagen, die Zweige wurden herab geschlagen, die Äste wurden abgebrochen, der Rasen wurde gefurcht...

Was Widerstand leistete, wurde zermalmt, was fest war, wurde zerschmettert, was Leben hatte, wurde getötet. (232)

(The foliage was beaten down, the branches were beaten down, the boughs were beaten down, the grass was furrowed...

What offered resistance was crushed, what was firm was shattered, what had life was killed.)

Finally, the systematic repetition of the contrastive phrase 'kein mehr – sondern' (no more – instead) underpins this process of total reversal, of comforting, idyllic images being destroyed. For example:

Als sie zu dem Bächlein gekommen waren, war kein Bächlein da, in welchem die grauen Fischlein schwimmen, und um welches die Wasserjungfern flattern, sondern es war ein großes schmutziges Wasser. (234)

(When they came to the little brook, there was no little brook any more in which the grey fishes swim and where the dragonflies play, instead, there was a large expanse of filthy water.)

The import of such passages beleaguers, if not invalidates, the whole conception of the 'braunes Mädchen', the embodiment of caring, protective nature.

And here we reach a critical point: it would appear that the 'braunes Mädchen' as epitome of the fairy-tale register is not only endangered from without, that is, by the force of the realistic strand; far more critically, this figure is threatened from within, from within the fairy-tale mode itself. The tales told by the grandmother all signal that the key elements of the fairy-tale realm are defunct. In her first story, the magical maid disappears when the farmer conveys the message given to him by a mysterious voice in the forest: 'Sag der Sture Mure, die Rauh-Rinde sei tot' (217) (tell Sture Mure that rough bark is dead). If we read 'Rinde' as metonym, we may conclude that the forest is dead. In the third story, the mythical realm yields to a purely material domain. The 'blutiges Licht' (223) (bloody light), hidden in the 'Hart-Höhle' on the High Rock, turns out to be a carbuncle and is then sold in succession to a farmer, doctor, banker, to princes and kings. The original mythical entity ends up quite literally as the crown jewel of worldly establishment. This victory of social reality is also reflected in the second tale where the goblin runs off joyfully in the red jacket which the villagers have given him.

Of course, there are countless fairy-tales with similar motifs, but within the concentration of this *Novelle*, these three stories acquire an urgent sense of negativity. Their import becomes particularly acute if we read them in conjunction with the lament of the 'braunes Mädchen' as she departs for ever: 'Sture Mure ist tot, und der hohe Felsen ist tot'. 'Mure' is an Austrian expression denoting a mountain stream. Thus the three basic natural elements of the fairy-tale are dead: 'Rauh-Rinde', the forest, 'hohe Felsen', the rocks, 'Sture Mure', the water. In this sense, the final departure of the 'braunes Mädchen', the living embodiment of all the fairy-tale motifs in *Katzensilber*, is not simply the traditional return of the fairy back to her realm, but signals the end of that very realm itself. In other words, the fairy-tale mode, which so persistently informs the style of *Katzensilber*, pronounces its own demise.

Strikingly enough, Stifter's text anticipates this demythologizing interpretation. On the walks, the grandmother constantly mythologizes the surrounding landscape. At one point, she speaks of the secret treasures in the brooks, gold and shells containing precious pearls. Roughly a page later, the children fetch up some of the sand, and the text drives home its demythologizing point: the sand is not gold, but mere 'Katzensilber', myca, and:

Muscheln waren wenige zu sehen, und wenn sie eine fanden, so war sie im Innern glatt, und es war keine Perle darin. (226)

(There were few shells to be seen, and when they found one, it was smooth inside and there was no pearl there.)

This demythologizing force has far-reaching consequences. If the fairy-tale is pronounced dead, then *Katzensilber* calls itself radically into question. All those carefully built up layers of idyllic pictures, a world protected by benevolent nature against the threats of destruction, may then emerge as mere petrifications left behind by the dried-up stream of myth. Like those shells found by the children, they may be intact form containing nothing.

We do not think that in the case of *Katzensilber* one can speak of sustained ironization; but we would suggest that the collapse of the text from within points to a latent crisis of the creative imagination. Clearly, Stifter's efforts went into the poetic validation of the *Bürgertum*. *Katzensilber* follows *Berg-kristall* in the *Bunte Steine* collection, and in many ways it is the extension of that story: the Christmas dream becomes heightened into the dream world of the fairy-tale. But the text in its entirety suggests that it is written in the teeth of the knowledge that this particular mode is no longer tenable, given the socio-cultural context in which the story is set and for which it is written. It is highly telling that Stifter feels the urge to build up images of comforting security but then, through the chosen plot, destroys them as he does in so many of his works. And at almost every turn the stylistic battle intimates the problematic enterprise of writing a protective tale about a protected world. Perhaps one may highlight this point by suggesting that there is a striking analogy between one specific plot item and the overall narrative process: we find frequent references to the farm's greenhouses – 'Glashäuser' is virtually a *Leitmotif*. Here, the father grows delicate flowers. The hailstorm smashes the greenhouses and destroys the protected beauty of the flowers:

Da sahen sie, daß alle Fenster der Glashäuser zerstört waren, und daß im Innern an der Stelle, wo die Blumen in Töpfen und Kübeln gestanden waren, weiße Haufen von Schloßen lagen. (237)

(Then they saw that all the windows of the greenhouses were destroyed: inside where the flowers had stood in pots and buckets there lay white heaps of hailstones.)

Katzensilber is in many ways a narrative glasshouse, full of pretty, poetic flowers so dear to the nineteenth-century reader. But as we have seen, at crucial points the text turns in on itself and destroys its own glasshouse character. Like *Turmalin*, the story may be flawed by traditional aesthetic standards; but it is precisely this self-questioning, if not self-destructive, element which distinguishes *Katzensilber* from the unreflective products of nineteenth-century *Heimatliteratur*. The modern Austrian writer Gert Friedrich Jonke parodies that tradition, and one of his novels is appropriately entitled *Glashausbesichtigung* (Inspecting the Greenhouse).

iii. *The doubly woven text*

Analysis of *Turmalin* and *Katzensilber* reveals thematic and stylistic strands which persistently strain against each other, yet one cannot detect that the narrator is in control; as in the case of *Der Hochwald*, the contrasting conceptions and registers do not fully interact, but stand side by side in narrative irresolution, and the tensions threaten to tear the text asunder. In this section we wish to examine two stories in which those same tensions are developed into a sustained dialectic which constitutes the organizing centre of the text. We have chosen *Bergkristall* and *Kalkstein*: in both these works, Stifter as narrator is conscious of the various perspectives he employs, and creates that finely differentiated illumination which, to recall the phrase from the first version of *Abdias*, yields an image of 'doppelt geschlungenes Leben', (doubly woven life).

In typical Stifterian manner, the opening sections of *Bergkristall* introduce the setting. The narrative first focuses on the valley of Gschaid and registers both the landscape and mindscape of this isolated community. The mountain which dominates the valley is rendered in all its geological and topographical details. There follows a description of the neighbouring valley with its village of Millsdorf, which is more accessible and prosperous than Gschaid. Finally we meet the main characters. We hear that the shoemaker of Gschaid has been bold enough to marry a woman from Millsdorf. They have two children, Konrad and Sanna, but for the inhabitants of Gschaid the children and their mother are still aliens. One Christmas Eve, Konrad and Sanna go over the narrow pass to visit their grandparents in Millsdorf. They have done so many times before, but this time they are overtaken by a snowstorm on their way back, and lose their way. They spend the night on the mountain. They would fall asleep and freeze to death if it were not for the thunderous cracking in the ice at midnight and spectacular movements of light in the sky. Entranced, they stay awake, and next morning they are found by rescue parties from both Gschaid and Millsdorf. The happy outcome serves to integrate them fully into the village community.

The outline of the events would suggest that the story with its reassuring circular movement from security into threat and back to security belongs to the category of *Heimatliteratur*: that it is one of those tales which celebrate sturdy peasant life and uphold equally sturdy moral values. The original version *Der heilige Abend* (Christmas Eve, 1845) may indeed be very close to that tradition. Tellingly, it was published at Christmas and was an enormous success. Heckenast intended to publish an illustrated edition immediately, but Stifter felt there was room for improvement. It took him seven years to revise and complete the second version. At first sight, the two versions appear to be very similar, but on closer analysis, seemingly slight changes emerge as more than stylistic tinkering: they deepen the implications of *Der heilige Abend*, and in particular they engage the interpretative issue with far greater urgency. In this context the discursive introduction to *Bergkristall* is of crucial importance. Here, the narrator reflects on the meaning of Christmas Eve. According to German folklore, this is the night when the Christchild comes and leaves presents for the children. It is a time, then, when material facts are suffused with spiritual significance. Stifter sees this as a glorious fiction which only children in their paradisally intact imagination can fully experience. But so strong is the spell of that magic that even in old age, within the barrenness of adult reality, man will be able to recapture some of that glory. The fiction of the Christchild is 'ein heiteres glänzendes feierliches Ding' (a serene, shining, solemn thing) which

durch das ganze Leben fortwirkt, und manchmal noch spät im Alter bei trüben schwermütigen oder rührenden Erinnerungen gleichsam als Rückblick in die einstige Zeit mit den bunten schimmernden Fittichen durch den öden, traurigen und ausgeleerten Nachthimmel fliegt. (*BSt*, 161f.)

(continues to exert its influence throughout a whole life and which, as we in advanced years recall our dark, melancholy, or emotional memories, figures as a backward glance into times gone by, a glance which flashes through the barren, sad, empty night sky on colourful, shimmering wings.)

As in the opening section of *Abdias*, we note the central juxtaposition of two perspectives, of 'heiter' and 'trüb': the one intimates transcendence, the poetry of the 'colourful shimmering wings' – the other acknowledges the wasteland of facticity, the prose of the 'empty night sky'. As we shall see, in his telling of the tale, Stifter draws on both these perspectives: he celebrates the poetic principle, yet gives full weight to the prosaic principle. In this context the conclusion of the discursive introduction acquires particular significance:

Weil dieses Fest so lange nachhält, weil sein Abglanz so hoch in das Alter hinauf reicht, so stehen wir so gerne dabei, wenn Kinder dasselbe begehen, und sich darüber freuen. – – (163)

(Because this festival is so lasting, because its radiance reaches so far into old age, we enjoy taking part when the children celebrate it and rejoice in it.)

The second half of this passage is not there in the first version; the addition of 'so stehen wir so gerne dabei' poignantly summarizes the narrative self-consciousness, the controlled dialectic of poetic and prosaic within *Bergkristall*. Of course, the story is Stifter's bestseller and has been seen by generations of readers as the perfect Christmas story. Yet in its amazing counterpoint, *Bergkristall* is an example of that secret boldness which Thomas Mann discerned in the finest of Stifter's achievements.

For the purposes of analysis it is helpful to separate the two narrative strands. We wish to begin with the poetic perspective, that which celebrates the essence of Christmas, the vision of a divinely underwritten, redeemed humanity. This sense of reconciliation emerges most clearly at those points in the story which tell how dividedness is transformed into harmony and cohesion. Initially, the children and their mother are foreigners within Gschaid. But the crisis brings about a change in attitude

– the villagers go out to rescue Konrad and Sanna, and in the end we read: 'sie wurden von nun an nicht mehr als Auswärtige, sondern als Eingeborene betrachtet...Auch ihre Mutter Sanna war nun eine Eingeborene von Gschaid' (210) (from this time on they were no longer seen as foreigners, but as natives...Sanna, their mother, too, became a native of Gschaid). This strand would corroborate the notion (expressed in the preface to *Bunte Steine*) of the 'gentle law' whose workings sustain the community. If thematically the story shows a reconciliation between outsiders and community, we should note that that reconciliation is prefigured by the narrative voice in the opening description of Gschaid: here we sense a conciliatory humour that affirms the community and its values. The shortcomings are noted: the father sees himself very much as a self-made man, proud of his solid house with its 'Prachtbetten, schöne geglättete Kästen mit Kleidern' (170) (splendid beds, beautiful clothes cupboards of smooth wood). The ethos of the self-made man even informs the villagers' attitude to the mountain – 'als hätten sie ihn selber gemacht' (165) (as though they had made it themselves). But within this perspective, the community, for all its faults, is validated. Particularly the ending of the story upholds the intrinsic value of this community. Here, Stifter organizes his material very carefully. When the children are found, the bell of the village church rings out, announcing the consecration. The members of the rescue party sink to their knees and pray: the 'Wandlungsglöcklein' is linked with the motif of 'Wandlung', transformation, and thus prefigures the changed attitude of the villagers who now welcome both mother and children into their community.

The account of the events on the mountain heightens this theme of harmony and cohesion into a metaphysical dimension. As the crisis occurs on Christmas Eve, the night when according to the Christian calendar Christ was born to love mankind and to conquer death, the reader will clearly entertain the expectation that the forces of death will not prevail – and the story fulfils this expectation. Naive faith is vindicated: at the critical point of midnight when the children are on the brink of death, Stifter builds into his account both explicit and implicit ciphers of salvation. The children, we are told, would fall asleep and freeze to death 'wenn nicht die Natur in ihrer Größe ihnen beigestanden wäre' (200) (if nature in her greatness had not come to their rescue); and the following paragraph which describes the extraordinary movement of light is shot through with images that evoke the biblical promise of salvation. Amid the stars, a light begins to spread in one great shining arch:

Dann standen Garben verschiedenen Lichtes auf der Höhe des Bogens wie Zacken einer Krone, und brannten. Es floß helle durch die benachbarten Himmelsgegenden, es sprühte leise, und ging in sanftem Zucken durch lange Räume. (200)

(Then sheaves of different light stood at the high point of the arch like the points of a crown, and they flamed. The light flowed brightly through neighbouring expanses of sky, it flashed gently and moved with quiet flickerings through vast spaces.)

Clearly, the splendour of this light links in the reader's mind with the brightly lit skies over Bethlehem, with the notion of the divine crown, and the arch may even recall that other emblem of salvation, the rainbow in the Old Testament. Thus, both the term 'beigestanden' and the images suggest that nature is the symbol and agent of divine providentiality. This import is, of course, reinforced when the rescue party offers a prayer of thanks and above all when Sanna says to her mother: 'ich habe heute nachts, als wir auf dem Berge saßen, den Heiligen Christ gesehen' (210) (I saw last night as we sat there on the mountain the Holy Christ). Only on a naive reading can Sanna's words be taken at their face value – but, as the opening of *Bergkristall* suggests, Stifter knows and exploits the powerful appeal of innocent faith: he makes the reader stand vis-à-vis the text as the adult stands vis-à-vis the wonder of a child's Christmas – 'so stehen wir so gerne dabei'.

If *Bergkristall* operated only on this level of the 'heiteres glänzendes feierliches Ding', then it could well be regarded as an artistically refined version of *Heimatliteratur*. The emphasis on reconciliation, embracing the familial, the natural and the religious spheres, is in many ways characteristic of that tradition. It is thus no surprise that the story proved such a success. In 1860 Berthold Auerbach published a tale entitled *Joseph im Schnee* (Joseph in the Snow), which would seem to be heavily indebted to Stifter's story: when a little boy gets lost in the snow on Christmas Eve, this crisis serves to bring his parents together, to unmask human falsity, to make right relationships possible. It is this type of *Heimatliteratur*, with its sentimentality and moral-cum-religious special pleading, which Stifter's modern compatriots, Thomas Bernhard and Gert Friedrich Jonke parody. Bernhard turns the isolated valleys of Austria into negative idylls, and Jonke's *Geometrischer Heimatroman* not only mocks the orderly ethos, but by implication the rigid narrative order of *Heimatliteratur*.

Such critical illuminations are essentially prefigured by *Bergkristall*. Indeed, the very beginning of the story, with the description of the village of Gschaid, complicates the interpretative issue. The village, we are told, constitutes a closely knit world, 'eine eigene Welt' (164), in which everybody knows everybody else, in which there is a whole community of stories which register the life and lineage of each person. This sounds like an unequivocal affirmation of the kind of story which serves the intactness of village life. But no sooner has the idyll been established than it is called into question – the narrator refers to the many stories told about the mountain:

Dieser Berg ist auch der Stolz des Dorfes, als hätten sie ihn selber gemacht, und es ist nicht so ganz entschieden, wenn man auch die Biederkeit und Wahrheitsliebe der Talbewohner hoch anschlägt, ob sie nicht zuweilen zur Ehre und zum Ruhme des Berges lügen. (165)

(This mountain is also the pride of the village, as though they had made it themselves, and one cannot be quite certain – with all respect for the honesty and truthfulness of the inhabitants of the valley – that they do not sometimes tell lies in honour and celebration of the mountain.)

Here unmistakably there is a hint of falsity, of stories told that either domesticate or sensationalize the mountain. What is implied is a critique of *Heimatliteratur* and of the kind of imagination that creates, and is reinforced by, such literature. Under this aspect, the work ethos of the community comes in for narrative criticism. There are strong traces of this in *Der heilige Abend*, but the critical implications are far more consistently sustained in the second version. The father-in-law's criterion for human achievement is material success: 'ein rechter Mensch müsse sein Gewerbe treiben, daß es blühe und vorwärts komme' (174) (a decent man must apply himself to his craft that it may flourish and prosper). The shoemaker even outdoes his father-in-law: he possesses a large book in which he registers all his business transactions, and gradually this book emerges as the emblem of a book-keeping way of life. The property motif gathers momentum – we are told: 'um dem Schwiegervater zu trotzen, kaufte er mit erübrigten Summen nach und nach immer mehr Grundstücke so ein, daß er einen tüchtigen Besitz beisammen hatte' (174) (in order to compete with his father-in-law he used his spare money to buy more and more land so that he had accumulated a goodly property). In the light of such remarks, the statements about the constancy and permanence of the villagers acquire an ominous undertone: 'Sie sind sehr stetig, und es bleibt immer beim alten' (164) (they are utterly constant and everything always stays the same). At the end of the story, the villagers may sink to their knees and celebrate the moment of 'Wandlung', but the closing paragraphs, in their formulation, undercut that notion. We read that the children become 'das Eigentum des Dorfes' (210) (the property of the village), hard-earned property which 'man sich von dem Berge herab geholt hatte' (210) (they had fetched down from the mountain). The first version has merely 'Eingeborene' – 'natives' – and is thus devoid of critical implications.

Furthermore, on this interpretative level, we note that such key concepts as trust, loyalty, obedience are made to ring hollow. Sanna's relationship to her brother is defined as follows:

Sanna hatte viel Glauben zu seinen Kenntnissen, seiner Einsicht und seiner Macht, und gab sich unbedingt unter seine Leitung, gerade so wie die Mutter sich unbedingt unter die Leitung des Vaters gab, dem sie alle Einsicht und Geschicklichkeit zutraute. (176)

(Sanna had great faith in his knowledge, his wisdom and his strength and surrendered unconditionally to his leadership just as the mother unconditionally surrendered to the leadership of the father to whom she ascribed all wisdom and skill.)

Yet precisely that faith in 'Leitung' – in the ability to lead – takes the children to the very brink of disaster, for in the blizzard the boy's authority is without foundation. The textual layering here is quite superb. Page after page is shot through with the word 'Weg' (path) – but that path has, of course, been lost. As in other works which we have discussed, the insistent linguistic presence highlights the absence of substantiation. Take the following typical example: Konrad says

ich kann heute die Bäume nicht sehen, und den Weg nicht erkennen, weil er so weiß ist. Die Unglücksäule werden wir wohl gar nicht sehen, weil so viel Schnee liegen wird...Aber es macht nichts. Wir gehen immer auf dem Wege fort, der Weg geht zwischen den Bäumen, und wenn er zu dem Platze der Unglücksäule kömmt, dann wird er abwärts gehen. (186)

(Today I cannot see the trees or make out the path because it is so white. We will not see the Column because there will be so much snow...But it does not matter. We will follow the path, the path leads between the trees, and when it comes to the site of the Column, it will lead downhill.)

This textual layering, which on the one hand posits authority and on the other hollows it out, also informs the use of dialogue. Sanna accepts Konrad's words in the monotonous refrain of 'Ja, Konrad'. We are reminded of the exchanges between the grandfather and the boy in *Granit*. There, such speech acts of faith are ultimately vindicated, but in *Bergkristall* they emerge as speech acts of bad faith: with each 'Ja, Konrad' the children move closer into disaster. Clearly, Stifter is here by implication critical of authority and of the ethos of obedience. And one must remember the ramifications: mother and daughter have the same name, and Sanna accepts Konrad's authority as unconditionally as her mother submits to the authority of her husband.[29]

As regards the depiction of nature, the perspective of the 'empty night sky', the prosaic principle, is particularly prominent. This is a stylistic register which makes no compromises with common reader expectations of a 'good story'. It is first at work in the opening sections where Stifter uses scientific and quasi-scientific language to describe painstakingly the geological and topographical details of the mountain. Again, one perceives the gulf that separates Stifter from *Heimatliteratur*. The work of Rosegger, Auerbach, Ganghofer – for all its fondness for descriptions of nature – has none of the scrupulous absorption in objective processes that characterizes Stifter's descriptive genius. Thus in *Joseph im Schnee*, for example, nature exists merely as the backdrop and the catalyst: there is no fundamental sense of her existing as a power in her own right.

When *Bergkristall* recounts how the children move inexorably into the snow and ice, we hear a stylistic register which highlights the sheer otherness of nature. For some twenty pages, the narrative refuses to poeticize. There are, of course, the diminutives which aim to stress the innocent helplessness of the children, and there is the occasional simile or metaphor which intimates the children's perception of the surroundings. But, in the main, we find sentences which in themselves enact the 'otherness' of which they speak by pushing the principle of abstraction totally beyond the limits of contemporary literary language. For example:

Jenseits wollten sie wieder hinabklettern. Aber es gab kein Jenseits. (193)

(Beyond, on the other side, they wanted to climb down again. But there was no Beyond.)

As they struggle through the snow we read: 'Endlich gelangten sie wieder zu Gegenständen' (190) (At last they reached objects again). And the snow is described as follows:

alles war, wenn man so sagen darf, in eine einzige weiße Finsternis gehüllt, und weil kein Schatten war, so war kein Urteil über die Größe der Dinge. (189)

(everything was, if one may say so, shrouded in one great white darkness, and because there were no shadows, there could be no judgment as to the size of things.)

The oxymoron 'weiße Finsternis', of which Stifter is so apologetically aware, challenges all the normal categories and distinctions enshrined in human speech. The snow and ice is something elemental beyond the reach of language; this sense reverberates in the comment on the silence which not even the church bells can breach: 'nur zu den Kindern herauf kam kein Laut, hier wurde nichts vernommen; denn hier war nichts zu verkündigen' (199) (but no sound reached the children, here nothing was heard, because here there was no message to proclaim).

Midnight is indeed the critical point, not only in terms of the plot-line (the rescue of the children from certain death), but in terms of the narrative act itself: in the phrase 'wenn nicht die Natur in ihrer Größe ihnen beigestanden wäre' (if nature in her greatness had not helped them) the two perspectives that lie at the heart of *Bergkristall* intersect. If we stress the anthropomorphizing metaphor in the verb 'helped', then the 'greatness' of nature is a moral agency, synonymous with magnanimity. But the metaphor cannot banish that other interpretative possibility encapsulated in the phrase 'hier war nichts zu verkündigen'. Within this perspective, 'greatness' stands in the non-figurative sense of sheer vastness, nature is not the agency of divine intervention: it simply *is*, a material totality, neither hostile nor friendly to man, but radically and essentially other. One may perceive the critical balance of this section in the story by comparing the two versions. In *Der heilige Abend*, we read:

das Eis des Gletschers krachte hinter ihnen in der majestätischen Einöde
der Nacht – – dreimal hörten sie es, als ob es durch die entferntesten
Adern liefe, und tief in die Festen des Berges sprengte – – dann war es
still und immerfort still – – *Urf*, 66)

(The ice of the glacier cracked behind them in the majestic wilderness
of the night – – three times they heard it, as though it ran through the
furthest veins, and forced its way into the fastness of the rock – – then
it was quiet and remained quiet – –.)

The dashes suggest the overwhelming power of the scene and
they leave the question open whether we are to read the thrice
repeated cracking in the ice as a divinely ordained event.
Tellingly, this version only comments: 'wenn ihnen nicht von
Seite der Seele Hilfe gekommen wäre, die sie rettete' (65) (if
they had not received help from the agency of their soul which
saved them). *Bergkristall* closes the gaps of these dashes and
at one level posits the notion of metaphysical causation by
prefacing the description of the cracking in the ice by that
narrative commentary – 'if it had not been for the fact that
nature in her greatness had helped them'. But on another level,
the passage also suggests that ultimately these may be but
natural processes, beyond all moral and religious reason-giving.
Far more urgently than in the first version, the biblical connotations of the images describing the light in the sky are here
countermanded by narrative reflections on other possible interpretations of these phenomena. The narrator conjectures:

Hatte sich nun der Gewitterstoff des Himmels durch den unerhörten
Schneefall so gespannt, daß er in diesen stummen herrlichen Strömen
des Lichtes ausfloß, oder war es eine andere Ursache der unergründli-
chen Natur, nach und nach wurde es schwächer. (*BSt*, 200)

(Whether the static electricity in the sky had been so pent up by the
unprecedented snowfall that it discharged in these silent and glorious
streams of light, or whether it was another cause within the in-
scrutability of nature, gradually it grew weaker.)

As the style of this passage suggests, Stifter would ideally wish
to fuse scientific fact and religious meaning, in keeping with
the preface to *Bunte Steine*, which sees the natural scientist as

the interpreter of God's creation. But such is the impact of the snow and ice description that one may read that previously quoted phrase 'Aber es gab kein Jenseits' as a metaphorical statement on the narrative act itself: within the perspective of the 'colourful shimmering wings' of imagination, there *is* a Beyond. But within the perspective of the narrator's meticulous observation of the natural world, there are only mighty phenomena – and no Beyond. The greatness is not there for the benefit of man: it is not even concerned with him. *Bergkristall* is thus not very far removed from *Abdias*.

The story concludes, of course, on a harmonious, if not idyllic, note. There is the happy ending, and the narrator contrasts the children's perception with the villagers' gossipy and sensational accounts of what happened:

Die Kinder aber werden den Berg nicht vergessen, und werden ihn jetzt noch ernster betrachten, wenn sie in dem Garten sind, wenn wie in der Vergangenheit die Sonne sehr schön scheint, der Lindenbaum duftet, die Bienen summen, und er so schön und so blau wie das sanfte Firmament auf sie hernieder schaut. (210)

(But the children will not forget the mountain, and they will look at it more seriously when they are in the garden, when, as in the past, the sun shines very beautifully, the linden tree gives off its scent, the bees hum, and the mountain looks down on them, as beautiful and blue as the gentle firmament.)

The idyllic aim is overt, but the *willed* naivety of these concluding lines emerges once we realize that the narrator here echoes almost literally the words spoken by Konrad on the mountain when he strives to comfort his sister:

Wir sind auf dem Berge, Sanna, weißt du, den man von unserm Garten aus im Sonnenscheine so weiß sieht...Erinnerst du dich noch, wie wir oft nachmittags in dem Garten saßen, wie es recht schön war, wie die Bienen um uns summten, die Linden dufteten, und die Sonne von dem Himmel schien? (191)

(We are on the mountain, Sanna, you know the one we can see from our garden, standing white in the sunshine...Do you still recall how, often of an afternoon, we would sit in the garden, and it was beautiful, and the bees would hum around us, and the linden trees would give off their scent and the sun would shine down from the sky?)

We have seen how problematic Konrad's voice of reassurance is, and this lends a precariousness to these closing lines. Furthermore, within the willed naivety, there reverberates the emphasis on 'noch ernster'. In the case of Sanna, the category of 'ernst' is that of religious perception and interpretation. And Stifter the narrator partakes of this in so far as his stance enacts that phrase in the opening section – 'so stehen wir so gerne dabei'. But while telling a moving Christmas tale, he has also recounted a story which in many ways is 'noch ernster', a story of nature dwarfing man.[30]

In so far as *Bergkristall* embodies the threat of the 'weiße Finsternis' which cancels out all human notions and accommodating images of nature the story points forward to the horrific vision of that late piece *Aus dem Bayrischen Walde*. For several days Stifter found himself imprisoned in a blizzard. The whole landscape, all the familiar landmarks were buried in snow. The experience of lost orientation, of lost meaning, was totally traumatic. For months Stifter was haunted by this vision of the monstrous whiteness, 'das Bild des weißen Ungeheuers' (*M*, 595). But just as in *Ein Gang durch die Katakomben* the experience of total destruction at the hands of some monstrous power yields to faith, so, too, *Aus dem Bayrischen Walde* ends with Stifter finding his way back to a contained, meaningful world which his bourgeois poetic imagination so cherished (the notion of 'eingebürgert' is crucial):

Jedoch Monate lang, wenn ich an die prachtvolle Waldgegend dachte, hatte ich statt des grün und rötlich und violett und blau und grau schimmernden Bandes, nur das Bild des weißen Ungeheuers vor mir. Endlich entfernte sich auch das, und das lange eingebürgerte edle Bild trat wieder an seine Stelle. (*M*, 594f.)

(Yet for months, whenever I thought of that splendid forest region, instead of seeing the ribbons of green and red and violet and blue and grey shimmering before me, I could only see the image of that white monster. Finally that faded too, and the long-established, noble image took its place.)

In conclusion, we would suggest that *Bergkristall*, in its counterpoint of transcendent energies, the 'colourful shimmering wings', interacting with the 'empty night sky' of facticity, anticipates that other famous snow journey in German literature,[31] that other foray into the 'Chaos von weißer Finsternis': the chapter entitled 'Snow' in Thomas Mann's *Der Zauberberg* (The Magic Mountain) –

Diese Welt in ihrem bodenlosen Schweigen hatte nichts Wirtliches, sie empfing den Besucher auf eigene Rechnung und Gefahr, sie nahm ihn nicht eigentlich an und auf, sie duldete sein Eindringen, seine Gegenwart auf eine nicht geheure, für nichts gutstehende Weise, und Gefühle des still bedrohlichen Elementaren, des nicht einmal Feindseligen, vielmehr des Gleichgültig-Tödlichen waren es, die von ihr ausgingen.[32]

(This world in its limitless silence had nothing hospitable about it, it received the visitor at his own choice and risk, it neither welcomed nor accepted him: it tolerated his intrusion, his presence, in a disturbing way which did not bode well. And it radiated feelings of the elemental, the quietly threatening, feelings not so much of hostility as of deathly indifference.)

Common to both Stifter's and Mann's description of the snow is the sense that man ventures into this realm at his peril: that the world of snow and ice is nature beyond the control – indeed even beyond the comprehension – of man. Hence both scenes acquire an existential implication in respect of the nature of man and of his place within the natural order of things. Both texts emerge with a conclusion that affirms the worth of man – and the dignity of those constructs, metaphors, and values by which he seeks to live. Hans Castorp is allowed to dream his dream of perfect humanity. And in *Bergkristall*, confronted by the elemental world of snow and ice, Sanna sees the Christ himself in the night sky. But both texts also intimate that the world of facts may not underwrite the promise of that vision.

A similar counterpoint is at work in *Kalkstein*. Here, the narrative probes not so much the workings of the 'Naturgesetz', but rather concentrates on that other conceptual pillar

of the preface to *Bunte Steine*: the 'Sittengesetz', the moral
law. As we shall see, the creative Stifter raises complex issues
which the discursive Stifter is prone to set aside.

Kalkstein is a double frame narration. On the opening page,
the narrator recalls how he and some friends once pondered
on the various factors that might determine a man's character
and his way of life. One of the friends then proceeds to recount
how he, in his capacity as land surveyor, made the acquaintance
of a priest in the barren region of the Kar. He had met the
man many years before at a luncheon and had even then been
struck by his withdrawn behaviour. The surveyor subsequently
spends several months in the Kar. During a thunderstorm he
shelters for the night in the priest's house and next day observes
how he guides the local schoolchildren across the dangerously
flooded meadow. Some time later, the priest tells him his life
story, which is marked by his lack of practical abilities and by
the powerful memory of an early erotic experience. Many years
later, the priest dies, and his will reveals that he has saved for
years in order to provide a new school so that in future the
children will no longer have to cross that easily flooded
meadow. His estate is far too modest: but others are so moved
that they contribute, and in the end the school is built.

Clearly, the story celebrates the good life – good understood
in two senses, as morally good and as existentially rooted. The
narrative patiently records the present circumstances of the
priest's life, the region he inhabits, the house where he lives.
And briefly, at the centre of the frame, and extending over a
few pages, the man himself vouchsafes us a glimpse both of
his past and of his inner life. The structural and thematic
similarities with Grillparzer's *Der arme Spielmann* are striking
– although Stifter's story lacks the catastrophic implications
of Grillparzer's tale. Beneath the surface of the orderly life
there is pain and anguish, but, as in so many of Stifter's works,
they largely function as catalysts of spiritual growth. There
can be no doubt that *Kalkstein* in many ways is a simple moral
tale which upholds the modest, but profoundly good, life of the

priest. Over the years, he has emerged from pain and depri-vation to find meaning in his service to the community as epitomized in his ceaseless concern for the welfare of the children. The selfless spirit of the priest's life recalls the key tenets of the preface to *Bunte Steine* which advocates the values of 'Gerechtigkeit Einfachheit Bezwingung seiner selbst Ver-standesgemäßheit Wirksamkeit in seinem Kreise' (9) (justice, simplicity, the overcoming of self, rationality, effective work within one's community). In this sense, then, the priest stands as the very embodiment of the 'gentle law', and Stifter builds into the surveyor's account powerful stratagems of persuasion which ensure that the reader will assent to the figure of the priest. There is, for example, the striking correlation of the landscape and the priest. Initially, the surveyor finds the region 'terrible' – 'eine fürchterliche Gegend' (*BSt*, 58) – because the monotonous sequence of limestone hills does not gratify man's sensuous and imaginative energies: there is no 'Abwechs-lung und Erquickung' (59) (variation or refreshment). But the priest's love for the region gradually prevails, and when the surveyor leaves he is at pains to spell out his revision of that early judgment:

Es ergriff mich nämlich beinahe eine tiefe Wehmut, als ich von der Gegend schied, welche mir, da ich sie zum ersten Male betreten hatte, abscheulich erschienen war. (107)

(In fact, something close to profound melancholy overcame me as I took my leave of this region which had appeared repulsive to me when I first entered it.)

His revision is in the spirit of the priest's own comment on the area: 'die Leute sagen...die Gegend sei häßlich, aber auch das ist nicht wahr, man muß sie nur gehörig anschauen' (103) (people say the region is ugly, but that is not true: you just have to look at it properly).

Kalkstein urges the reader to 'look properly' at both the landscape and the figure of the priest. Both are inconspicuous, and both gradually reveal their intrinsic value. The priest's austere life may initially strike us as 'fürchterlich': like the landscape that surrounds it, it lacks 'Abwechslung und Erquickung'. But the story is so conceived that the reader comes to appreciate the inner beauty of the priest, his moral substance. (One is strongly reminded of the central thematic concern in *Brigitta*.) Let us look at some of these stratagems of persuasion: when the priest guides the children across the dangerously flooded meadow into safety, the visual effects are so arranged as to evoke the figure of Christ. His 'suffer the little children to come unto me' is concretely enacted:

Die nassen Kinder drängten sich um den nassen Pfarrer, sie küßten ihm die Hand, sie redeten mit ihm, er redete mit ihnen, oder sie standen da, und sahen zutraulich zu ihm hinauf. (80)

(The soaking children crowded round the soaking priest, they kissed his hand, they talked with him, he talked with them, or they simply stood there and looked trustingly up at him.)

This grouping – 'der Pfarrer in der Mitte der Kinder' (79) (the priest amidst the children) – becomes a central metaphor in the story. It persuades us to focus on the sheer innocence and goodness of the priest when he later recounts his life and when finally his will is disclosed. Clearly, we are asked to admire the moral achievement of this man who has learnt to overcome and who serves God by serving the community, by cherishing the divine life as embodied in the children. To the very end of *Kalkstein*, Stifter ensures that we shall not lose sight of this didactic aim: the priest's estate is of course far too small to finance the building of a new school, but others respond, and the school is built. Thus the forces of divine Reason are seen to be at work everywhere, as the preface to *Bunte Steine* suggests, and the story ends on a note of almost triumphant didacticism:

Aber wie das Böse stets in sich selber zwecklos ist und im Weltplane keine Wirkung hat, das Gute aber Früchte trägt, wenn es auch mit mangelhaften Mitteln begonnen wird, so war es auch hier. (114)

(But as evil is always inherently purposeless and has no effect within the overall design of the world, whereas good bears fruit, however small the means with which it is begun, so it proved to be the case here.)

In this sense, then, *Kalkstein*, like *Granit*, is a modest, rural restatement of key notions of eighteenth-century Enlightenment thought: the faith in man's perfectibility, the faith in theodicy. Despite all their inadequacies, the landscape, the priest, the villagers, and the surveyor ultimately emerge as servants of Reason's design, of a divinely underwritten world. At one point the priest says of the landscape: 'sie ist, wie sie Gott erschaffen hat' (60) (it is as God created it), and the phrase poignantly echoes those voices on the opening page of the story which hold that 'Gott habe die Menschen erschaffen, wie er sie erschaffen habe' (55) (God has made men as he has made them).

Yet the total effect of *Kalkstein* is not simply to be subsumed under this didactic purpose. Thomas Mann spoke of the story's 'stiller Gewagtheit' (quiet boldness),[33] and, as Stopp and others have shown,[34] the work generates a symbolic import which modifies the resolute didactic intention. From the start, the text is shot through with elements which point not in the moral direction, but in the direction of psychological analysis. In this context a look at the original version, *Der arme Wohltäter*, (The poor Benefactor), is highly revealing. Here, the opening page tells us that the story will function both as a moral tale and as a psychological study. We hear that the surveyor told the story of the priest in such a way 'daß wir begriffen, daß der Mann nicht nur diese Handlung unternehmen konnte, sondern daß er sie unternehmen mußte' (*Urf*, 209) (that we understood that the man not only was able to behave the way he did but also that he had to so behave). The moral category of *Können* is quite explicitly juxtaposed with the psychological category of *Müssen*. In *Kalkstein* this phrase has disappeared, but its essence is not abandoned: the psychological issue is discreetly – but also frequently – hinted at.[35] As narrators, both the surveyor and the priest betray little interest in psychological processes: nevertheless their accounts constantly invite the reader to probe beneath the surface of the moral tale. From the start, the surveyor registers the repressive aspects of the priest's behaviour. He describes their first meeting:

Lächelnd und freundlich saß er da, er hörte aufmerksam alles an,...als ob ihn eine Pflicht dazu antriebe...und obwohl er nicht groß war, so richtete er sich nie vollends auf, als hielte er das für unschicklich. (*BSt*, 57)

(He sat there, smiling and exuding friendliness, he listened attentively to everything,...as though duty demanded it...and although he was not large, he never sat fully upright, as though he felt it to be unseemly.)

The initial strangeness of the man – the shabby black clothes, the embarrassed attempt to hide the fine white linen of his cuffs – intrigues the narrator: 'dieser Eigenheiten willen fiel mir der Mann auf' (57) (the man caught my attention because of these peculiarities). The reader, of course, is equally intrigued: but we have to wait for some thirty pages before the psychological issue is taken up. But even at this point, when the priest embarks on his life story, the psychological issue is forced into second place. The priest prefaces his story as follows:

Bemerken Sie wohl, ich erzähle es nicht, weil es wichtig ist, sondern damit Sie sehen, wie alles so gekommen ist, was jetzt ist, und damit Sie vielleicht geneigter werden, meine Bitte zu erfüllen. (86)

(Mark well that I tell it not because it is important, but in order that you understand how everything has come to be the way it is and that you may perhaps be the more inclined to fulfil my request.)

The original emphasis on 'unternehmen mußte' does not figure, and we are explicitly dissuaded from probing analysis: the story, as the life which it chronicles, is not important, it is only intended to serve a particular goal – that the surveyor will help to ensure that the priest's will is carried out. The surveyor, the immediate recipient of the priest's tale, heeds these words: from this point on he abandons his initial curiosity. But the reader is free to listen to the priest's account and to perceive the factors that explain 'how everything has come to be the way it is', to understand, in the terms of the first version, why the priest had to ('mußte'), arrive at the ethos of his present life.

From the priest's story there emerge two central strands: first, there is his incapacity to meet the demands of practical living, of the material world as represented by his family's business tradition. Second, there is his one and only erotic experience: as a young man he is powerfully attracted to the girl next door. His shy declaration of love is expressed in the peach which he invitingly puts three times by the garden fence. The third time he encourages the girl to take it. She does so, and from then on they meet regularly until one day the girl's mother destroys the relationship: ' "Johanna, schäme dich." Wir schämten uns wirklich und liefen auseinander' (100) ('Johanna, you should be ashamed of yourself.' We were genuinely ashamed and ran from each other). Some time later, he learns that the girl has moved to another town and is about to become engaged. 'Ich meinte damals, daß ich mir die Seele aus dem Körper weinen müsse' (101) (I thought at that time that I would have to weep the soul out of my body). This outline of the past events suggests a tragic love story which, in the overall context of the work, functions as the basis for moral growth. But the symbolic import of the priest's account focuses less on the pain of thwarted love than on the blight inherent in the Christian view of sexuality. The contrast with the first version is significant in this respect: in *Der arme Wohltäter* the account is more particularized. There is not only the peach, but the girl gives the boy plums, nuts, and cake in return. Sexual desire is more overt – after their separation the boy watches 'begierig' (*Urf*, 257) (cravingly) as the girl passes by. Moreover, in the frame more is made of the presence of a pretty young woman in the priest's house, and, as in this version he is a Protestant, the narrator can at one point inquire if he is married. By comparison, the account in *Kalkstein* is stylized: the details are reduced, but at the same time are heightened into symbolic units. The garden, the quasi-seduction by means of the peach, the *Leitmotif* of shame, amount to a reworking of the key elements that make up the story of Adam and Eve.

This emerges most clearly from the correlation of the peach, its 'roten Wange' (*BSt*, 99) (red cheek) with the red flush in the cheeks of both the boy and the girl after their separation: 'mir brannten die Wangen vor Scham' (100) (my cheeks were burning with shame), and 'sie ging mit geröteten Wangen und mit niedergeschlagenen Augen vorüber' (100) (she went past, her cheeks flushed and her eyes downcast). The compounding of innocent sexual longing and the sense of shame reverberates powerfully within the strict self-discipline of the celibate priest who is so tellingly described as 'ängstlich reinlich' (61) (anxiously clean), who cannot part with the linen, yet is so anxious to hide it:

Ich habe nämlich noch immer das schöne Linnen, das ich mir in der Stube in unserem Gartenflügel angeschafft hatte. Es ist ein sehr großer Fehler, aber ich habe versucht, ihn durch noch größeres Sparen an meinem Körper und an anderen Dingen gut zu machen. Ich bin so schwach, ihn mir nicht abgewöhnen zu können. (104)

(I still have the beautiful linen which I had accumulated in the parlour of the garden wing of our house. It is a very grave fault, but I have tried to make up for it by even greater economies in respect of bodily comfort and other matters. But I am too weak to be able to do without it.)

The linen enshrines not only the memory of the girl, but of sexuality *per se*. In his life of willed austerity, the priest strives to exorcise that memory, but he retains the emblem of denied sexuality in the white linen worn next to the body. This sublimated need gives a dark relief to the good life that the story chronicles and celebrates: it gives the lie to the priest's remark: 'an alles gewöhnt sich der Mensch, und die Gewohnheit wird dann sehr leicht, sehr leicht' (72) (man can get used to anything, and the habit then becomes very easy, very easy). We may ask whether the priest as teller of his tale is aware of such implications. The answer is that we cannot know. As we have seen, the *Kalkstein* version suppresses the psychological issue as much as possible, but in no other work has Stifter exploited the ambivalence of silence so superbly. The priest tells his tale as a chain of unexplicated, uninterpreted facts. At no stage does he analyse or make suggestive links. This would indicate total naivety. On the other hand, Stifter makes the priest utter phrases which suggest that this is much more a case of willed naivety. There is, for example, the moment when the priest first describes the girl:

Diese Frau hatte auch ein Töchterlein, ein Kind, nein es war doch kein Kind mehr – ich wußte eigentlich damals nicht, ob es noch ein Kind sei oder nicht. (98)

(This woman had a little daughter, a child: no, she was no longer a child – actually, at that time, I did not know whether she was still a child or not.)

This is by any standards an intriguing example of ambiguity. Towards the end of his account, the priest refers to the fact that he has been able to sacrifice everything but the linen – 'eine Sünde gegen dieses Sparen' (104) (a sin against this abstemiousness), and he adds: 'ich kann es dam Zwecke nicht entziehen' (104) (I cannot divorce it from its function). What, we may ask, is the precise purpose of the linen? The text does not answer this question, for the priest does not define the 'Zweck'. The surveyor is quite unaware of such interpretative difficulties. He who initially is so perceptive in respect of the priest's strange behaviour stops reflecting and is content to measure surfaces only, as he does in his professional capacity. Thus he blithely continues: 'Ich wußte nun, weshalb er sich seiner herrlichen Wäsche schämte' (104) (I now knew why he was ashamed of his splendid linen). After the priest's death he buys the linen, and he and his wife cherish it as a memento of the priest's 'tiefen dauernden und zarten Gefühle' (114) (profound, lasting, tender feeling). In other words, Stifter makes here the most innocent interpretation prevail: both the linen and the priest are remembered as emblems of 'Schönheit und Reinheit' (114) (beauty and purity). And this interpretation is largely that of any conservative critic who would stress the priest's ability to overcome both the handicap of being a slow learner and the loss of the girl; who would read the priest's posthumous achievement as a triumph of the 'gentle law', a moral victory over the painful constraints of his life.

By contrast, a sceptical critic would dissect the moral achievement and, invoking the reductive tenets of materialistic determinism, he would trace this moral capacity back to, and equate it with, the dictates of a socio-psychological need. In such an analysis, the priest would stand as a slow learner who always has been, and still is, determined to make good at all costs. Thus, his school project would emerge as a final attempt to live up to the achievement ethos of his family for whom 'Bauen' (building) had emblematic value; his concern for the children would be viewed as pure surrogate for the denied experience of sex and, by extension, of family life. Finally, his shame-burdened love for fine linen would be seen as the fetishism of a life atrophied in its obedience to contemporary socio-moral values.

Such contrasting interpretative possibilities are in fact anticipated on the opening page of *Kalkstein*. Here, various voices discuss whether the primitive levels in man are ultimately sanctified by the overriding presence of Reason, or whether man may be determined by these primitive levels, in which case all his higher aspirations are subordinated to the promptings of those baser needs. Some maintain that man is determined by circumstances, others invoke the mysterious wisdom of God: 'man könne nicht wissen, wie er die Gaben verteilt habe' (55f.) (one cannot know how he has distributed human gifts). This lengthy debate enacts in essence the juxtaposition in the original version of the moral category *Können* and the psychological category *Müssen*. And in our view, *Kalkstein* sustains these two strands throughout. It does so mainly by using two narrators. The priest does not interpret or, at most, hedges his interpretative bets by making ambiguous statements. But both the facts and the symbolic import of his story convey an overwhelming sense of *Müssen*, deriving both from the social and the sexual circumstances of his life. Even his will in the very opening lines invokes that modal verb: 'ich muß' (111). The surveyor, on the other hand, emphasizes the priest's purity and in his final comment invokes the workings of divine providence. He highlights the moral capacity and thus is the pillar of *Kalkstein* as a moral tale. In this sense we would argue that the story illuminates in equal measure the moral achievement, the *Können*, and the psychological necessity, the *Müssen*. It weighs up the triumph of sublimation against the price of sublimation. It shows us a priest who does embody, however modestly, the moral law – and at the same time it suggests that this achievement is bought at the price of forfeiting vitality.

There is, then, an unforgettable astringency, reminiscent of Grillparzer's *Der arme Spielmann*, to the portrayal of the priest: the story refuses to be either sentimental or grandiloquent. The priest is an isolated figure in spite of the years of patient service to his flock. The final sentence refers to the possibility that people, standing by the grave of the priest, may do so 'mit einem Gefühle, . . . das dem Pfarrer nicht gewidmet worden ist, da er noch lebte' (115) (with an emotion that had not been extended to the priest when he was alive). There is an acknowledgment of the morally good life, but not much more than that – perhaps because that life is lived on such a tight rein that it invites little affection. Time and again, *Kalkstein* conveys the sense of rigidity which informs the priest's behaviour and speech patterns. For example, when the surveyor meets him again in the Kar region, the priest remembers:

'Ja, ich bin derselbe Mann,' antwortete er, 'ich bin vor acht Jahren zu der hundertjährigen Jubelfeier der Kircheneinweihung nach Schauendorf gegangen, weil es sich gebührt hat, ich bin bei dem Mittagessen geblieben, weil mich der Pfarrer eingeladen hat, und bin der erste nach dem Essen fortgegangen, weil ich vier Stunden nach Hause zurück zu legen hatte. Ich bin seither nicht mehr nach Schauendorf gekommen.' (60)

('Yes, I am the same man,' he answered, 'eight years ago I went to the

centenary celebrations of the consecration of the church at Schauendorf
because it was fitting; I stayed to lunch because the priest invited me,
and I was the first to leave after the meal because I had a four-hour
journey to get home. Since then I have not been to Schauendorf again.')

The pedantic cadence of listing, the threshold repetition of the
syntactical structure 'weil' highlights an austere discipline
which has no relationship to vitality or spontaneity. The priest
may be close to nature, indeed the story itself (and traditional
criticism of it) makes this point frequently: but in a fundamental sense he has removed himself from the vital forces of
nature.

In this context, the scene of the thunderstorm is crucially
important. While the elemental forces rage, the priest sits
calmly at his table. He says that it is his 'Gewohnheit' (custom)
to do so. The powerful description of the storm precedes the
priest's life story by some twenty pages, but the link is there:
from earliest childhood on, the priest has pitted the calm
determination of 'Gewohnheit' against the ravages of life. In
other words, just as it is his 'Gewohnheit' to sit out thunderstorms, so too, metaphorically, it is his willed custom to sit out
the storms of feeling and passion, of individuation. And this
battle lasts until the thunderstorm of life is over. The text
drives this point home when it echoes the key motifs of the
priest's life at the hour of his death. We read: 'Er war wie
gewöhnlich, und redete gewöhnliche Worte. Endlich schlief er
sanfte ein es war vorüber' (109) (He was as usual and he spoke
usual words. Finally he went gently to sleep and it was over).
Clearly 'es war vorüber' links with the phrase 'es ist vorüber'
which the priest pronounces at the end of the thunderstorm.

In conclusion, we would suggest that the two strands of
Kalkstein, the moral tale and the psychological study, are
reflected in the colour symbolism of the story. On the one hand
we have the dominating pattern of black and white which
lends itself to the contours of a moral tale that advocates purity
and renunciation. This is further reinforced by the *Leitmotiv*
of 'blau': time and again the priest's clear blue eyes are

mentioned, and thus, gradually, blue emerges as the colour of supreme serenity. On the other hand, we find the colour red in all its shades from pink to fiery crimson. It occurs in the description of the thunderstorm, and it links with the peach, its 'soft, red cheek', with the 'flushed cheeks' of the young lovers and finally with the red ribbon which the priest has tied round the white linen. Red, then, is the colour of *Kalkstein* as a psychological study, the tale of sexuality and passion. And thus, just as the two colour schemes interact, so, too, the two strands of *Kalkstein* are interwoven. In order to match this composite nature of the text, the critic must acknowledge the white of innocence and willed purity, but he must also be alert to the full spectrum of colours that go to make up that white.

7 · CONCLUSION: STIFTER AND THE REALIST TRADITION

L'observation scientifique consiste à décrire *sans interpréter, à ne jamais donner une signification aux choses*.

(Alain Robbe-Grillet, 1959)

(Scientific observation consists in describing *without interpreting, in never giving meaning to things*.)

Puisque c'est avant tout dans [la] présence [du monde] que réside sa réalité, il s'agit donc, maintenant, de bâtir une littérature qui s'en rende compte...Décrire les choses, en effet c'est délibérément se placer à l'extérieur, en face de celles-ci. Il ne s'agit plus de se les approprier ni de rien reporter sur elles.

(Alain Robbe-Grillet, 1963)

(Since it is above all in the presence of the world that its reality resides it is now necessary that we build a literature which will face this fact ...Indeed, to describe things is deliberately to place oneself outside – and opposite them. It is no longer a question of appropriating them, of attributing anything to them.)

We have attempted in our analysis of various examples of Stifter's prose to make a case in stylistic and structural terms for his art. Two remarks by J. P. Stern will serve to clarify our undertaking. Stern has insisted on Stifter's concern to offer a painstaking description of integral being beyond individuation:

Not that these descriptive passages are lacking in tension, even in a strange narrative energy. But the source of that tension is the anxiety lest anything be forgotten, the fear lest even all these things should not be enough to ward off the blow.[1]

Stern comments on these 'things', describing them, rightly, not just as contingent objects but, as it were, as things in a Rilkean sense, units of being, ciphers for a rightness and integrity that is denied to man. He observes: 'and so they ['die Dinge'] become not symbols of human value and dignity, but fetishes of Stifter's own fears'.[2] Here he raises the vital interpretative issues, but with more than a hint of invoking the notion of the pathological Stifter. Not, of course, that he succumbs to that simple, post-Freudian, biographical heresy which equates literary interpretation with the tracing of psychological 'causes'. But even he, supremely sensitive reader that he is, would seem to have no other account to offer than that of pathological provenance. On the other hand, while invoking such factors as fear, anxiety, he does also speak of a 'strange narrative energy'. We hope that our analysis has gone some way towards explicating that narrative energy: and that, in the process, we have provided some kind of answer to T. J. Reed's criticism of *Der Nachsommer* (and, by implication, of the whole of Stifter's work): 'The worthy occupations seem brittle, their motives anxiety rather than harmony. Stifter's unruffled repetitions start to seem a slow-motion hysteria.'[3]

But we are still left with the issue with which we began our study: how are we to place, to locate Stifter's art, or, to put the matter polemically, how is he to be defended against the charge of being a provincial writer? One possibility is to pursue a sociological argument which can, at the very least, have the virtue of rescuing Stifter from being dubbed a literary backwoodsman. Even Glaser's vituperative study suggests that *Der Nachsommer* is the very paradigm of a particular kind of (bourgeois) utopian thinking.[4] Similarly, one should mention the arguments advanced by Otto Brunner and Carl Schorske,[5] both of whom stress the extent to which the somewhat rarefied ambience of Risach's estate has to do with the waning of that particular socio-economic ethos in which the house sheltered both family and employees alike. Moreover, there are other aspects within the sociological reading of Stifter that need to be mentioned: most obviously the fact that he was not entirely unaware of the world outside the Bohemian forests. He did experience Vienna, did acquire some sense of the challenge, of the stresses and strains of urban life. In *Wien und die Wiener*, to which we have referred in our opening chapter, he speaks of the 'adventurousness and multiplicity of the enormous city' ('Abenteuerlichkeit und Mannigfaltigkeit der ungeheuren Stadt' (*M*, 294)), whereby he admits to his own fascination with the pretence, the gloss, the surfaces of modern city life. Not that he is uncritical, of course, but the critique is wonderfully perceptive, as in the extraordinary passage about money:

...das Geld, ein Ding, erst harmlos erdacht zur Bequemlichkeit der Menschen, ein hohler unbedeutender Vertreter der wahren Güter, um sie, die großen, plumpen, unbequemen nicht allerorts mitführen zu dürfen – dann sachte wachsend in mählicher Bedeutung, unsäglichen Nutzen gewährend, Dinge und Völker mischend in steigendem Verkehr, der feinste Nervengeist der Volksverbindungen – endlich ein Dämon, seine Farbe wechselnd, statt Bild der Dinge selbst Ding werdend, ja einzig Ding, das all die anderen verschlang. (290)

(money, a thing, initially a harmless invention for the convenience of men, a hollow, insignificant representative of genuine goods which meant that one did not have to carry them, the large, clumsy, uncomfortable things, with one. Then gradually gaining in cumulative importance, of remarkable usefulness, mediating between things and people in ceaseless commerce, the subtlest nerve of links between peoples – and finally a demon, changing its colours, instead of being an image of things now a thing in its own right, indeed becoming the only true thing, one which devoured all others.)

The denunciation entailed in this passage is hardly surprising, coming from Stifter. But what is surprising is the analytical sharpness and intelligence: the insights are not dissimilar to those advanced by Karl Marx or Georg Simmel about money and market fetishism. All of which helps to cast a new light on Stifter's painstaking litany of things and objects, to reveal it as, by implication at least, the attempt to resist the devaluations and abstractions of modern life.[6]

Now clearly Stifter, in his literary work, has very little to say about urban life, about the great city – beyond voicing a number of unambiguous hints that it is something questionable and threatening, the source of inauthentic living. That Stifter should turn away from the city to the world of the country, of the village community, that he should praise its solidity and integrity is anything but remarkable.[7] It would unite him with a whole conservative strand in German culture, one whose disastrous consequences are well known. But Stifter is not the unproblematic apologist for the virtues of the agrarian world. He is, as we have already argued, no writer of *Heimatliteratur*, of cosy idylls. It has often been suggested that the fondness for the idyll in nineteenth-century German literature is symptomatic of the lack of bourgeois emancipation, of a protective rather than a creative, enterprising ethos. But the intact idyll is precisely what Stifter cannot deliver: his idyll is made under stress, and it shows, in its cracks and fissures, the signs of this stress. We have no wish to deny that Stifter is part of Austrian *Biedermeier* conservatism, part of a profoundly bourgeois ethos. But in another sense, his work can be seen within a larger (European) format: for in its desperate attempt to reconcile individual and totality, centre and frame, it enacts vital conflicts within the ethos of bourgeois individualism. The attempted exorcism only serves to define the conflict more clearly, to provide an insistent intimation of discontinuity and stress.

We do not wish to pursue the sociological argument any further. More important, in our view, is the (related) issue of the extent to which Stifter's work, far from being peripheral to the conditions of nineteenth-century European prose fiction, is central to them. One important issue is the whole question of scientism. It has often been suggested that nineteenth-century realism has profoundly to do with the inroads of science, of scientific inquiry, into man and his emotional and psychological territory. The point has been made that, where the theory of mid-nineteenth-century European realism envisages a fusion of the artistic and the scientific enterprise, its German counterpart is concerned to advocate poetry rather than prose, symbolism rather than documentation.[8] In one sense, of course, one can see how such a generalization would apply to Stifter: but in other respects it proves less than adequate. We know that he planned a novel about Kepler, to be called *Die Sterne* (The Stars). He spoke in a letter of wishing to take the figure of Kepler and 'diesen Mann poetisch behandeln'⁹ (and treat this man poetically). He was unremittingly concerned to describe the circumstantial world as a totality, as a process, one which obeyed the objective laws of its own being, which was not to be dictated to by man, which was anything but an extension of him, a foil or background for his experience. Not for nothing does Stifter in the preface to *Bunte Steine* (and in the *Kirchschlag* letters and in the *Sonnenfinsternis* essay) identify the mature (i.e. reverently objective) human perspective as being that of the 'Forscher' or scientist. And the scientific mind, he insists, is concerned with laws, with generalities – and not with aberration or particularity.¹⁰ Not, of course, that Stifter succeeded in being a 'scientist' in his literary work. Certainly, in terms of his aesthetics, he was wedded to notions of harmony, totality, wholeness derived from German classicism. Hence his titanic attempt to fuse the two undertakings: to combine a circumstantial description of the real world, a detailed listing (almost in a spirit of scientific documentation) with a sacramental sense of the (human) value inhering in that documentable and listable world. Hence his ceaseless attempt to place at the centre of the documentable and listable world a unit of individual (and individuated) human interest. But this constellation brings with it the risk of disjunction between frame and centre, between the totality of matter on the one hand and the holiness of the heart's affections on the other.

In this sense, then, Stifter is anything but the simple celebrator of the retreat into an intact, reassuring natural world. We should never forget that he was a contemporary of Darwin's, that he shares with the latter both a commitment to scientific inquiry and a passionate concern to relate human existence to the totality of organic matter. Dolf Sternberger in a suggestive essay has demonstrated the centrality of Darwin's work for the imaginative life of the nineteenth century.¹¹ And he draws attention to the twofold appeal of the Darwinian law of natural selection: at one level, it claimed causal authority in its demonstration of the patterned functioning of evolving life; at another, it was a human construct, a heuristic tool that allowed man's quest for order and meaning to find an adequate explanation of natural phenomena while locating precisely that exercise of the human intelligence within the greater necessity of biological being. Sternberger writes:

Darum auch steht die Natürliche Zuchtwahl stets im Zwielicht zwischen Eigenmacht und Machtmittel oder – wissenschaftlich gesprochen – zwischen objektivem Gesetz, besser wirkender Kraft einerseits und bloßem heuristischen Prinzip, bloßer Annahme zum Zwecke der bestmöglichen Erklärung andererseits. Halb Naturkraft, halb Werkzeug – genau besehen, beides zugleich –, dienlich und doch auch Bewunderung, wenn nicht gar Verehrung, jedenfalls Unterwerfung fordernd, erfüllt die Natürliche Zuchtwahl auf das genaueste die Funktion, die zuvor getrennten Gestalten der organischen Natur zur bruchlos fortgleitenden Reihe wechselnder Bilder zusammenzuschließen.[12]

(Hence it is that Natural Selection stands somewhere in a twilight zone between a force in its own right and a tool, or – methodologically speaking – between an objective law, energy functioning more efficiently, on the one hand, and on the other, simply a heuristic principle, a mere assumption in the service of the best possible explanation. Half natural force, half an implement – on closer examination, it is both at once – functional, yet also demanding admiration, if not reverence, certainly submission, Natural Selection completely fulfils the function of uniting hitherto separate units of organic nature into a sequence of uninterrupted progression.)

Man, then, is both the product of this law and also its maker. He is both object and subject, both creature and creator. Sternberger reminds us that the great bestseller of the second half of the nineteenth century in Germany was Ludwig Büchner's *Kraft und Stoff* (Energy and Matter), a work which combined materialistic determinism with a strange elation at man's ability to say and perceive his determined status. *Kraft und Stoff* appeared in 1855 (four years before Darwin's *Origin of the Species*). A passage such as the following could, one feels, well have come from Stifter's pen:

Was ist das ganze Leben und Streben des Menschen gegenüber diesem ewigen, widerstandslosen, nur von eiserner Notwendigkeit oder unerbittlicher Gesetzmäßigkeit getragenen Gange der Natur? Das kurze Spiel einer Eintagsfliege, schwebend über dem Meer der Ewigkeit und Unendlichkeit.[13]

(What does all man's living and striving amount to in the face of this eternal, irresistible rhythm of nature, sustained as it is by iron necessity or implacable laws alone? The brief play of a gnat hovering above the sea of eternity and infinity.)

Stifter's scientism, his attempt to assimilate to the undertaking of the artist that of the 'Forscher' emerges, then, not as a parochial effusion, but as something that touches the very nerve centre of nineteenth-century German intellectual life. His life's work is part of a strand in German culture that extends at least as far back as Goethe's *Die Wahlverwandtschaften* (1808), that takes in Georg Büchner's anguished reckoning with materialist thinking, the ruthless historical pathos of Friedrich Hebbel (despite his notorious antagonism to Stifter), that looks forward to Marx and the Naturalist writers at the turn of the century, to Haeckel's *Natürliche Schöpfungsgeschichte* (1868), to the upheaval in ethical thinking enshrined in Paul Rée's *Der Ursprung der moralischen Empfindungen* (1877) and *Die Entstehung des Gewissens* (1885) and in Bölsche's *Das Liebesleben in der Natur* (1898–1902).[14] And we would do well to recall that these issues are by no means confined to Germany alone. In a recent article Gillian Beer has examined (to quote her title) 'plot and the analogy with science in later nineteenth-century novelists'.[15] The novelists in question are George Eliot, Hardy, and Zola. She draws attention to the ways in which plot, in their fictions, is invested with a sombrely deterministic authority in that it is made to enshrine a necessary organization of experience beyond the control and the comprehension of the individual. The upshot of this is 'a painful play of energies between the scrupulous disclosures of law and the passionate needs of human beings'.[16] Gillian Beer shows most persuasively that such a realization that plot must recognize (and convey) the design of the material world has profoundly to do with the impact of science upon the moral and aesthetic imagination. She writes:

Man had always been at the centre of fiction, but in their texts Lyell and Darwin showed that it was possible to have plot without man and regardless of him...This displacing and localizing of man both in terms of time and space was one of the challenges of scientific theory for nineteenth-century novelists.[17]

It is a challenge to which Stifter was particularly alive.

In its key values and concepts, Stifter's oeuvre belongs unmistakably in the mainstream of nineteenth-century European thought. Yet what prevents him from being known and esteemed outside specialist German circles is the fact that his art is intimately involved in – indeed inseparable from – that particularly German kind of bourgeois realism which is so markedly different from the prose literature of, for example, nineteenth-century England. The issues are many and complex, and we can only hope to sketch them in here. But they are essential to an adequate understanding of Stifter's creative achievement, for they highlight both the limitation and the importance of his vision.

At the outset it is helpful to recapitulate the factors that separate the literature and the society of the German-speaking lands from their English counterparts. Several studies have helped to crystallize this difference. Raymond Williams in *The Country and the City*[18] makes the point that England witnesses a remarkably early development of agrarian capitalism, that the process is well under way by the late eighteenth century when the extension of the enclosures finally completes the demise of the medieval form of common land and open strip farming. At one point[19] Williams refers to George Eliot's famous essay on *The Natural History of German Life* (which embodies her enthusiastic response to W. H. Riehl's attempt at a cultural and spiritual geography of Germany).[20] Williams criticizes George Eliot for attempting to transfer the German social model to the (very different) English social experience. Riehl's view of Germany highlights the 'individualized land', the particularism of Germany in the mid-nineteenth century. It is a particularism which produces the 'home town' ethos of which Mack Walker has written.[21] The home towns were pre-industrial urban groupings, dominated by a particular density of civic, economic, and familial relationships. They were based on a guild economy and were fiercely protective of their own autonomy and individuality. Within such a framework individualism was confirmed (rather than contradicted) by social and cultural institutionalization in a way that was scarcely the case in England. And this helps to account for the very different flavour of German realism when compared with its English counterpart. The concern for spiritual community is particularly strong (for 'Gemeinschaft' rather than 'Gesellschaft' to employ the famous terms from Tönnies). Moreover, individual existence is felt to be relatable to – and susceptible of – cultural and conceptual definitions and is not the begetter of individuated psychology in the sense of European realism. All this explains why, when German writers of the 1830s and 1840s attempt to write historical and social novels, they often produce works in which the characters seem to be not so much individuals in their own right as bearers of certain cultural and social values. In, for example, Gutzkow's *Wally die Zweiflerin* (1835), in Immermann's *Die Epigonen* (1823–35) and *Münchhausen* (1838–9) we have not so much a realism of palpable event and vital incident as a realism that explores the historicity of certain values, ideas, and cultural concepts.

All this may sound very rarefied and forbidding. But with later writers of the German nineteenth century the tradition bears fruit in a way that has too long gone unrecognized. In Keller and Raabe over and over again we feel that the characters are metaphors for a particular social ethos, that their ideas and values, their speech and behaviour habits have vitally to do with the notion of community which they carry around with them. If they seem cardboard figures, this is because we the readers bring expectations of individuated realism to bear which are simply out of tune with the kind of realism that was appropriate in a society where the country (understood as 'nation') *was* the regions with their characteristically urban version of 'Gemeinschaft' enshrined in the home town ethos. Not, of course, that we should make the mistake of seeing the literature that emerges from the German speaking lands as devoid of the stresses and strains that we associate with European realism. But the tensions are expressed through a different kind of *mimesis*. What is lacking in external conflict is made up for by spiritual and conceptual conflict. And Stifter manifestly belongs within this literary tradition. No one attempted more passionately than he to establish a seamless union between the individual self, the familial unit, the tightly knit local community, and the total community of the organic world. Yet in his hands the attempted exorcism of individuation became more and more problematic. The implicitly didactic thrust of his splendid descriptive prose collides with his impulse to create characters whose affective needs simply refuse to be assuaged by notions of gradualness and continuity. The structural and stylistic dislocations have to do with the tensions at the heart of bourgeois thought.

It is, in our view, in such terms that Stifter is a key figure within the tradition of nineteenth-century German prose. Moreover we would want to claim that his work (like the tradition to which it belongs) is part of the ambience that produced European realism: and that European realism cannot adequately be understood without a sense of Stifter's amazing undertaking.

The argument about Stifter's relationship to the phenomenon of literary realism has so far proved fairly unedifying. There is, for example, the somewhat turgid exchange between Zenker and Reuter in the periodical *Neuere deutsche Literatur*,[22] the burden of which can be summarized as follows:

(a) realism is the artistic depiction of the totality of social experience at any given time, a depiction which is truthful in so far as it stresses the historical dynamic, the impulse for change which any and every society embodies.

(b) was Stifter a realist by these criteria? Perhaps, in many of his works, he was too much in love with a static world? Alas, it is difficult not to see this argument as a desperate attempt on the part of the critics to legitimate their particular literary predilections in terms of that ideology of realism which alone confers the cachet of respectability. Not, admittedly, that non-Marxian criticism has made much headway in clarifying the relationship of Stifter's art to literary realism. J. P. Stern sees Stifter as part of that particular German tradition which expresses a re-interpretation of the common signs, values, and postulates on which realism is grounded.[23] Marianne Ludwig argues that Stifter is a realist in the precise sense that he has a particular closeness to things (res).[24] Yet one feels that her argument is too simplified. Of course, the world of things, objects, and humble circumstance, is, for Stifter, true, whereby truthfulness is to be understood in the sense of the Bishop's reflections in Grillparzer's *Weh dem, der lügt!* (Woe unto the Liar):

> Wahr ist die ganze kreisende Natur,
> Wahr ist der Wolf, der brüllt, eh er verschlingt.[25]

> (Truth is found in the whole circling nature,
> Truth is found in the wolf who roars before he devours.)

But this notion of truthfulness is not a precept for realism as we commonly understand it. What it implies is that man is not true because he is individuated, whereas objects, plants, animals are true because they have an integrity of being and purpose.

Realism, as Stern has argued,[26] inhabits that middle ground between the realm of the inner life, of psychology on the one hand and on the other the density of public circumstances, of institutional, economic, corporate pressures. Realism takes for granted that man is housed in the circumstantial density of the objective world, and that these circumstances are implicated in his humanity or lack of it, just as his humanity or inhumanity are unthinkable without the admixture of social and public existence. If man is so placed in that middle ground, he is so for good or ill. And the good or ill is the point – and is the centre of the moral concern of realism. But Stifter is interested in whether man is housed or not, whether he is part of the necessary chain of being or not. He is, one might say, exploring the ontological bases of realism – rather than the workings of these ontological conditions in the specific praxis of a given community or family.

Those conditions, conditions of interrelationship between individual and communality, particularity and totality, centre and frame are, in much of Stifter, in a state of disequilibrium, on occasion even of irreconcilability. Hence the extraordinary way in which things and humble circumstances become, in Stifter's hands, either the very emblems of intact being or the palpable facts of clutter, of unregenerate matter. Much depends on their relatability (and relatedness) to the human centre, on the weight and significance which we attribute to that centre. In that wide evaluative oscillation to which things are subject in Stifter we find an indication of the extent to which his oeuvre is a radical and fissured version of the realist's undertaking. In one sense he is the high priest of things; in another he is the painstaking cataloguer of clutter. Realism is both about the way in which man's humanity is abstract and shapeless without a relationship to palpable objects and circumstances and also about the sense in which things, facts can function as obstacles, as resistances, as constrictors of (but therefore also as definers and parameters of) man's selfhood and humanity. In Stifter, that dual sense of the thing as extension of man and obstacle to man is polarized to the point where either things quite simply *are* values or they are irrelevant bits and pieces.

The passages in which Stifter exhorts man to heed the wisdom of things are legion. But we should recall remarks that suggest the other pole. In a letter to Heckenast he says that the daily routine in his administrative job produces a hideous clutter in his mind. The formulation is telling:

Lieber teuerster Freund, wenn Sie nur wüßten, wie mir ist! Durch das Heu den Häckerling die Schuhnägel die Glasscherben das Sohlenleder die Korkstöpsel und Besenstiele, die in meinem Kopfe sind, arbeitet sich oft ein leuchtender Strahl durch, der all das Wust wegdrängen und einen klaren Tempel machen will, in welchem ruhige große Götter stehen.[27]

(Best and dearest friend, if only you knew how I feel. Through the hay, the chaff, the cobbler's nails, the bits of glass, the leather soles, the corks, plugs, and broomhandles that are all inside my brain a clear shaft of light often manages to force its way which promises to get rid of all the rubbish and create a clear temple in which great, calm gods can stand.)

One has the sense very powerfully that the demands of the job mean that he is constantly surrounded by alien things: 'wenn ich dann in meine Amtsstube trete, stehen wieder Körbe voll von jenen Dingen für mich bereitet, die ich mir in das Haupt laden muß' (when I then step into my office there are always baskets waiting for me, full of things which I have to load into my head).[28] And this produces the sombre – indeed, in the context of so much of Stifter's work, heartbreaking – reflection: 'ich glaube, daß sich die Dinge an mir versündigen' (I think that things are sinning against me).[29] One might end with a more light-hearted version of the theme of resistant, hostile things in Stifter. In 1841 he writes a wonderfully funny letter to his wife in which he reports how he is getting on while left (in Amalia's absence) to the tender mercies of Franzi in the kitchen:

Am vergangenen Sonntag schwangen wir uns gar auf Zwetschgenknödl, die Franzi sagte, sie könne dieselben machen, aber als ich einmal zufällig in die Küche kam, so zog sie den Teig so seltsam auf dem Brette hin und her, und knetete mit ihren ungeschickten Fingern in den Zwetschgen herum, daß mir gleich aller Appetit verging, und wirklich, als sie die Knödel auf den Tisch brachte, so sahen sie gar nicht, wie Knödl aus, sondern sie lagen in der Schüssel, wie ausgeschundene Frösche in einer unheimlichen bleichen Flüssigkeit schwimmend.[30]

(Last Sunday we even rose to the level of prune dumplings, which Franzi said she could make. But when I once went by chance into the kitchen, she was tugging the dough this way and that on the board so oddly and was kneading the prunes with her clumsy fingers that I lost all appetite. And truly, when she served the dumplings, they did not look a bit like dumplings: they lay in the dish like flayed frogs, swimming in a mysterious pale fluid.)

We have already had occasion to mention Flaubert's *Bouvard et Pécuchet*, a novel in which objects congeal into banal clutter. It is worth remembering that a number of critics – notably Erich Heller[31] – have suggested that realism always is a volatile phenomenon, embracing on the one hand a profound love for the material world and on the other a loathing for that material world which it seeks to redeem by an aesthetic labour of love, transforming it into form and style. Flaubert wanted to write a novel that would be all style, form – in a word, art, and no content: and the will to aesthetic transformation and validation is unmistakably present in his Austrian contemporary. Stifter's art is the supreme example of that 'justification of the world as an aesthetic phenomenon' of which his great admirer, Nietzsche so often spoke.[32]

All of which brings us back to the point we made in our survey of responses to Stifter's art: that he has been denigrated for being the boring cataloguer of humble objects and circumstances and has been praised for the purity and integrity of his art. The painstaking cataloguer or the utopian maker? In one sense, this reflects modern uncertainties about art; art can be justified as a documentary medium, or it can be praised for its ability to transcend the given, the known. This modern irresolution is the inheritance – and radicalization – of the tension at the heart of literary realism: that between matching and making, between solidity of specification and the formal control of aesthetic statement. Perhaps Stifter is not such a parochial figure after all.

If Stifter's treatment of things enacts a dialectic extending either side of the middle ground of realism, this is not the only sense in which the strange tenor of his work partakes of the whole problematic of nineteenth-century European prose.

There is, for example, the unremitting debate about objectivity and subjectivity in the epic form. The demand for narrative objectivity that recurs throughout the second half of the nineteenth century can, paradoxically, lead to a greater subjectivity of narrative effect. The worship of objectivity hastens the demise of the authoritatively evaluating, judging narrator. And his place is taken by the viewpoints of the characters, by a pluralism of subjective perspectives. (There is also the paradox that the naturalists' dispassionate reportage style can often sound more like a mood picture than a scientific dossier.) Stifter's massive, dispassionate constatation of circumstances, equally, does not feel like reportage: if he (like Rilke) espouses the ontological integrity of things, it also follows (as with Rilke) that things are only redeemed by the human act of saying them, by their being brought into the realm of human discourse and value-ascription. Stifter, like Rilke, oscillates between the virtue of depersonalized saying and the sense that only man can do this reverent saying. Stifter's things are not the same as what Stern has described as the realist's 'emblems of plenty'.[33] They are emblems of value, ontological value, and when they are not underwritten by this metaphysic of validation, then they become inert 'Plunder', so much dead weight. All this prevents Stifter from simply succumbing to the inwardness, the 'Verinnerlichung', of so much nineteenth-century German prose.[34] For Stifter's art is sustained by the desperate attempt to make things and circumstances be the bearer and vessels of (inward) value.

In the foregoing remarks we have endeavoured to demonstrate the stature of Stifter's oeuvre when viewed in the context of nineteenth-century European prose writing. Yet, when we recall that Stifter was contemporary with Dickens and Flaubert, the nagging question of his provincialism returns. We have tried to suggest that, compared with other prose writers of his age, Stifter is not some kind of primitive backwoodsman. But it still could be objected that Stifter is and remains a backwoodsman because his essentially conservative cast of mind (in political, ethical, and aesthetic terms) means that if he ever achieved modernity it was by inadvertence and not by virtue of an articulate – and articulated – intelligence. A recent volume of essays by Karl Heinz Bohrer can help us to focus this problem.[35] Bohrer reminds us that the category of the sudden and the momentary is a cornerstone of modern aesthetics. (Baudelaire, some four years before the appearance of *Witiko* speaks in a famous essay of the cardinal importance of 'the transient, the fleeting, the contingent'.)[36] Bohrer argues that within modern aesthetics we find a 'Verabsolutierung des "Jetzt" zum erscheinenden Augenblick, zur poetologischen Struktur der "Epiphanie"',[37] (absolutizing of the 'now' as phenomenal moment into the poetological structure of the 'epiphany'), a repudiation of general laws in favour of subjective truths, or, to quote Bohrer again, a 'Verschließung der Individualität gegen die übrigen Menschen in einem solipsistischen Akt und als die Absage gegen jede Gesetzlichkeit'[38] (individuality closing itself off from the rest of mankind in a solipsistic act, in the repudiation of any kind of law or system). One must concede that such an aesthetic (with all its attendant ethical implications) would have been anathema to Stifter. And this would seem to make him a resolutely old-fashioned writer, poles apart from modern aesthetic developments. Yet we would do well to remember that such modernist aesthetics rely for their workings on the negative intimation of all that is sequential and processual. 'Suddenness' can only exist as an intrusion upon norms of gradualness and regulated growth. And however determinedly Stifter may have set his face against the ethical and aesthetic acknowledgment of the sudden, yet his art knows of more than those gradual processes which so often engage his descriptive genius.

ABBREVIATIONS OF PERIODICALS

ASNS	*Archiv für das Studium der neueren Sprachen*
DU	*Der Deutschunterricht*
DVjS	*Deutsche Vierteljahrsschrift für Literaturwissenschaft und Geistesgeschichte*
EG	*Etudes Germaniques*
Euph.	*Euphorion*
FMLS	*Forum for Modern Language Studies*
GLL	*German Life and Letters*
GQ	*German Quarterly*
GRM	*Germanisch-Romanische Monatsschrift*
JES	*Journal of European Studies*
LuK	*Literatur und Kritik*
MLQ	*Modern Language Quarterly*
MLR	*Modern Language Review*
Neophil.	*Neophilologus*
OGS	*Oxford German Studies*
VASILO	*Vierteljahrsschrift des Adalbert-Stifter-Instituts des Landes Oberösterreich*
WW	*Wirkendes Wort*
ZfdP	*Zeitschrift für deutsche Philologie*

NOTES

1 BIOGRAPHICAL INTRODUCTION

1 For a discussion of Stifter's class background see Martin Tielke, *Sanftes Gesetz und historische Notwendigkeit*, Bern, 1979, pp. 58f.

2 We are greatly indebted to Jean-Louis Bandet's admirable discussion of Stifter's biography (*Adalbert Stifter: Introduction à la Lecture de ses Nouvelles*, Klincksieck, 1974, pp. 15–43).

3 J. P. Stern, *Re-interpretations*, London, 1964, p. 249.

4 Stifter to Fanni Greipl, 20 August 1835.

5 H. Landesmann to Moritz Hartmann, 18 April 1845, quoted in M. Enzinger, *Adalbert Stifter im Urteil seiner Zeit*, Vienna, 1968, p. 173.

6 Stifter to Amalia Stifter, 3 November 1866.

7 Stifter to Amalia Stifter, 28–30 June 1863.

8 Stifter to Heckenast, 25 May 1848.

9 *SW*, vol. 16, p. 43.

10 ibid., p. 223.

11 ibid., p. 62.

12 Stifter to Heckenast, 17 July 1844.

13 *SW*, vol. 16, p. 184, from the article entitled 'Bildung des Lehrkörpers' which appeared in the *Wiener Bote*.

14 Kurt Vancsa, *Die Schulakten Adalbert Stifters*, Nürnberg, 1955.

15 Stifter to Heckenast, 13 May 1854.

16 Stifter to Heckenast, 6 March 1849.

17 *SW*, vol. 16, p. 7.

18 ibid., p. 8.

19 Stifter to Heckenast, 11 February 1858.

20 Stifter to Louise von Eichendorff, 24 June 1854.

21 Claudio Magris, *Der habsburgische Mythos in der österreichischen Literatur*, Salzburg, 1966.

22 Roy Fuller, 'A normal enough Day: Franz Kafka and the Office' in J. P. Stern (ed.), *The World of Franz Kafka*, London, 1980, pp. 191–201.

23 Stifter to Heckenast, 3 February 1852.

24 Stifter to Heckenast, 16 February 1847.

25 Arthur Schopenhauer, *Die Welt als Wille und Vorstellung* (Zürcher Ausgabe) vol. 4, p. 559.

26 ibid., p. 576.

27 ibid., p. 560.

28 Stifter to Heckenast, 1 June 1865.

2 STIFTER CRITICISM

1 For a discussion of Stifter scholarship see Herbert Seidler, 'Adalbert Stifter Forschung', *ZfdP* 91 (1972) pp. 113–57 and 252–85; Stern, *Re-interpretations*, pp. 358–62; Johann Lachinger, 'Einleitung' in *Stifter-*

Symposion (ed. Johann Lachinger) Linz, 1978, pp. 7–9; Ursula Naumann, *Adalbert Stifter* (Sammlung Metzler) Stuttgart, 1979.

2 Moriz Enzinger, *Adalbert Stifter im Urteil seiner Zeit*, Vienna, 1968.

3 ibid., p. 84.

4 Stifter to Heckenast, 29 September 1854.

5 See Fritz Krökel, 'Nietzsches Verhältnis zu Stifter', *VASILO* 9 (1960) pp. 106–20.

6 E. Bertram, *Nietzsche: Versuch einer Mythologie* (reprinted) Bonn, 1965, pp. 247ff.

7 E. Bertram, *Studien zu Adalbert Stifters Novellentechnik* (reprinted) Dortmund, 1966.

8 E. Bertram, 'Nietzsche die Briefe Adalbert Stifters lesend', *Ariadne* 1 (1925) pp. 7–26.

9 E. Lunding, *Adalbert Stifter*, Copenhagen, 1946.

10 K. G. Fischer, *Adalbert Stifter: Psychologische Beiträge zur Biographie*, Linz, 1961; Michael Kaiser, *Adalbert Stifter: Eine literaturpsychologische Untersuchung seiner Erzählungen*, Bonn, 1971; Fritz Klatt, 'Stifter und das Dämonische', *Dichtung und Volkstum* 40 (1939) pp. 276–95; W. Muschg, *Studien zur tragischen Literaturgeschichte*, Berne/Munich, 1965, pp. 180–205; John Reddick, 'Tiger und Tugend in Stifters *Kalkstein*: Eine Polemik', *ZfdP* 95 (1976) pp. 235–55; Urban Roedl, *Adalbert Stifter: Geschichte seines Lebens* (reprinted) Bern, 1958; Urban Roedl, *Adalbert Stifter* (Rowohlts Monographien) Reinbek bei Hamburg, 1965.

11 Enzinger, *Stifter*, p. 47.

12 J. W. Storck, ' "Unter Witikos Banner"? Bemerkungen zu Adalbert Stifters böhmischem Geschichtsbild' in *Stifter-Symposion* (ed. Lachinger) pp. 70–9.

13 Julius Kühn, *Die Kunst Adalbert Stifters*, Berlin, 1943, p. 282.

14 Arno Schmidt, ' "Der sanfte Unmensch": Einhundert Jahre Nachsommer' in Schmidt, *Dya na Sore*, Karlsruhe, 1958, pp. 194–229.

15 Arno Schmidt, 'Die Handlungsreisenden' *Texte und Zeichen* 2 (1956), pp. 296–9. For a discussion of Schmidt's reactions to Stifter see Josef Huerkamp, 'Steine des Anstoßes: Später Nachtrag zu Arno Schmidts Angriffen auf Adalbert Stifter', *VASILO* 28 (1979) pp. 43–7.

16 See Lachinger, 'Einleitung' in *Stifter-Symposion* (ed Lachinger) p. 9.

17 Walther Rehm, *Nachsommer: Zur Deutung von Stifters Dichtung*, Munich, 1951; Emil Staiger, *Adalbert Stifter als Dichter der Ehrfurcht* (reprinted) Zurich, 1952.

18 H. A. Glaser, *Die Restauration des Schönen; Stifters Nachsommer*, Stuttgart, 1965.

19 Hermann Bahr, 'Adalbert Stifter: Eine Entdeckung' in H. Kindermann (ed.), *Essays von Hermann Bahr*, Vienna, 1962, pp. 88–125 (it should be noted, however, that Bahr not only celebrates Stifter's perfectly chiselled prose but also equates it with the ideology of 'conservative revolution'); Curt Hohoff, *Adalbert Stifter: seine dichterischen Mittel und die Prosa des 19. Jahrhunderts*, Düsseldorf, 1949.

20 See especially Kaiser's study mentioned in note 10 above.

21 Rudolf Wildbolz, *Adalbert Stifter: Langeweile und Faszination*, Stuttgart, 1976, p. 145.

22 Thomas Mann, *Die Entstehung des Doktor Faustus*, in Mann, *Das essayistische Werk* (ed. Hans Bürgin), Fischer Bücherei, Frankfurt am Main and Hamburg, 1968, p. 157.

3 THEME AND STRUCTURE

1 Stifter to Leo Tepe, 26 December 1867.

2 'Nachgelassene Blätter' in *Mappe, Schilderungen, Briefe* (Winkler Ausgabe) p. 601.

3 For two very different views of the 'Vorrede' see F. J. Stopp, 'Die Symbolik in Stifters *Bunten Steinen*', *DVjS* 28 (1954) pp. 165–93; and Eugen Thurnher, 'Stifters "sanftes Gesetz"' in *Unterscheidung und Bewahrung* (Festschr. Kunisch) Berlin, 1961, pp. 381–97.

4 J. G. Herder, *Sämtliche Werke* (ed. Suphan), vol. 14, Berlin, 1909, p. 213.

5 On the stylistic tensions between the particular and the general see Friedbert Aspetsberger, 'Stifters Erzählung *Nachkommenschaften*', *Sprachkunst* 6 (1975) pp. 238–60; and K. K. Polheim, 'Die wirkliche Wirklichkeit: Adalbert Stifters *Nachkommenschaften* und das Problem seiner Kunstanschauung' in *Untersuchungen zur Literatur als Geschichte* (Festschr. Benno von Wiese) Berlin, 1973, pp. 385–418.

6 Herder, *Sämtliche Werke*, vol. 14, p. 234.

7 On the narrative issue see W. Preisendanz, 'Die Erzählfunktion der Naturdarstellung bei Stifter', *WW* 16 (1966) pp. 407–18.

8 Michael Böhler, 'Die Individualität in Stifters Spätwerk: Ein ästhetisches Problem', *DVjS* 43 (1969) p. 665. See also Gerhard Bauer, 'Die "Auflösung des anthropozentrischen Verhaltens" im modernen Roman', *DVjS* 42 (1968) pp. 677–701.

9 We owe this formulation to Joachim Müller, *Adalbert Stifter: Weltbild und Deutung*, Halle (Saale), 1956, p. 67.

10 *Duineser Elegien*, Elegy 2.

11 J. P. Stern, *Idylls and Realities*, London, 1971, pp. 109ff.

12 Herder, *Sämtliche Werke*, vol. 14, p. 245.

13 Stifter to Heckenast, 13 October 1849.

14 *Mappe, Schilderungen, Briefe* (Winkler Ausgabe) p. 915.

15 See for example Hermann Kunisch, *Adalbert Stifter: Mensch und Wirklichkeit*, Berlin, 1950; Werner Hoffmann, *Adalbert Stifters Erzählung 'Zwei Schwestern'*, Marburg, 1966; and Friedrich Sengle, *Biedermeierzeit*, vol. 3 (*Die Dichter*), Stuttgart, 1980, pp. 978ff. The finest discussion of the rewriting of the *Mappe* is to be found in Jean-Louis Bandet's study *Adalbert Stifter*, pp. 333–43.

16 Jens Tismar, *Gestörte Idyllen*, Munich, 1973.

17 Walter Benjamin, 'Das Kunstwerk im Zeitalter seiner technischen Reproduzierbarkeit' in Benjamin, *Lesezeichen*, Leipzig, 1970, pp. 378ff.

18 *Die Mappe meines Urgroßvaters (Studienfassung)*, Winkler Munich, 1950,

p. 388. See Franz Koch, 'Dichtung des Plunders', *ASNS* 186 (1949) pp. 1–27.

19 Heinrich Böll, *Werke (Essayistische Schriften und Reden I, 1952–63)*, Cologne, n.d., p. 311.

20 Stifter to Karl Donberger, 7 December 1850.

21 See Wolfgang Iser, *Der Akt des Lesens*, Munich, 1976. We have in mind here a more profound hiatus than that which serves a pedagogic intention (see Klaus Amann, *Adalbert Stifters 'Nachsommer': Studie zur didaktischen Struktur des Romans*, Vienna, 1977, pp. 60ff.), and we endorse the argument advanced by Hans Piechotta in his study *Aleatorische Ordnung*, Giessen, 1981, pp. 31–44.

22 Quoted in Enzinger, *Adalbert Stifter im Urteil seiner Zeit*, p. 132.

4 THE TRAGEDY OF INDIVIDUATION

1 Raymond Williams, *The English Novel from Dickens to D. H. Lawrence*, St Albans, 1974, pp. 62–77.

2 ibid., p. 70.

3 Roy Pascal, 'Des Landschaftsschilderung in Stifters *Hochwald*' in L. Stiehm (ed.), *Adalbert Stifter: Studien und Interpretationen*, Heidelberg, 1968, pp. 57–68.

4 See Jean-Louis Bandet's telling discussion of the moral irresolution (*Adalbert Stifter*, pp. 148–53). Martin Tielke (*Sanftes Gesetz*, pp. 43ff.) overlooks the irresolution: but he comments very acutely both on the personification of nature and on the fact that human beings are likened to natural phenomena (the girls to flowers, Gregor to a rock etc.).

5 On the deliberate 'picture making' see Tielke, *Sanftes Gesetz*, pp. 33ff.

6 A number of critics have insisted on the spiritual significance of Abdias's life story. See for example Benno von Wiese, 'Adalbert Stifter: *Abdias*' in *Die deutsche Novelle von Goethe bis Kafka*, vol. 2, Düsseldorf, 1962, pp. 127–48; Peter Schäublin, 'Stifters *Abdias* von Herder aus gelesen', *VASILO* 23 (1974) pp. 101–13 and *VASILO* 24 (1975) pp. 87–105; H. R. Klieneberger, 'Stifter's *Abdias* and its Interpreters' *FMLS* 14 (1978) pp. 332–44.

7 Peter Märki criticizes the story for insufficient motivation (*Adalbert Stifter: Narrheit und Erzählstruktur*, Bern, 1979, pp. 47–8).

8 Aphorism 52 of *Betrachtungen über Sünde, Leid, Hoffnung und den wahren Weg* in M. Brod (ed.), *Hochzeitsvorbereitungen auf dem Lande und andere Prosa aus dem Nachlaß* New York and Frankfurt am Main, 1953, p. 44.

9 One is reminded of Franz Kafka, that other writer of letters to the father, and of his famous repudiation 'zum letzten Mal Psychologie!' (*Hochzeitsvorbereitungen*, p. 51). See Erich Heller's discussion of this aphorism (and of *Der Prozeß* as a novel beyond individuation and, hence, character) in Heller, *Kafka* (Fontana Modern Masters) London, 1974, pp. 104f.

10 See Burkhard Bittrich, 'Das Eingangskapitel von Stifters *Hagestolz*',

VASILO 8 (1959) pp. 92–8; and Herbert Seidler, 'Adalbert Stifter' in K. K. Polheim (ed.) *Handbuch der deutschen Erzählung*, Düsseldorf, 1981, pp. 263–5.
11 Stifter to Heckenast, 17 July 1844.

5 RECONCILIATIONS

1 'Stammbuchblatt' in *Mappe, Schilderungen, Briefe* (Winkler Ausgabe) p. 913.
2 Stifter to Heckenast, 11 February 1858.
3 See Krökel, 'Nietzsches Verhältnis zu Stifter', pp. 106–20; and Glaser, *Die Restauration des Schönen*. For a discussion of *Der Nachsommer* as a totally hermetic text, see Thomas Keller, *Die Schrift in Stifters 'Nachsommer'*, Cologne/Vienna, 1982.
4 Amann, *Adalbert Stifters 'Nachsommer'*; Marie-Ursula Lindau, *Stifters 'Nachsommer: Ein Roman der verhaltenen Rührung*, Bern, 1974; Christine Oertel Sjögren, *The Marble Statue as Idea: Collected Essays on Adalbert Stifter's 'Der Nachsommer'*, Chapel Hill, 1972.
5 Sjögren (*Marble Statue*, p. 25) endorses Risach's version, which, in our view, does not do justice to the text.
6 See for example the collection of essays entitled *Problems of the Self*, Cambridge, 1973.
7 Stern (*Re-interpretations*, pp. 289ff.) speaks of the hiatus which separates the *Novelle* of passion from the gradual unfolding of the 'Nachsommer' world. Herbert Kaiser (*Studien zum deutschen Roman nach 1848*, Duisburg, 1977, p. 150) refers to Risach's narration as the vital 'Nahtstelle' where the historicity of an individual life interlocks with the ahistorical generality of the 'Rosenhaus' utopia.
8 Hermann Kunisch, *Adalbert Stifter: Mensch und Wirklichkeit*, Berlin 1950. See also note 15 to Chapter 3.
9 Stifter to Heckenast, 16 February 1847.
10 For a discussion of this narrative process see Jean-Louis Bandet, *Adalbert Stifter*, pp. 142–3; and Friedbert Aspetsberger, 'Die Aufschreibung des Lebens: Zu Stifters *Mappe*', *VASILO* 27 (1978) pp. 11–38.
11 Robert Musil, *Der Mann ohne Eigenschaften*, Hamburg, 1965, p. 39.

6 NARRATIVE AND STYLE

1 See Walther Hahn, 'Zeitgerüst und Zeiterlebnis bei Stifter: *Granit*', *VASILO* 22 (1973) pp. 9–16; Uwe Ketelsen, 'Geschichtliches Bewußtsein als literarische Struktur: Zu Stifters Erzählung aus der Revolutionszeit – *Granit* (1848–1852)', *Euph.* 64 (1970) pp. 306–25.
2 Stern, *Idylls and Realities*, pp. 109ff.
3 Herder, *Sämtliche Werke*, vol. 14, p. 234. The original reads: 'Wie unser Gang ein beständiges Fallen ist zur Rechten und zur Linken und dennoch kommen wir mit jedem Schritt weiter: so ist der Fortschritt der Cultur in Menschengeschlechtern und ganzen Völkern.'

4 Franz Kafka, *Brief an den Vater* (Fischer Bücherei) Frankfurt am Main, 1975, pp. 10–11.
5 Stifter to Heckenast, 23 January 1852.
6 Stifter to Heckenast, 8 June 1861.
7 Reclam, Stuttgart, 1961, p. 605.
8 ibid., p. 50.
9 See H. Blumenthal, 'Stifters *Witiko* und die geschichtliche Welt', *ZfdP* 61 (1936) pp. 393–431; H. Pfotenhauer, 'Die Zerstörung eines Phantasmas: Zu den historischen Romanen von Stifter und Flaubert', *GRM* 27 (1977) pp. 25–47; Ferdinand Seibt, 'Stifters *Witiko* als konservative Utopie', in *Deutsche und Tschechen: Beiträge zu Fragen der Nachbarschaft zweier Nationen*, Munich, 1971, pp. 23–39; Martin Selge, 'Die Utopie im Geschichtsroman: wie man Adalbert Stifters *Witiko* lesen kann', *DU* 27 (1975), Heft 3, pp. 70–85. For a discussion of the essentially unhistorical character of *Witiko* see Hans Piechotta, *Aleatorische Ordnung*, Giessen, 1981, p. 163.
10 See Hans Dietrich Irmscher, *Adalbert Stifter: Wirklichkeitserfahrung und gegenständliche Darstellung*, Munich, 1971, pp. 286ff.
11 Heinz Schlaffer, 'Epos und Roman, Tat und Bewußtsein: Jean Pauls *Titan*' in *Der Bürger als Held*, Frankfurt am Main, 1973, pp. 15–50.
12 From the 'Antwort auf eine Rundfrage' which appeared in *Die Welt im Wort*, 21 December 1933. Reprinted in Mann, *Das essayistische Werk: Miszellen* (ed. Hans Bürgin) (Fischer Bücherei) Frankfurt am Main and Hamburg, 1968, pp. 186f.
13 Eva Arts, *Studien zur Erzählkunst Adalbert Stifters: Der Aufbau der vier späten Erzählungen*, Vienna, 1976, pp. 243ff.; Herbert Seidler 'Adalbert Stifters späte Erzählungen im Rahmen des bürgerlichen Realismus' in *Stifter Symposion* (ed. Lachinger), Linz, 1978, pp. 44–7; R. Wildbolz, *Adalbert Stifter*, p. 134. See also Curt Hohoff, *Adalbert Stifter*, pp. 76f.
14 Leo Tepe to Adalbert Stifter, 17 October 1867, in *SW*, vol. 24, p. 144.
15 Stifter to Leo Tepe, 31 October 1866.
16 Ian Watt, *The Rise of the Novel*, Harmondsworth, 1968, p. 135.
17 Stifter to Leo Tepe, 12 March 1867.
18 T. W. Adorno, 'Über epische Naivetät' in R. Tiedemann (ed.), *Noten zur Literatur*, Frankfurt am Main, 1981, p. 37.
19 See note 1 to Chapter 4.
20 H. Himmel, *Adalbert Stifters Novelle 'Bergmilch': Eine Analyse*, Cologne, 1973.
21 Eve Mason, 'Stifter's *Turmalin*: A Reconsideration' *MLR* 72 (1977) pp. 348–58. See also G. H. Hertling, ' "Wer jetzt kein Haus hat, baut sich keines mehr". Zur Zentralsymbolik in Adalbert Stifters *Turmalin*', *VASILO* 26 (1977) pp. 17–34.
22 Joachim Müller ('Stifters *Turmalin*: Erzählhaltung und Motivstruktur. Ein Vergleich beider Fassungen', *VASILO* 17 (1968) pp. 33–44) suggests that there is a greater optimism to the second version. In our view, the understatement of the personal tragedy does not amount to optimism.

23 Konrad Steffen, *Adalbert Stifter: Deutungen*, Basel and Stuttgart, 1955, p. 149.

24 'Stifter's *Turmalin*', pp. 349–52.

25 Stifter to Louise von Eichendorff, 31 March 1853.

26 Eve Mason, 'Stifter's *Katzensilber* and the Fairy-tale Mode', *MLR* 77 (1982), pp. 114–29.

27 ibid., p. 120.

28 Quoted in Enzinger, *Adalbert Stifter im Urteil seiner Zeit*, p. 79.

29 For a political interpretation of the child in Stifter's work as symbolic of the acquiescent citizen see Tielke, *Sanftes Gesetz*, p. 35.

30 See Larry D. Wells, 'Adalbert Stifter: *Bergkristall*', *VASILO* 19 (1970) pp. 141–7.

31 See R. Struc, 'The Threat of Chaos: Stifter's *Bergkristall* and Thomas Mann's "Schnee"', *MLQ* 24 (1963) pp. 323–32.

32 Thomas Mann, *Der Zauberberg* (Fischer Bücherei) Frankfurt am Main and Hamburg, 1975, p. 501.

33 Thomas Mann, *Die Enstehung des Doktor Faustus*, in Mann, *Das essayistische Werk* (ed. Hans Bürgin) (Fischer Bücherei) Frankfurt am Main and Hamburg, 1968, p. 157.

34 For a discussion of the symbolic value of the landscape in *Kalkstein* see F. J. Stopp, 'Symbolism in Stifter's *Kalkstein*', *GLL* 7 (1953–4) pp. 116–25. The discussions of Stifter's predilection for symbolic writing are legion. See especially Stopp, 'Die Symbolik in Stifters *Bunten Steinen*'; Herbert Seidler, *Studien zu Grillparzer und Stifter*, Vienna, Cologne, Graz, 1970; Sjögren, *Marble Statue*.

35 In our discussion of these hints we are especially indebted to Reddick, 'Tiger und Tugend in Stifters *Kalkstein*: Eine Polemik'.

7 CONCLUSION

1 Stern, *Re-interpretations*, p. 295.

2 ibid., p. 297.

3 T. J. Reed, 'The "Goethezeit" and its Aftermath' in Malcolm Pasley (ed.), *Germany: A Companion to German Studies*, London, 1972, pp. 534f.

4 Glaser, *Zur Restauration des Schönen*. See also Tielke, *Sanftes Gesetz*.

5 Otto Brunner, 'Das "ganze Haus" und die alteuropäische "Ökonomik"' in *Neue Wege der Verfassungs– und Sozialgeschichte*, Göttingen, 1968, pp. 103–27; Carl Schorske, 'The Transformation of the Garden' in *Fin-de-Siècle Vienna: Politics and Culture*, London, 1980, pp. 279–321.

6 See Gundel Mattenklott, *Sprache der Sentimentalität*, Frankfurt am Main, 1973. As with the studies mentioned in note 4 above, this is a fierce onslaught on Stifter which, however much it condemns his solutions, does at least suggest that he is confronting problems of European dimensions.

7 See W. H. Riehl's discussion of the ritualized and non-individuated forms of peasant life in *Land und Leute*, Stuttgart, 1861. See also

George Eliot's enthusiastic discussion of Riehl in 'The Natural History of German Life', *Westminster Review* 66 (July, 1856), pp. 51–79.

8 See for example *Realismus und Gründerzeit: Manifeste und Dokumentation zur deutschen Literatur 1848–1880* (ed. Max Bucher et al.) Stuttgart, 1976, pp. 46–7; and Hans Dietrich Irmscher, *Adalbert Stifter: Wirklichkeitserfahrung und gegenständliche Darstellung*, Munich, 1971, p. 341.

9 Stifter to Heckenast, 29 July 1858.

10 For a discussion of Stifter's 'scientism' see Martin Selge, *Adalbert Stifter: Poesie aus dem Geist der Naturwissenschaft*, Stuttgart, 1976.

11 Dolf Sternberger, *Panorama oder Ansichten vom 19. Jahrhundert* (reprinted) Frankfurt am Main, 1974.

12 ibid., pp. 95f.

13 Quoted by Sternberger, p. 112.

14 See Roy Pascal's admirable discussion of late nineteenth-century scientism in *From Naturalism to Expressionism*, London, 1973, pp. 42ff.

15 *Comparative Criticism* 2 (1980), pp. 131–49.

16 ibid., p. 136.

17 ibid., p. 135.

18 St Albans, 1975.

19 ibid., p. 300.

20 See note 7 above.

21 Mack Walker, *German Home Towns*, Ithaca and London, 1971.

22 Edith Zenker, 'War Stifter Realist?', *NDL* 4 (1956) Heft 10 (October), pp. 97–109; and H. H. Reuter, 'Stifter war Realist', *NDL* 5 (1957) Heft 9 (September), pp. 120–9. See Zenker's reply pp. 129–36.

23 Stern, *Re-interpretations*.

24 Marianne Ludwig, *Stifter als Realist*, Basel, 1948.

25 *Weh dem der lügt*, Act I.

26 See his discussion of the 'middle distance' in Stern, *On Realism*, London, 1973, pp. 122ff.

27 Stifter to Heckenast, 13 May 1854.

28 ibid.

29 ibid.

30 Stifter to Amalia Stifter, 25–28 August 1841.

31 Erich Heller, 'Die realistische Täuschung' in Heller, *Die Reise der Kunst ins Innere*, Frankfurt am Main, 1966, pp. 105–19.

32 Nietzsche, *Die Geburt der Tragödie*, paras 5 and 24.

33 Stern, *On Realism*, p. 5.

34 See Wilhelm Dehn's indispensable study *Ding und Vernunft: Zur Interpretation von Stifters Dichtung*, Bonn, 1969, especially pp. 119ff.

35 Karl Heinz Bohrer, *Plötzlichkeit: Zum Augenblick des ästhetischen Scheins*, Frankfurt am Main, 1981.

36 Charles Baudelaire, 'The Painter of Modern Life', in Baudelaire, *Selected Writings on Art and Artists* (ed. and trans. P. E. Charvet), Cambridge, 1981, p. 403.

37 Bohrer, *Plötzlichkeit*, p. 63.

38 ibid.

SELECT BIBLIOGRAPHY

The bibliography makes no claim to exhaustiveness. For a fuller compilation see Eduard Eisenmeier, *Adalbert-Stifter-Bibliographie*, Linz, 1964ff. We list here studies that relate specifically to our argument.

Amann, Klaus, *Adalbert Stifters 'Nachsommer': Studie zur didaktischen Struktur des Romans*, Vienna, 1977

Arts, Eva, *Studien zur Erzählkunst Adalbert Stifters: Der Aufbau der vier späten Erzählungen*, Vienna, 1976

Aspetsberger, Friedbert, 'Stifters Erzählung *Nachkommenschaften*', *Sprachkunst* 6 (1975) pp. 238–60

'Die Aufschreibung des Lebens: Zu Stifters *Mappe*', *VASILO* 27 (1978) pp. 11–38

Aust, Hugo, *Literatur des Realismus*, Stuttgart, 1977

Bahr, Hermann, 'Adalbert Stifter: Eine Entdeckung' in H. Kindermann (ed.), *Essays von Hermann Bahr*, Vienna, 1962, pp. 88–125

Bandet, Jean-Louis, 'La Structure reconstituée: Remarques sur la Composition du *Nachsommer*', *EG* 26 (1971) pp. 46–54

Adalbert Stifter: Introduction à la Lecture de ses Nouvelles, Klincksieck, 1974

Bertram, Ernst, *Studien zu Adalbert Stifters Novellentechnik*, 1907 (reprinted) Dortmund, 1966

Bittrich, Burkhard, 'Das Eingangskapitel von Stifters *Hagestolz*', *VASILO* 8 (1959) pp. 92–8

'Das Liebesgespräch in Stifters *Prokopus*', *VASILO* 16 (1967) pp. 78–83

Blackall, Eric, *Adalbert Stifter: A Critical Study*, Cambridge, 1948

Bleckwenn, Helga, 'Künstlertum als soziale Rolle: Stifters Berufswahl', *VASILO* 28 (1979) pp. 35–42

Blumenthal, Herbert, 'Stifters *Witiko* und die geschichtliche Welt', *ZfdP* 61 (1936) pp. 393–431

'Adalbert Stifter und die deutsche Revolution von 1848', *Dichtung und Volkstum (Euph)* 41 (1941) pp. 211–37

Böhler, Michael, 'Die Individualität in Stifters Spätwerk: Ein ästhetisches Problem', *DVjS* 43 (1969) pp. 652–84

Borchmeyer, D., 'Ideologie der Familie und ästhetische Gesellschaftskritik in Stifters *Nachsommer*', *ZfdP* 99 (1980) pp. 226–54

'Stifters *Nachsommer* – eine restaurative Utopie?', *Poetica* 12 (1980) pp. 59–82

Buch, Hans Christoph, *Ut pictura poesis: Die Beschreibungsliteratur von Lessing bis Lukács*, Munich, 1972

Dehn, Wilhelm, *Ding und Vernunft: Zur Interpretation von Stifters Dichtung*, Bonn, 1969

Dittmann, Ulrich (ed.), *Adalbert Stifter: Brigitta. Erläuterungen und Dokumente*, Stuttgart, 1970

Adalbert Stifter: Abdias. Erläuterungen und Dokumente, Stuttgart, 1971

Domandl, S., *Adalbert Stifters Lesebuch: Die geistigen Strömungen zur Jahrhundertmitte*, Linz, 1977

Ehrentreich, A., 'Zur Gestalt der Novelle bei Adalbert Stifter', *GRM* 23 (1935) pp. 192–204

Enzinger, Moriz, *Adalbert Stifters Studienjahre (1818–1830)*, Innsbruck, 1950

Gesammelte Aufsätze zu Adalbert Stifter, Vienna, 1967

Adalbert Stifter im Urteil seiner Zeit, Vienna, 1968

Fischer, K. G., *Adalbert Stifter: Psychologische Beiträge zur Biographie*, Linz, 1961

Adalbert Stifters Leben und Werk in Briefen und Dokumenten, Frankfurt am Main, 1962

Frey, Eleonore, 'Dinge und Beziehungen: Zu Stifters *Brigitta*', *Orbis Litterarum* 24 (1969) pp. 52–71

Gelley, Alexander, 'Stifter's *Der Hagestolz*: an Interpretation', *Monatshefte* 53 (1961) pp. 59–72

George, E. F., 'The Place of *Abdias* in Stifter's Thought and Work', *FMLS* 3 (1967) pp. 148–56

Gillespie, G., 'Space and Time seen through Stifter's Telescope', *GQ* 37 (1964) pp. 120–30

Glaser, H. A., *Die Restauration des Schönen: Stifters Nachsommer*, Stuttgart, 1965

Godden, C., 'Two Quests for Surety: A comparative Interpretation of Stifter's *Abdias* and Kafka's *Der Bau*', *JES* 5 (1975) pp. 341–61

Greiner, Ulrich, *Der Tod des Nachsommers*, Munich, 1979

Gump, Margaret, *Adalbert Stifter*, New York, 1974

Hahn, Walther, 'Zeitgerüst und Zeiterlebnis bei Stifter: *Granit*', *VASILO* 22 (1973) pp. 9–16

Hein, A. R., *Adalbert Stifter: Sein Leben und seine Werke*, Prague, 1904

Hermand, Jost, *Die literarische Formenwelt des Biedermeier*, Giessen, 1958

Hertling, G. H., ' "Wer jetzt kein Haus hat, baut sich keines mehr". Zur Zentralsymbolik in Adalbert Stifters *Turmalin*', *VASILO* 26 (1977) pp. 17–34

Heselhaus, Clemens, 'Wiederherstellung. Restauratio-Restitutio-Regeneratio', *DVjS* 25 (1951) pp. 54–81

Hoffmann, Werner, *Adalbert Stifters Erzählung 'Zwei Schwestern'*, Marburg, 1966

'Zur Interpretation und Wertung der ersten Fassung von Stifters Novelle *Das alte Siegel*', *VASILO* 15 (1966) pp. 80–96

Hohoff, Curt, *Adalbert Stifter: Seine dichterischen Mittel und die Prosa des 19. Jahrhunderts*, Düsseldorf, 1949

Höllerer, Walter, *Zwischen Klassik und Moderne*, Stuttgart, 1958.

Huerkamp, Josef, 'Steine des Anstoßes: Später Nachtrag zu Arno Schmidts Angriffen auf Adalbert Stifter', *VASILO* 28 (1979) pp. 43–7

Hunter, Rosemarie, 'Wald, Haus und Wasser, Moos und Schmetterling:

Zu den Zentralsymbolen in Stifters Erzählung *Der Waldgänger'*, *VASILO* 24 (1975) pp. 23-36

Irmscher, Hans Dietrich, *Adalbert Stifter: Wirklichkeitserfahrung und gegenständliche Darstellung*, Munich, 1971

Jennings, Lee B., *The Ludicrous Demon: Aspects of the Grotesque in German post-Romantic Prose*, Berkeley, 1963

Kaiser, Gerhard, 'Stifter – dechiffriert?' *Sprachkunst* 1 (1970) pp. 273-317

Kaiser, Michael, *Adalbert Stifter: Eine literaturpsychologische Untersuchung seiner Erzählungen*, Bonn, 1971

Keller, Thomas, *Die Schrift in Stifters 'Nachsommer'*, Cologne/Vienna, 1982

Ketelsen, Uwe, 'Geschichtliches Bewußtsein als literarische Struktur: Zu Stifters Erzählung aus der Revolutionszeit – *Granit*, 1848–1852', *Euph.* 64 (1970) pp. 306-25

Killy, Walther, *Wirklichkeit und Kunstcharakter*, Munich, 1963.

Klatt, Fritz, 'Stifter und das Dämonische', *Dichtung und Volkstum (Euph.)* 40 (1939), pp. 276-95

Klieneberger, H. R., 'Stifter's *Abdias* and its Interpreters', *FMLS* 14 (1978) pp. 332-44

Koch, Franz, 'Dichtung des Plunders', *ASNS* 186 (1949) pp. 1-27

Kohlschmidt, Werner, 'Leben und Tod in Stifters *Studien'*, *Euph.* 36 (1935) pp. 210-30

Korff, F. W., *Diastole und Systole: Zum Thema Jean Paul und Stifter*, Bern, 1969

Kraft, Peter, 'Adalbert Stifter aus der Sicht Walter Benjamins', *Die Rampe*, 1979, Heft 2, pp. 45-67

Krökel, Fritz, 'Nietzsches Verhältnis zu Stifter', *VASILO* 9 (1960) pp. 106-20

Kühn, Julius, *Die Kunst Adalbert Stifters*, Berlin, 1943

Kunisch, Hermann, *Adalbert Stifter: Mensch und Wirklichkeit*, Berlin, 1950

Lachinger, Johann, 'Adalbert Stifters *Abdias*: Eine Interpretation', *VASILO* 18 (1969) pp. 97-114

(ed.), *Stifter-Symposion*, Linz, 1978

Lange, Victor, 'Stifter: *Der Nachsommer*' in B. von Wiese (ed.), *Der deutsche Roman*, vol. 2, Düsseldorf, 1963, pp. 34-75

Lindau, Marie-Ursula, *Stifters 'Nachsommer': Ein Roman der verhaltenen Rührung*, Bern, 1974

Ludwig, Marianne, *Stifter als Realist*, Basel, 1948

Lunding, Erik, *Adalbert Stifter*, Copenhagen, 1946

Magris, Claudio, *Der habsburgische Mythos in der österreichischen Literatur*, Salzburg, 1966

Märki, Peter, *Adalbert Stifter: Narrheit und Erzählstruktur*, Bern, 1979

Martini, Fritz, *Deutsche Literatur im bürgerlichen Realismus*, Stuttgart, 1962

Mason, Eve, 'Stifter's *Turmalin*: A Reconsideration', *MLR* 72 (1977) pp. 348-58

'Stifter's *Katzensilber* and the Fairy-Tale Mode', *MLR* 77 (1982) pp. 114-29

Mattenklott, Gundel, *Sprache der Sentimentalität: Adalbert Stifter*, Frankfurt am Main, 1973

Mayer, G. 'Adalbert Stifters *Nachsommer*: Gestaltbegriff und Werkstruktur' in J. Thunecke (ed.), *Formen realistischen Erzählkunst* (Festschr. Jolles) Nottingham, 1979, pp. 120–7

Mettenleiter, Peter, *Destruktion der Heimatdichtung*, Tübingen, 1974

Mettler, Heinrich, *Natur in Stifters frühen Studien*, Zurich, 1968

Mühlher, Robert, 'Natur und Mensch in Stifters *Bunten Steinen*', *Dichtung und Volkstum (Euph.)* 40 (1939) pp. 295–304

Müller, Joachim, *Adalbert Stifter: Weltbild und Dichtung*, Halle (Saale), 1956
 'Stifters späte Erzählungen', *VASILO* 9 (1960) pp. 79–93
 'Stifters Humor', *VASILO* 11 (1962) pp. 1–20
 Neue Beiträge zum Grillparzer und Stifter Bild, Graz and Vienna, 1965
 '*Die Pechbrenner* und *Kalkstein*: Strukturanalyse einer Urfassung und einer Endfassung der *Bunte Steine*', *VASILO* 15 (1966) pp. 1–22
 'Stifter *Turmalin*: Erzählhaltung und Motivstruktur. Ein Vergleich beider Fassungen', *VASILO* 17 (1968) pp. 33–44

Müller K.–D., 'Utopie und Bildungsroman: Strukturuntersuchungen zu Stifters *Nachsommer*', *ZfdP* 90 (1971) pp. 199–228

Muschg, W., 'Das Farbenspiel von Stifters Melancholie' in *Studien zur tragischen Literaturgeschichte*, Bern, 1965, pp. 180–204
 'Die Landschaft Stifters' in *Pamphlet und Bekenntnis*, Olten, 1968, pp. 171–89

Naumann, Ursula, *Adalbert Stifter* (Slg. Metzler) Stuttgart, 1979

Oertel, Christine, 'Stifters Erzählung *Der fromme Spruch*', *Monatshefte* 42 (1950) pp. 231–6

Pascal, Roy, *The German Novel*, Manchester, 1956

Pfotenhauer, Helmut, 'Die Zerstörung eines Phantasmas: Zu den historischen Romanen von Stifter und Flaubert', *GRM* 27 (1977) pp. 25–47

Piechotta, Hans, *Aleatorische Ordnung*, Giessen, 1981

Polheim, K. K., 'Die wirkliche Wirklichkeit: Adalbert Stifters *Nachkommenschaften* und das Problem seiner Kunstanschauung' in V. J. Günther (ed.), *Untersuchungen zur Literatur als Geschichte* (Festschr. v. Wiese) Berlin, 1973, pp. 385–418

Preisendanz, Wolfgang, 'Die Erzählfunktion der Naturdarstellung bei Stifter', *WW* 16 (1966) pp. 407–18

Rath, Rainer, 'Zufall und Notwendigkeit: Bemerkungen zu den beiden Fassungen von Stifters Erzählung *Der arme Wohltäter, Kalkstein*', *VASILO* 13 (1964) pp. 70–80

Reddick, John, 'Tiger und Tugend in Stifters *Kalkstein*: Eine Polemik', *ZfdP* 95 (1976) pp. 235–55

Rehm, Walther, *Nachsommer: Zur Deutung von Stifters Dichtung*, Munich 1951

Roedl, Urban, *Adalbert Stifter: Geschichte seines Lebens* (reprinted) Bern, 1958
 Adalbert Stifter (Rowohlts Monographien) Reinbek bei Hamburg, 1965

Rosei, Peter, 'Versuch über Stifter', *LuK* 11 (1976) pp. 161–7

Schäublin, Peter, 'Stifters *Abdias* von Herder aus gelesen', *VASILO* 23 (1974) pp. 101–13 and 24 (1975) pp. 87–105

Schlaffer, Hannelore and Heinz, *Studien zum ästhetischen Historismus*, Frankfurt am Main, 1975

Schmidt, Hugo, 'Eishöhle und Steinhäuschen: Zur Weihnachtssymbolik in Stifters *Bergkristall*', *Monatshefte* 54 (1964) pp. 321–35

Schuller, Marianne, 'Das Gewitter findet nicht statt, oder die Abdankung der Kunst: Zu Adalbert Stifters Roman *Der Nachsommer*', *Poetica* 10 (1978) pp. 25–52

Schwarz, Egon, 'Zur Stilistik von Stifters *Bergkristall*', *Neophil* 38 (1954) pp. 260–8

Seibt, Ferdinand, 'Stifters *Witiko* als konservative Utopie' in *Deutsche und Tschechen: Beiträge zu Fragen der Nachbarschaft zweier Nationen*, Munich, 1971, pp. 23–39

Seidler, Herbert, *Studien zu Grillparzer und Stifter*, Vienna, Cologne, Graz, 1970

'Adalbert Stifter Forschung', *ZfdP* 91 (1972) pp. 113–57 and 252–85

'Adalbert Stifter' in K. K. Polheim (ed.), *Handbuch der deutschen Erzählung*, Düsseldorf, 1981, pp. 258–70

Selge, Martin, 'Die Utopie im Geschichtsroman: wie man Adalbert Stifters *Witiko* lesen kann', *DU* 27 (1975) Heft 3, pp. 70–85

Adalbert Stifter: Poesie aus dem Geist der Naturwissenschaften, Stuttgart, 1976

Sengle, Friedrich, *Biedermeierzeit*, Stuttgart, 1971–80

Silz, Walter, 'Stifter's *Abdias*' in *Realism and Reality*, Chapel Hill, 1954

Sjögren, Christine Oertel, *The Marble Statue as Idea: Collected Essays on Adalbert Stifter's 'Der Nachsommer'*, Chapel Hill, 1972

Staiger, Emil, *Adalbert Stifter als Dichter der Ehrfurcht* (reprinted) Zurich, 1952

Steffen, Konrad, *Adalbert Stifter: Deutungen*, Basel and Stuttgart, 1955

Stern, J. P., *Re-interpretations*, London, 1964

Idylls and Realities, London, 1971

Stiehm, Lothar (ed.), *Adalbert Stifter: Studien und Interpretationen*, Heidelberg, 1968

Stillmark, Alexander, 'Stifter contra Hebbel', *GLL* 21 (1967–8) pp. 93–107

'Stifter's Symbolism of Beauty: The Significance of the Flower in his Works', *OGS* 6 (1972) pp. 74–92

'Stifter's early Portraits of the Artist', *FMLS* 11 (1975) pp. 142–64

'Stifter's *Letzte Mappe*: The Idea of Wholeness' in C. P. Magill (ed.), *Tradition and Creation* (Festschrift E. M. Wilkinson) Leeds, 1978, pp. 162–76

Stopp, F. J., 'Symbolism in Stifter's *Kalkstein*', *GLL* 7 (1953–4) pp. 116–25

'Die Symbolik in Stifters *Bunten Steinen*', *DVjS* 28 (1954) pp. 165–93

Struc, Roman, 'The Threat of Chaos: Stifter's *Bergkristall* and Thomas Mann's "Schnee"', *MLQ* 24 (1963) pp. 323–32

Thurnher, Eugen, 'Stifters "sanftes Gesetz"' in Unterscheidung und Bewahrung (Festschrift H. Kunisch) Berlin, 1961, pp. 381–97

Tielke, Martin, Sanftes Gesetz und historische Notwendigkeit, Bern, 1979

Tismar, Jens, Gesörte, Idyllen: Eine Studie zur Problematik der idyllischen Wunschvorstellungen, Munich, 1973

Vancsa, Kurt, Die Schulakten Adalbert Stifters, Graz, 1955

Wagner, Karl, '"Patriarchalisches Streben"? Ein sozialgeschichtlicher Versuch über Stifters Nachsommer', VASILO 29 (1980) pp. 139–65

Weidinger, Rosemarie, 'Adalbert Stifter und die Naturwissenschaften', VASILO 3 (1954) pp. 129–38 and 4 (1955) pp. 1–12

Weiss, Walter, 'Adalbert Stifters Der Waldgänger' in A. Haslinger (ed.), Sprachkunst als Weltgestaltung (Festschrift H. Seidler) Salzburg, 1966, pp. 349–71

Wells, Larry, 'Adalbert Stifter: Bergkristall', VASILO 19 (1970) pp. 141–7

Widhammer, Helmuth, Die Literaturtheorie des deutschen Realismus, Stuttgart, 1977

Wiese, Benno von, 'Adalbert Stifter: Brigitta' in Die deutsche Novelle von Goethe bis Kafka, vol. 1, Düsseldorf, 1956, pp. 196–212

'Adalbert Stifter: Abdias' in Die deutsche Novelle von Goethe bis Kafka, vol. 2, Düsseldorf, 1962, pp. 127–48

Wildbolz, Rudolf, Adalbert Stifter: Langeweile und Faszination, Stuttgart, 1976

Wodtke, F. W., 'Mensch und Schicksal in Adalbert Stifters frühen Studien', WW 12 (1962) pp. 12–28

INDEX

249